The Deconstruction of Narcissism and the Function of the Object

The Deconstruction of Narcissism and the Function of the Object addresses the topic of narcissistic suffering and presents an innovative take on its psychoanalytic treatment through the deconstruction of its solipsism.

Presenting a new approach which builds on intuitions described by Freud and Winnicott, René Roussillon introduces the project of reconstructing what remains of "narcissistic" and solipsistic propositions in the theories of narcissism. Roussillon's work explores his views on narcissism, its multiple pathological manifestations and its connection to the concept of the object. Spanning topics such as sexualization and desexualization in psychoanalysis, the symbolizing function of the object, transference and associativity, this new approach to treatment provides more satisfactory therapeutic results than current practice which seeks to analyze narcissistic impasses from an intrapsychic perspective alone.

This book will be of interest to psychoanalytic and psychodynamic clinicians.

René Roussillon is Professor Emeritus of Clinical Psychology and Psychopathology at the University of Lyon, France. He was awarded the Bouvet Prize in 1991 and the Sigourney Award in 2016. He is the author of 15 books translated into 10 languages. Roussillon is also a training member of the Société Psychanalytique de Paris and the Groupe Lyonnais de Psychanalyse Rhône-Alpes.

Psychoanalytic Ideas and Applications Series

Series Editor: Silvia Flechner

For more information about this series, please visit: https://www.routledge.com

The Deconstruction of Narcissism and the Function of the Object

Explorations in Psychoanalysis

René Roussillon

Routledge
Taylor & Francis Group

LONDON AND NEW YORK

Cover image: enjoynz / Getty Images

First published 2023
by Routledge
4 Park Square, Milton Park, Abingdon, Oxon OX14 4RN

and by Routledge
605 Third Avenue, New York, NY 10158

Routledge is an imprint of the Taylor & Francis Group, an informa business

British Library Cataloguing-in-Publication Data
A catalogue record for this book is available from the British Library

Library of Congress Cataloging-in-Publication Data
Names: Roussillon, René, author.
Title: The deconstruction of narcissism and the function of the
object: explorations in psychoanalysis / René Roussillon.
Description: Abingdon, Oxon; New York, NY: Routledge, 2023. |
Series: IPA psychoanalytic ideas and applications | Includes
bibliographical references and index. |
Identifiers: LCCN 2022007351 (print) | LCCN 2022007352 (ebook) |
ISBN 9781032056869 (hardback) | ISBN 9781032056876 (paperback) |
ISBN 9781003198710 (ebook)
Subjects: LCSH: Narcissism. | Psychoanalysis.
Classification: LCC BF575.N35 R683 2023 (print) | LCC BF575.N35
(ebook) | DDC 155.2/3—dc23/eng/20220616
LC record available at https://lccn.loc.gov/2022007351
LC ebook record available at https://lccn.loc.gov/2022007352

ISBN: 978-1-032-05686-9 (hbk)
ISBN: 978-1-032-05687-6 (pbk)
ISBN: 978-1-003-19871-0 (ebk)

DOI: 10.4324/9781003198710

Typeset in Palatino
by codeMantra

Contents

Preface

One of the greatest difficulties facing psychoanalytic practice today lies in the difficulty of analyzing the forms of narcissistic suffering that threaten a person's sense of identity and which I propose to call "narcissistic-identity suffering". Many of the most influential works by the psychoanalysts who came after Freud, those at the root of the most prominent currents of modern psychoanalysis (M. Klein, W. RBion, D. W. Winnicott, J. Lacan, A. Green, M. and W. Baranger, H. Kohut, T. Ogden, etc.), encountered this issue and attempted to develop theoretical models and even technical developments in an effort to make progress in the treatment of this difficulty.

The psychoanalyst who tries – and how can one not try in the current context of psychoanalytic practice – to take into account these different contributions and working hypotheses must either join one of the "schools" generated from them or else try to cobble together "his" own personal model by combining whatever aspects of them seem most relevant to him for his practice.

Drawing on the most heuristic aspects of the concepts of various influential authors, this book proposes to explore a different approach that is based both on identifying the paradoxes at the core of the impasses of narcissistic regulation and on an attempt to deconstruct these paradoxical impasses by tracing them back to their archaic and infantile sources and the relational contexts in which they were formed.

The central hypothesis underlying this approach is that narcissism, in its most pathogenic manifestations, presents itself as "solipsistic", self-generated and as having made itself "all by itself", thereby erasing the traces of its own history. I propose to re-establish what the organization of narcissism owes to the significant objects with which it was constructed. In doing so, my aim is an opposition to the impasses created by the narcissistic postulate of the self-generation of psychic processes. I seek to deconstruct this narcissistic postulate by highlighting what the subject owes to the relational systems in which he or she has been immersed through an exploration of the responses and reactions with which his or her attempts at communication, drive impulses and affects were confronted during childhood.

This fundamental hypothesis could also be formulated in a simple sequence that identifies the basis of the three forms of reflexivity: to a very large extent, "we hear as we have been heard", "we see as we have been seen" and "we feel as we have been felt".

If we have been well heard, we hear ourselves well, if we have been properly felt, we feel well, and if we have been well seen, we see ourselves well. Conversely, if we have been badly heard, we hear ourselves badly, if we have been badly seen, we see ourselves badly, if we have been badly felt, we feel badly. Ultimately, if we are not heard, we do not hear ourselves or no longer hear ourselves, if not seen, we do not see ourselves or no longer see ourselves, if not felt, we do not feel ourselves or no longer feel ourselves.

We thus seek to bring about what has not happened, to make heard what has not been heard, to show what has not been seen, to make felt what has not been felt.

The starting point for this set of hypotheses came to me after a careful reading of Freud's article "Mourning and melancholia". I was struck by the fact that Freud did not refer to melancholia as a problem of the "lost object" as it is often characterized, but as a problem of the "disappointing object".

A "lost" object is an object that is now absent, whereas a disappointing object is disappointing in its way of being present. The object evoked by Freud is "a narcissistic object", a point which becomes clear if we think of the "self-mirror" function of the mother described by Winnicott. "Disappointment" comes from this "mirror" function.

In Freud's article, the result of this "narcissistic disappointment" is an incorporation of the object. Freud specifies, in *Inhibitions, Symptoms, and Anxiety* in 1926, that the ego tends to "assimilate", that is to say, to act as if this came from itself, what it was confronted with, and particularly if it found itself powerless in the face of what it was confronted with. This is the process that leads to the postulate of self-generation.

Self-generation has been explored in relation to delusions of self-generation, but less emphasis has been placed on the self-generation of psychic processes. The first forms of the ego, the skin-ego described by Anzieu, for example, are presented as "bags", "containers" (Bion) or "envelopes" (Anzieu). But the primitive ego tends to consider that what comes and felt as "internal" is of the "ego", regardless of the way in which "it entered" inside. If the object was incorporated following an experience of traumatic disappointment, it will thus be treated as coming from the ego and not from the incorporation of the object. It will be "assimilated" as Freud writes.

Freud's hypotheses, clarified later by the contributions of the analysts I have mentioned, open up a working hypothesis for the clinic. It is a matter of helping to "disincorporate" the internalized object by trying to go back to the primary narcissistic disappointments at the origin of the incorporation, putting the object that has been erased by the process of assimilation in the picture again, and thus contributing to its externalization.

But Freud's reflections open up another way of understanding and working with what he called "narcissistic neuroses" at the time. In his analysis, Freud confronts the question of destructiveness, which is also one of the most characteristic features of many clinical pictures of narcissistic-identity suffering. In *Mourning and Melancholia*, Freud evokes the hatred that emanates from the subject and is directed toward the object, as well as its reversal against the ego when it has incorporated the object. The subject attacks the incorporated object and with it the ego that now holds it. This is an important reference point in the working-through of destructiveness, but it is often not enough. It must be complemented by the remark that Freud makes in passing in *Group Psychology and the Analysis of the Ego* in 1921. In the appendix of the text, Freud evokes what becomes of the hatred expressed by the object for the subject when the object is subsequently incorporated. He comes back to it in 1923 in *The Ego and the Id* in the chapter devoted to the dependent relationships of the ego, when he speaks of the "severe and cruel" superego that unleashes its attacks against the ego. The superego then carries the incorporation/identification of the object, as Freud indicates, once again in passing and without going into it any further.

Thus, there can be an incorporated "destructiveness" coming from the destructiveness of the object, where the subject is traversed by movements of negativism and destructiveness that are the exact image of those he had to endure from the significant objects in his history. Ferenczi would later describe "identification with the aggressor" in the same manner but without specifying the link with incorporation.

In Freud's writings, destructiveness is often closely connected to the issue of the compulsion to repeat, but the latter is not always explored thoroughly in light of Freud's final propositions on the subject. During his exile in London, Freud wrote a few small notes which, in the context of his facing the end of his life, take on an almost testamentary value. In one of them, he returns to the subject of repetition and proposes two remarks, which, although not entirely new, are this time affirmed with new conviction. In the first, he emphasizes the fact that repetition compulsions refer to the earliest experiences. According to what he emphasizes in *Constructions in Analysis*, the earliest experiences are undoubtedly those from "when [the child] could still hardly speak".

In the second he proposes an "explanation" for this repetition and notes, soberly: "(Explanation: weakness of the power of synthesis)". He thus implicitly links compulsive repetition, the compulsion to repeat and psychic integration through the function of synthesis. What is repeated is what is not integrated, and repetition seems to aim for an attempt at integration that is liable to attack the ego, which does not make space for it.

The exile of integration "attacks" what is refused at its reception. Destructiveness does not aim fundamentally at "destruction" – it is above all aimed at integration. And if we accept Winnicott's reflections on primary destructiveness – reflections that include, as I propose in this book, the "response" of the environment to the processes of the subject – the object and then the self that is subjected to this constraint of integration must be able to "survive" (Winnicott) this destructiveness in order for the psychical topography to deepen and reshape itself. Destructiveness appears as a test of the consistency of the object and the ego, a test of endurance.

Actual destruction is its drama, and transformation its happy outcome.

These are the main lines of force of the reflections presented in this book, which takes up the clinical and theoretical argumentation underlying this set of hypotheses in greater detail.

Series Editor's Foreword

The Deconstruction of Narcissism and the Function of the Object: Explorations in Psychoanalysis

By René Roussillon

The Publications Committee of the International Psychoanalytic Association continues, with the present volume, the series «Psychoanalytic Ideas and Applications».

The aim of this series is to focus on the scientific production of significant authors whose works are outstanding contributions to the development of the psychoanalytic field and to set out relevant ideas and themes, generated during the history of psychoanalysis, that deserve to be known and discussed by present-day psychoanalysts.

The relationship between psychoanalytic ideas and their applications needs to be put forward from the perspective of theory, clinical practice and research, to maintain their validity for contemporary psychoanalysis.

The Publication's Committee's objective is to share these ideas with the psychoanalytic community and with professionals in other related disciplines, to expand their knowledge and generate a productive interchange between the text and the reader. The IPA Publications Committee is pleased to publish René Roussillon's book *The Deconstruction of Narcissism and the Function of the Object: Explorations in Psychoanalysis*.

René Roussillon is a prominent figure in French Psychoanalysis and has a lifetime of contributions in the field. He is Professor Emeritus of Clinical Psychology and Psychopathology at the University of Lyon 2 (France). He has published numerous books and papers published in international reviews. He has received the Bouvet Prize 1991 and the Sigourney Award in 2016. The IPA Publications Committee has already published one of his books: *Agony and Symbolization*, which has kindled much interest in the psychoanalytic community.

The main goal of René Roussillon in this book is to expose his views on narcissism and its multiple pathological manifestations and its connection to the concept of the object. It provides an original contribution to the topic of narcissistic pathologies. The author proposes the notion of "deconstruction" of narcissistic functions. In his view, the work of deconstruction will allow for a restoration of the place of benevolent objects in the psychic life of the subject.

Another important aspect of the author's original contribution is his view that paradoxes and impasses frequently encountered in different manifestations of narcissistic pathologies are result of a process of incorporation of a disappointing object that undermines the psychic impact of other important historical objects. Through the book, Professor Roussillon examines the multiple facets of these impasses and paradoxes and addresses key clinical considerations in the psychoanalytic treatment of these patients. Clinical vignettes illuminate the theoretical concepts proposed by the author as well as his recommendations to help overcome these impasses.

The reader has only to look at the table of contents to appreciate the richness of the content of the book, as one can value the different angles from which the author studies and reflects on his perspective on narcissistic pathologies. Some of the themes studied in this volume, to name a few, are narcissism and paradoxes, dissecting primary narcissism, destructiveness and complex forms of the "survival" of the object and the symbolizing function of the object.

There is little doubt that this book would be of much interest to the psychoanalytic community. It is important to make the work of René Roussillon accessible to English-speaking psychoanalyst and psychoanalytic-oriented clinicians. It is a significant contribution to the study of narcissism and its connexion to the concept of the object by an esteemed author. It will be helpful from both theoretical and clinical perspectives.

This book is a remarkable contribution to the study of narcissism both theoretically and clinically. Its availability to the English readership is a significant contribution to the creation of bridges between different psychoanalytic cultures. One should be thankful to Dr. Roussillon for his insights and his creative contributions.

Gabriela Legorreta
Series Editor
Chair, IPA Publications Committee

1 Working-through and its various models

Introduction: one way of looking at the problem

In the practice of psychoanalysis, the concept of working-through is a fundamental one, although it must be acknowledged that Freud described it in detail on only two occasions: in 1914, in his famous paper "Remembering, Repeating and Working-through" (Freud 1914)[1] and in 1926, in *Inhibitions, Symptoms and Anxiety* (1926 [1925]).[2]

It is a fundamental concept and perhaps even one that defines the specificity of psychoanalytic practice, insofar as, much better than any other, it differentiates psychoanalysis from the kinds of psychotherapy that are based on suggestion; Freud himself emphasized this element. Although it appeared as long ago as 1914, at a time when the overall conception of psychoanalysis was focused on recovering forgotten memories – so that it could now almost be seen as a somewhat outdated way of looking at psychoanalytic practice – it has travelled through the years and remained a feature of the various models and conceptions of how psychoanalysis is carried out.

It was no doubt not by mere chance that a Congress of the International Psychoanalytical Association was devoted to an in-depth examination of the topic.[3] This was an indication that it involves a concept of the practice of psychoanalysis in which psychoanalysts who belong to different traditions can still acknowledge one another as such; it is, therefore, a fundamental concept, one which is common to the various ways in which psychoanalysis is actually practiced.

On the face of it, the concept of working-through would seem to be simple enough. Nevertheless, if psychoanalysts belonging to different traditions see in what the concept attempts to define an important element of their practice as psychoanalysts, that apparent simplicity may well mask a whole series of complex levels upon which it functions. Any attempt to think about the concept must therefore try to expand on these.

In this chapter, I shall focus on exploring that diversity in an attempt to describe the various modalities in which working-through can operate.

DOI: 10.4324/9781003198710-1

These depend on the kind of psychoanalytic work required by different transference situations and different modes of mental functioning.

My main hypothesis is that, in different ways and involving issues that may also be very different, working-through is part and parcel of every psychoanalytic endeavor (which in itself may follow different models and patterns). To put it as simply and as clearly as possible, and using what in Freud's own vocabulary is accepted by all psychoanalysts, I would remind the reader that when he introduced the concept of working-through in 1914, he linked it very closely to the idea of resistance. In 1926, he went on to describe five kinds of resistance that he organized into three main categories: ego-resistances (of which there are three types), resistances arising from the id and resistances coming from the super-ego.

Following the indications described by Freud, I shall, therefore, explore the models of working-through as they pertain to each of these groups, *viz*:

- ego-resistances, of which there are three types: repression resistance, transference resistance and resistance involving the gain from illness;
- resistances arising from the id (linked to the compulsion to repeat and the need to symbolize);
- resistances coming from the super-ego (expressed through the unconscious sense of guilt, which Freud later replaced by the need for punishment, or through ways in which subjectivity may become alienated…).

Each of these five types of resistance demands a different kind of psychoanalytic work; each requires working-through, and here too the form that this may take and the issues involved in it will be different in each case.

Working-through in 1914: the first model, with the three kinds of ego-resistance

Before exploring the complex nature of the concept, I shall discuss the way in which Freud treated it in 1914, the way in which it was understood by psychoanalysts of that period.

At that time, Freud saw the concept of working-through in the light of his vision of psychoanalytic treatment as based on remembering repressed events from the past and on the resistance that the patient sets up against remembering. This enabled Freud to contrast psychoanalysis with other conceptions of psychotherapy based on hypnosis and suggestion; these are carried out without any resistance being shown, and no working-through is, therefore, called for. It is the rejection of suggestion and hypnosis that renders working-through necessary. In both cases, the idea is to enable what was repressed to be discharged; in this context, this means uncovering the repressed material completely, bringing it into the mental sphere and thereby integrating it. The difference lies both in the means employed and in the connection between those means and the quality of the firm sense of engagement that is thereby established.

In psychoanalysis, that sense of engagement is based on an alliance with the secondary processes, which is what working-through calls upon. It is because the analysand's ego is treated with respect in psychoanalytic technique that the paths leading to repressed memories have to be worked through; hypnosis and suggestion simply short-circuit that work by making do with a conviction based on the quasi-hallucinatory force with which the initial situation returns.

Remembering is, therefore, contrasted with this modality in which past experiences are brought back in a manner that involves the compulsion to repeat (a concept, indeed, which appears for the first time in Freud's 1914 paper) and the process-related forms that this can take on: enactments and actualization in the transference of the repressed past. This, in summary, is the description of the psychoanalytic process that arises from Freud's 1914 paper.

Between the return of past events enacted in the transference and remembering *stricto sensu*, there is already one form of resistance: transference. That resistance is linked to the *Agieren* itself – an enacted form of the return of a past event that does not enable it to be experienced as a memory.

It is this resistance that must first of all be worked through. The psychoanalyst suggests an interpretation (later, Freud would say a "construction", which is a more accurate way of putting it – the idea of a hypothesis is brought out much more clearly), which behaves like a thought-in-waiting directed toward the repressed content, acting like an attractor for this.

The work can then be carried out fragment by fragment, "piece by piece", as Freud put it, in a very gradual manner, in order to open up a path from these thoughts-in-waiting to repressed feelings and to the scenes and memories that portray them and express them. This work imposes on the psychoanalyst what Freud called "a trial of patience" (1914, p. 155). It is at this point that the analysis comes up against the second type of resistance: repression.

The slow pace of psychoanalytic work stands in contrast to any conception of the return of past experiences involving catharsis or immediate abreaction – an example of this would be the kind of instantaneous resolution that we find in Hitchcock's *Marnie*. It is based on a conception of the way in which secondary processes function, with small quantities at a time, and also on the acknowledgement of the need for processing loss. Any hope of "identity of perception" in the actualization of the transference has to be abandoned and let go of, as well as the transference enactments to which it gives rise.

The work of analysis then comes up against the third kind of ego-resistance that Freud mentioned: that involving the "gain from illness" (in his 1926 paper, Freud writes "(secondary) gain from illness"). The patient has to give up identity of perception and agree simply to make do with identity of thinking, i.e. a representative and symbolic equivalent of the initial experience.

Nevertheless, since nobody can be killed in his or her absence or as an effigy, there is a further crucial issue at stake in this work. Since resistance also actualizes past experience, making it present and active, it plays just as important a role as its gradual lifting. As Donnet (1967)[4] put it, there is an "antinomy of resistance": it both acts as a brake on the work being done and is a necessary element of the quality of that work. Processing resistance requires a great deal of effort on the part of the mind, subjectively enhancing the analysis and giving full value to what is at stake in it. It is because resistance exists, actualizing repression in the treatment and making it tangible, that the issues involved in that repression and the repressed contents can be detected and recognized in the analysis. It is because all of this requires work – and therefore time, patience and effort – that the outcome of an analysis will lead to a sense of engagement based on the subjective appropriation of the content of that analysis; the amount of energy put into it bears witness to this.

It is, however, only under certain conditions that this kind of work becomes possible. Freud described these factors as his discoveries progressed. A certain kind of mental functioning is required in both analysand and analyst:

- repression must involve memories or ideational contents that have at one time been conscious then subsequently repressed;
- the work is simply that of "insight" – to put it briefly, a transference neurosis has to be set up; this is an intermediate area between the historical neurosis and the psychoanalytic situation;
- resistance here is above all that of the preconscious ego (the only resistance that Freud described in his 1914 paper).

The psychoanalyst's work can, therefore, be seen as being able to guess, thanks to the patient's free associations, what unconscious representations structure the sequence of associations. It then becomes possible to reconstruct the actual past experiences that are hidden behind these representations; those that are activated in and by the transference can thereupon be communicated to the analysand.

The situation and conception of the issues involved in working-through changed when Freud, as he was writing *Beyond the Pleasure Principle* (1920),[5] began to think that unconscious resistances could stand in the way of the lifting of resistance and that the work of analysis could come up against the resistances of the unconscious super-ego (and its possible distortions) or those that he called in 1926 "resistances arising from the id", i.e. those that are linked to failures in the transformation of drive-related urges coming from the id.

Working-through these resistances thus took on quite another aspect and the theory behind the work of psychoanalysis became much more complex. In addition to processing the ego-resistances – what we could call the "classic" kind of psychoanalytic work – other quite different forms of that work would henceforth be developed; this, of course, is an ongoing theme in contemporary psychoanalysis.

Briefly, there are three main models of the work that is done during an analysis, corresponding to the three main types of resistance described by Freud. All of these models can be found in every analysis, although they may vary in proportion, with one or another of them predominating at any one time.

The first is the one that I have just described – the difference being that henceforth it is seen as being only part of the work required of the psychoanalyst; it is not the only model, even though it does have some *in situ* relevance to neurotic states. It corresponds to the idea of "insight" with respect to a repressed ideational complex. As I have pointed out, the aim of working-through in this case is to lay the groundwork for enabling the return of the repressed to make its way back through the associative plethora of those preconscious structures that are its derivatives. When there is a sufficient degree of indications that the repressed element is ready, working-through enables the reasons for and issues behind its earlier repression to be explored "piece by piece". Psychoanalysts expect this kind of work to enable the repressed element to be accepted and stabilized, thanks to the effort put into how it can be expressed.

The earlier phase of repression – repression *stricto sensu* – may also be the effect of a "primal repression" (Freud 1915, p. 148; 1926, p. 94). As the work of the analysis digs deeper – and this may be a crucial element in, for example, transference situations in which the main issue has to do with narcissistic problems and the sense of identity – that primal repression will also have to be processed. This leads to the second model of the work of psychoanalysis.

The work of "becoming conscious" and resistances arising from the id: a second model of working-through – by means of play

This model can be deduced from various papers that Freud wrote between 1923[6] and 1926. In these, he described clinical situations in which unconscious material had not been represented and subsequently repressed, since it had never at any time reached consciousness. It had not been transformed or represented symbolically in such a way as to enable it to "become conscious" (Freud 1923, 1926). In the following section, I shall explore the implications of the third model based on the work not only of symbolization (the theme of this second model) but also on subjective appropriation.

I shall for the moment focus on the kind of processing that is typical of this second model of working-through. It is based on the work of transformation that is required for material to become conscious, i.e. on processing the resistance arising from the id.

This involves past experiences that are traumatic by nature or that have had a traumatic impact. The unconscious material is immediately counter-cathected before it becomes in any way possible to represent it consciously to any significant extent. Given the intense unpleasure, dread or agony to which they give rise, traumatic situations and relationships prevent the self from metabolizing the inner subjective experience that they produce. Primary defenses come almost automatically into play as soon as the dread, terror or threat of annihilation contained in the traumatic situation begins to be felt, even before there is any true possibility of experiencing the situation and representing it ideationally (Freud 1920; Winnicott 1974[7]). In so doing, that defense excludes from subjectivity the perceptual and sensory elements that might have enabled the subject-ego to construct a meaningful representation of what was experienced.

It could all the same be said – and, in Europe and English-speaking countries, some contemporary psychoanalysts such as Leowald (1980)[8] tend to follow this line – that, more generally, where there is no specific traumatic context, the "raw material", as Freud called it (1900a, 1920g, 1923b), that we find at the frontier between id and ego, where the ego can take over from the id, is by its very nature extremely complex (Leowald op. cit.). That raw material mixes together various perceptions, different feelings and several drive-related impulses that may well be in conflict with one another; it merges the self's subjective experience and drive-related involvement with the other person's responses to those impulses.

From the outset, then, there is such an entangled and condensed mixture of elements that they cannot be integrated as such, hence the fact that they often appear to be enigmatic and confused. In order for them to be integrated, they must gradually be de-condensed and transformed thanks to a to-and-fro movement between internal and external, through a series of transfers and transpositions.

Although life in general may offer opportunities for carrying out these transfers and transpositions, sometimes it is only through psychoanalysis and the specific setting that it provides that this work can be carried out (cf. Faimberg 1998).[9] Material that has not been de-condensed, transposed and transformed – this is the work of metaphorization typical of symbolic representation – cannot be brought into consciousness; it cannot "become conscious" (Freud 1926, p. 159). It is, therefore, subject to "primal repression" (ibid., p. 94) before any true subjectivation can occur.

Primal repression then draws into itself any subsequent repression or splitting; these are the only outward manifestations of what has taken place.

Often, therefore, in the course of an analysis, over and beyond processing secondary repression as I have described with respect to Freud's 1914 paper, there is another kind of work that consists in transforming that "raw material" into something that can become conscious and able to be integrated within the ego. Freud described the factors underlying this process in 1932,[10] in an aphorism that has become famous: *"Wo Es war soll Ich werden"* ["Where id was, there ego shall be": 1933 [1932], p. 80].

The model of working-through that is called upon here corresponds to what both analysand and analyst have to do in order for these transformations to take place. In this way, the primitive unconscious material that has never reached consciousness but which underlies secondary repression may be able to become conscious.

The first task is to facilitate the de-condensing of that raw material in the mind so that it can be represented piece by piece and detail by detail – in other words, to metabolize the resistance that is an integral part of the unconscious material (Freud 1923) and of the drive-related urges that are contained in it and shaped by it.

For that to occur, the specific issues relating to resistances arising from the id will have to be brought into the psychoanalytic situation. Here, too, there is an antinomy of resistance with which those psychoanalysts who deal with "borderline psychoanalytic situations" as I have called them (Roussillon 1991)[11] are familiar. These borderline situations are a threat to the psychoanalytic situation as such they push it to the very limit and constantly threaten disruption. They become manifest through transference situations typical of negative therapeutic reactions, delusional (Little 1981) or passionate transference patterns – and also in less obvious or less spectacular ways that correspond more to inertia, such as "cold" melancholia and masochism in functioning.

When it becomes possible to do so in the transference, the fragments and components that are activated therein in an almost hallucinatory way have to be separated out, as it were. In this way, the subjective experience involved can be acknowledged as a "psychic representation", enabling it to be integrated into the dimension of identity of thinking and of symbolization.

To put it briefly, the task is to enable what presents itself to the mind to be acknowledged as a "re-presentation" of something belonging to the past, not as actually occurring in the present. This requires drive-related impulses and traumatic experiences to be metabolized; the initial subjective experience has to be transformed into a representation that is able to "become conscious". All of this requires some work of (re)construction in which the analyst plays a direct role, such that some degree of personal involvement on his or her part is inevitable. I shall come back to this crucial point later.

As Freud pointed out in 1923, the ego requires "representations" if it is to do any work. It has to transform everything into mental representations, and in particular verbal ones: perceptions, sensations, drive-related impulses, affects – in other words, all the components of the "raw material" of the mind. This is the first step in the qualitative re-working of subjective experience.

It then has to explore the various mental aspects and facets of that experience in order to familiarize thinking with its primary uncanniness and thereby make its gradual integration a possibility.

This work of processing can be likened to the importance of play for children (Winnicott 1971)[12] because it has the same function as play at that stage in life: to bring under control difficult and potentially traumatic situations in order to symbolize them and prepare the way for their subjective appropriation or subjectivation. Transferring sensations, perceptions and drives and locating them in play objects – and therefore in the animism of childhood – means that they can be diffracted. This in turn enables their characteristic features to be explored, so that they become easier to grasp and their various aspects can be laid out for investigation. That is why there is a need for repetition in order to explore what is at stake fragment by fragment and "piece by piece" – just as when children play. Here, working-through and repetition go hand in hand. The psychoanalyst will have to differentiate this necessary and productive form of repetition, one that is part of what I have called the "constraints of symbolization" (Roussillon 1991, 1995[13]), from those other kinds of repetition that involve the return of the traumatic situation itself.

It is important to note that this kind of processing is often carried out by both protagonists working together. The analyst is, therefore, much more involved in the process and is potentially in a more compromising situation than is the case in the first model of working-through that I described earlier. Analysand and analyst both take part in this work, hence the fact that some authors have emphasized the inter-subjective aspects (Renik 2004)[14] of psychoanalytic treatment, co-thinking (Widlöcher 1995)[15] and co-construction (Author 1984). Ideational representation is not a "given", it has to be constructed and is the product of the work of the analysis.

This joint work, in "the overlap of two areas of playing" (Winnicott 1971, p. 38), enables the experience to be shared and libidinal elements to be revitalized. This is a necessary step if those experiences that the patient was unable to symbolize are to be bound together and integrated into the framework of the preconscious ego. I have suggested that this work should be described as being carried out "side-by-side", even though the situation as a whole remains dissymmetrical, insofar as each protagonist takes support from the other and the other's work. It is in this sense that Winnicott's aphorism "psychotherapy takes place in the overlap of two areas of playing" can be seen as particularly relevant.

The idea of working "side-by-side" in constructing meaning has also to do with something that I have been highlighting for some years now: work that is accomplished in parallel or in a "double" manner. Working-through takes place in a domain that is structured by two different vectors, that of the analysand and that of the analyst, which although distinct are linked together (through interplay) and require further connections to be made between them. Processing takes place between these two areas, as they are brought together and linked up. The analyst relies on his or her empathy toward what is taking place without the patient being able to give proper form to it, in order to make contact with and reconstruct, through portraying them, the subjective experiences that are involved in the pattern of the transference. A kind of shared symbolization will then take place; through the work of the analysis, what the patient had been unable to symbolize in the past with his or her primary objects will then be offered a second chance of being dealt with (Faimberg 2009).[16] As I have said, the analyst is part and parcel of that endeavor and will inevitably be compromised by it to some extent, in the sense that the threat of suggestion or even of narcissistic seduction will necessarily be present. Another kind of work will, therefore, be required as a result of what is involved in working-through the resistances arising from the id: processing on the one hand the inevitable seduction and suggestion that is part and parcel of analytical work, and, on the other, the transference links that may echo these elements with respect to the sexual and narcissistic seductions that the patient experienced with significant objects in the past.

In order to symbolize subjective experience, the analyst has to engage with it; that deep involvement represents a threat to subjective appropriation. It is possible to symbolize *for* the object (cf. corroborative dreams as an expression of compliance towards the analyst) – the work of symbolization carried out in such circumstances has in fact an alienating impact.

Freud saw this form of working-through, which involves not simply the work of symbolization but also that of subjective appropriation – the introjection of subjective experience – as being that of processing the resistances coming from the super-ego. If the shadow of the object (and of the analyst) falls on the analysis (Roussillon 2000), the impact of that shadow will have to be dealt with, as will the tendency of the mental apparatus to assimilate the shadow of the object (Freud 1926) – and, therefore, that of the analyst.

This leads to the third form of resistance and to the third model of working-through.

Working-through and resistances coming from the super-ego: the third model and what it involves

When, in 1923, Freud studied what was involved in negative therapeutic reactions, he emphasized that this had also to do with the person to whom the outcome of an analysis can be attributed. The work of psychoanalysis mobilizes a fundamental issue: that of the conditions under which the subjective appropriation by the analysand of that work can take place. Again, the question of seduction and suggestion in and through the analysis comes to the fore, as well as the specter of hypnosis that was already present in Freud's 1914 paper. It was not by chance that Freud, in several of his papers written during that period (and all through his exchange of correspondence with Ferenczi), discussed the idea of unconscious thought-transmission.

In his 1923 paper, again on the subject of the negative therapeutic reaction, Freud suggested that the unconscious sense of guilt that underlies this reaction may result from a "borrowed" identification, a hypothesis which also evokes the question of suggestion and seduction. When the work of analysis is carried out by both participants – Widlöcher's "co-thinking", and my own "co-construction" (Roussillon 1984)[17] – it becomes a matter of ensuring that no alienating suggestions are contained within it, that it is not rejected and that negativism is not exacerbated. Psychoanalysis can then be thought of as a "field", as suggested by the Barangers (1996).[18] This is all the more the case when we have to deal with transference situations in which narcissistic issues are very much to the fore.

It is, therefore, not enough merely to represent and symbolize the "raw material" of the mind. What has to be elucidated is to whom that symbolization is attributed and what kinds of subjective appropriation accompany the work of symbolization. As I have briefly pointed out, Freud noted that some dreams can be corroborative; the patient dreams "in compliance with the physician's words" (1923, p. 115). Here, the analyst replaces the super-ego that has to be seduced or passively submitted to.

Some kinds of super-ego may be alienating and, therefore, will have to be deconstructed. They rebel against the psychoanalytic process and entail resistances to it, thereby disrupting mental functioning.

This evokes, naturally enough, the "harsh and cruel" super-ego that Freud described in his 1923 paper; it disrupts mental functioning through treating representation as an act – that kind of confusion creates an impasse for the ego. There then arises a "pure culture of the death instinct" (1923, p. 53). Thus, the super-ego may demand too much of the ego and dispossess it of the benefits of its work of symbolization – or perhaps even refuse to set up the conditions under which the ego can carry out the work of symbolization. Toward the end of *Civilization and its Discontents (1929),*[19] Freud said that it is necessary to "lower its demands" (i.e. those of the super-ego) (Freud 1930 [1929], p. 143) and fight against its more extreme requirements. What also springs to mind here, of course, are the ideals that the super-ego imposes on the ego.

Analyzing and working-through the resistances coming from the super-ego imply going back to the way in which the "shadow" of the patient's parental objects "fell upon the ego", thus contributing to the construction of the super-ego. The shadow of the parental objects may, as Freud pointed out, also be that of their own super-ego. What must also be examined in the transference relationship is how the shadow of the ideals, the theories and the specific way in which the analyst functions (Brenman 2006)[20] may fall upon the analysis and upon the analysand (Mitchell 1997; Hanly

2009). That was already a major issue for Ferenczi in his exploration of the technique of psychoanalysis and in his denunciation of what he called the professional hypocrisy of some of his colleagues. It plays a significant part also in Anzieu's study of the principle of transitional analysis in individual psychoanalysis (Anzieu 1989)[21] and is a fundamental element of Winnicott's theory and of the analysis of psychic intrusions.

In the work of co-construction required by any working-through of the resistances of the id and of archaic material, analysts cannot avoid revealing something of how they themselves function and of their own ideals. Attempting to ignore this would imply the risk of isolating a counter-transference element and exacerbating the analysand's submissiveness (or, *mutatis mutandis*, rebellion) when faced with an alienating super-ego/ego ideal. The analyst's counter-attitude will inevitably be in collusion with transference issues that have to do with "resistances coming from the super-ego", such that no working-through of their past history will be possible.

On the other hand, taking on board the inevitable suggestion/seduction effect within the analysis will open up avenues to processing the historical dimension of the super-ego resistances, enabling some degree of gradual "transitionalization" of that instance to take place. A crucial element in the subjective appropriation of the analysis lies in the fact of enabling the super-ego also to be subjectively appropriated. It is for this reason that J-L Donnet, in a personal communication, suggested that Freud's aphorism should be modified so as to read "*Wo Es* und Uber-Ich *waren, soll Ich werden*" – "Where id and super-ego were, there ego shall be".

In my own clinical experience, the work that is facilitated by the capacity for play opens up the possibility for the processes of symbolization to unfold along a found-created dimension. In addition to this, one of the pivotal elements of the work of transitionalization of the super-ego depends on the analysand's capacity to say "no" to the analyst. This is a deep-rooted no that enables analysands to avoid the alienation arising from submission or rebellion; these usually indicate that the analysand is unable to say no in any authentic way – it is very much a superficial no, a no that, paradoxically, indicates compliance.

When the analysand does not have that capacity to say no, one of the forms that working-through will take is closely related to what we call negativism; this is another means by which analysands manage to preserve a sufficient degree of differentiation with respect to their analyst. The idea is to prevent the shadow of the analyst – the analyst's ideals, theories and *a priori* assumptions – falling on the analysand, and with it the risk of a re-sexualization of the latter's relationship to the super-ego.

In these clinical situations, working-through is superimposed on putting to the test both the analyst and his or her narcissism; these then have to "survive" (to use Winnicott's term) in order to make possible the work of differentiating me from not-me. That work is one of the crucial issues to be dealt with in the analysis and in the processing that the analytical situation encourages. If no "uncoupling" takes place between analysand and analyst, the coupling/uncoupling interplay between ego and super-ego – their entanglement/differentiation – cannot be worked through freely enough, so that it remains caught up in the constraints of the infantile dimension.

If that uncoupling cannot be carried out, all the analyst does is substitute for the past influence of the analysand's significant objects the present influence of his or her own ideals, value systems and *a prioris*. Thereupon, the analysis becomes a kind of machine for influencing or for suggesting, whatever the analyst's good intentions or professional ethics. Some degree of influence and suggestion coming from the analyst is anyway inevitable, because these elements do not depend exclusively on the analyst or on the precautions that he or she takes in order not to have an impact on the patient; they depend also on the form of the transference and on the function that this attributes to the analyst. Being sensitive to the effects of this tendency and of how it is expressed is part of what is involved in working-through the "resistances coming from the super-ego"; it then becomes possible to analyze those influences.

The sensitivity and attentiveness that are given to these issues enable what Winnicott called the "use of the object" to be analyzed – by which he meant the analysand's capacity to use the analyst and working-through in order to analyze the characteristic features of his or her own narcissism.

Conclusion

In the three "models" that I have described and the three transference situations that are part of them, working-through is always present, although its nature changes as the issues involved in it change through the interplay of the psychoanalytic encounter. Working-through is a fundamental feature of the psychoanalytic process; it is *the* element that gives enough time for the workings of the mind to be properly acknowledged, brought under control, explored and appropriated. Above all, it is *the* element that provides the proper conditions for the work of psychoanalysis not to be limited to the preconscious [Pcs.] system but to come into contact with the real unconscious issues that the various kinds of resistance both hide and reveal; in this way, true processing can lead to an authentic kind of engagement.

That is why working-through is the crucial concept of psychoanalytic technique, the concept that gives it its very foundation. It is thanks to the idea of working-through that psychoanalysis can avoid being simply another technique based on suggestion, no matter how sophisticated. That is a crucial issue for contemporary psychoanalysis.

Notes

1 Freud, S. (1914b). "Remembering, repeating and working-through (further recommendations on the technique of psycho-analysis, II)". *Standard Edition*, 12: 147.
2 Freud, S. (1926d [1925]). *Inhibitions, symptoms and anxiety*. Standard Edition, 20: 77.
3 IPA Congress, Berlin, July 2007.
4 Donnet, J.-L. (1967). "L'Antinomie de la résistance". *L'inconscient*, n° 4. PUF.
5 Freud, S. (1920). "Beyond the pleasure principle". *SE*, 18: 1–64.
6 Freud, S. (1923). *The ego and the id*. Standard Edition, 19: 3.
7 Winnicott, D.W. (1974). "Fear of breakdown". In C. Winnicott, R. Shepherd, & M. Davis (Eds), *Psychoanalytic Explorations*, 87–95. Cambridge, MA: Harvard University Press.
8 Loewald, H. (1980). *Papers on psychoanalysis*. London: Yale University Press.
9 Faimberg, H. (2009). "Après-coup et construction". *Revue Française de psychanalyse*, n° 5, special Congress issue, 473–486. PUF.
10 Freud, S. (1933a [1932]). *New introductory lectures on psycho-analysis*. Standard Edition, 22: 3.
11 Roussillon, R. (1991). *Paradoxes et situations limites de la psychanalyse*. Paris: PUF.
12 Winnicott, D.W. (1971b). *Playing and reality*. London: Routledge, 1999.
13 Roussillon, R. (1995). "La métapsychologie des processus". *Revue française de psychanalyse*, 1995, n° 5.
14 Renik, O. (2004). "Intersubjectivity in psychoanalysis". *International Journal of Psycho-Analysis*, 85: 1053–1056.
15 Widlöcher, D. (1995). Report read to the 55th Congress of French-speaking psychoanalysts, Revue française de psychanalyse, 1995, LIX (Special Congress issue): 1721–1787.
16 Faimberg, H. (2009). "Après-coup et construction". *Revue Française de psychanalyse*, n° 5, special Congress issue, 473–486. PUF.
17 Roussillon, R. (1984). "Construction de la scène primitive et co-construction du processus analytique, à propos de l'interprétation". *Bulletin de la Société Psychanalytique de Paris*, 1984: 27–44.
18 Baranger, W., & Baranger, M. (1996). "Processus et non-processus dans le travail analytique". *Revue française de psychanalyse*, LX, n° 4 (October–December 1996), 1223–1242.
19 Freud, S. (1930a [1929]). *Civilization and its discontents*. Standard Edition, 21: 59.
20 Brenman, E. (2006). *Recovery of the lost good object*. London: Routledge.
21 Anzieu, D. (1989). "Principe d'analyse transitionnelle en psychanalyse individuelle". In *Psychanalyse des limites*. Paris: Dunod, 2007.

2 The function of the object in the binding and unbinding of the drives

Destructiveness and violence are usually badly thought of and often have negative adjectives attached to them. They are nonetheless a necessary feature of life and of the various processes that make life possible. Without destructiveness, nothing can be created – the earlier state of something has to be destroyed if something new is to emerge. Both bodily metabolism and psychical metabolization imply the deployment of destructive procedures. The clinical problem of destructiveness is therefore not that of destructiveness per se but of the ways in which it is expressed and manifested – in other words, what becomes of it.

The problem of the outcome of destructiveness is that of the desired result. If destructiveness is employed in such a way as to promote or prolong life, if it serves creativeness, the immediate impression we have is that it will have a completely different effect from what would occur if actual destruction were its aim.

Nonetheless, that difference may be much more relative than might appear to be the case at first glance; there may well be significant differences depending on whether we look at manifest or latent issues and modalities. This could be the situation too depending on the length of time taken into consideration, or on a broadening of the context, or if survival of the species is a factor, for example. Absolute or "pure" destructiveness may perhaps not exist other than as a concept. Destructiveness cannot be looked upon as an "in-itself" invariant – and the same is broadly true of creativeness. In clinical work, it has to be analyzed in terms of its "meaning", the meaning that it has, not in any absolute sense, but for a given individual.

I shall therefore take as my starting point the idea that the clinical issue has to do with the ways in which destructiveness is manifested and how these link up with other drive-related tendencies.

The hypotheses that I shall attempt to explore can be expressed as several postulates:

1 Violence and aggressiveness should not be looked upon as a direct form of expression of a "destructive drive" or "destructive instinct".

DOI: 10.4324/9781003198710-2

There are always other factors that are not manifest, "unconscious" issues that have to do with something other than violence and aggressiveness: anxiety, suffering, helplessness, etc.

2 Every other feature of the workings of the human mind, destructiveness and the various forms that it may adopt should not be looked upon as if they were completely identical in or to themselves; they necessarily cast some kind of shadow, which "says" both more and less. I hope to clarify that point in the course of my exploration. I would suggest that there are three levels or "forms" that this articulation can have:

3 From a clinical point of view, it is always important to take into consideration how destructiveness is articulated, bound up and blended with that other great force with which it has to come to terms: creativeness and the love that lies behind it. This was initially part of my exploration of paradox, of paradoxicality and of "paradoxical logic", which is expressed in the course of psychoanalytical treatment mainly as a paradoxical transference underlying some kinds of negative therapeutic reaction. Subsequently, I presented a paper at the 1995 Monaco Congress on Violence[1] in which I explored:

1 The first level is that of "binding", the primary amalgamating of the drives. I would argue that what is usually called the "death drive" is in fact an indication that this binding has failed – leading to unbinding. We do need concepts that can describe what a moment of "pure" creativeness or of "pure" destructiveness might be, always assuming – but I personally am rather doubtful of this – that these are more than simply speculative abstractions.

2 The second level of articulation involves how the conflict of ambivalence is structured. This implies differentiating between love and hate, between tenderness and violence, and between creativeness and destructiveness. I emphasize both the idea of differentiation (binding is a mixture, not a differentiation) and that of setting up a kind of articulation characterized by conflict. Ambivalence implies a conflict between two antagonistic and contradictory tendencies with respect to the same object or the same process. The conflict of ambivalence is based on the acknowledgment of the simultaneous nature of those two antagonistic tendencies with respect to the same object.

3 The third level of articulation – I shall not go into any detail about this in this chapter, given that its clinical manifestations do not involve violence – has to do with the different ways in which the conflict is set up and dealt with; this in turn requires us to look at the pre-eminence, in these, of love or creativeness.

4 What I am now about to develop here follows on from some of my previous issue of pre-ambivalent primary guilt. I shall not go

into any detail about the findings that I presented in those articles (Roussillon 1995 op cit) but, since they are implicit in what I am now about to develop, I shall touch on some aspects of them, i.e. those that are directly relevant to this chapter.

Conflict and paradoxicality

Conflict has to do with drive-related impulses in a context of object relations, while paradox appears to be more specific to issues and deadlocks involving narcissism. Thus setting up a conflict of ambivalence implies a psychical structure governed by the pleasure/unpleasure principle, which in turn assumes that the individual is able to draw a sufficiently clear distinction between "good" and "bad", between experiences of pleasure and those of unpleasure. In the course of psychoanalytical treatment, the paradoxicality that I have just outlined produces a "borderline" or "extreme" situation in the analyzing space (Roussillon 1991).[2] This is manifested via a paradoxical transference and the predominance of the process of reversal. It gives rise to negative therapeutic reactions in which the more the treatment progresses, the worse the patient's condition seems to be.

On the other hand, some kinds of paradoxicality disrupt those differentiations and bring about a degree of confusion in the mind between the dimension of pleasure and that of unpleasure. They lead to a kind of psychical paralysis that Anzieu (1975a, 1975b),[3] for example, sees as a manifestation of the death drive. The most extreme example of this is Shakespeare's Richard III who, at the beginning of the play, puts it thus (I am summarizing): "Since I possess none of the attractiveness that appeals to human beings, let evil be my good". Here, "bad" does not clash with "good"; it actually becomes "good" in a kind of reversal that throws any difference into turmoil. It is on that basis that Richard III sets off on a whole series of murders.

When Freud (1916)[4] studied this play, he put Richard III in the category of character traits that are "exceptions". The individual is an outlaw, or rather above the law; having "paid" once and for all, from the very beginning. From birth, he or she was marked by evil, by the "devil" – doomed to be evil, that person will, like Richard III, "prove a villain". The paradoxical reversal of evil into good disorganizes the fundamental conflictuality based on the contrast between good and bad and the bringing into conflict of good and evil. Henceforth, nothing can counterbalance destructiveness, nothing can stand in its way – it is, in fact, treated as being the supreme "good". My hypothesis (Roussillon 1991, 1995)[5] is that, underlying the reversal of good into bad, there is a merging together of the two, a failure to differentiate the one from the other and therefore a paralysis of basic psychical functioning, of attributive judgment, which has its roots in the ability to differentiate between pleasure and unpleasure, in the ability to seek out pleasure and avoid unpleasure.

The negative therapeutic reaction and the logics of paradoxicality

The processual forms of negative therapeutic reaction, and of the outbursts of destructiveness and negativity/negativism that go hand in hand with this, are the particularly pernicious variations on the theme of "all or nothing" typical of the less civilized kinds of drive manifestation. Some examples of the way in which negativism can be expressed, taken from a classical form of psychoanalytical treatment, will enable us to see how negativity functions; they highlight the "paradoxical logic" to which they give rise in secondary processes.[6]

Here is a fairly recent example, taken from my own clinical work, of repeated awareness of the acuteness of some kinds of negativity in the course of an analysis.

The patient is a woman in her 50s; treatment follows the standard psychoanalytical procedure (three sessions per week, with the patient lying on the couch).

I am her fourth analyst. According to the patient, her three earlier attempts brought only slight changes to her mental functioning and clinical symptoms, the dominant feature of which is severe depression that borders on melancholia. From what the patient tells me, my impression is that her previous analysts had difficulty in "surviving" her destructiveness. Two of them ended up, as she put it, by "showing [her] the door", while the third "didn't have a clue", so that there was no possibility of anything happening.

So, when I began this treatment, I was "warned" that she was a very difficult patient, borderline, whose destructiveness was very poorly integrated. Indeed, it took months if not years of slowly "surviving" and processing her mechanisms before any kind of positive outcome could even be hoped for.

In the months preceding the most significant phase of the analysis, the patient's negativistic processes could begin to be approached. Our work led to the well-known formula that Bergeret (1984) has emphasized: "Faced with a glass that is half full, [the patient] sees one that is half empty". In the following session, she wanted to pick up on that statement in order to challenge it, but in fact said: "Yes, that's right, when a glass is full, I see it as being half empty". She then paused and burst out laughing as she heard herself modifying the saying and, in fact, making it even more inflexible instead of challenging it as she had set out to do. That proved to be a decisive step forward.

Later, some processing of her destructiveness began to be possible; this took different forms, the various versions of which I think may be useful to explain insofar as putting words on the different patterns of destructiveness in that patient represented the most significant part of the work of the analysis, enabling her to break free of the existential deadlocks in which she kept imprisoning herself.

Here is a list of the various formulations to which the analysis gave rise in the course of the many long months of working through that followed:

"What you say is good and correct. But it's worthless, and it's even bad for me in fact because I'm not the one who, all by myself, had the thought".

Therefore: "What I get from other people is worthless because it comes from someone else. The only things that are good and acceptable are those that I myself produce".

Or again: "Getting something from somebody else means that I wasn't able to produce it myself – and that means that I'm completely useless".

We can see in these statements the necessity of a kind of self-engendering, which implies rejection of any form of dependence. Here are some more examples:

"What I have is worthless, because I have it. It is only what someone else has and I don't that is good; only what I do not possess is of any value". (This, of course, is one form that destructive envy may take on.)

I owe it to Groucho, of the Marx Brothers, for helping me to find a particularly opposite way of expressing the reverse situation: "I don't want to belong to any club that will accept people like me as a member".

So, "What I have is bad because I have it; everything that I possess is bad or worthless because I possess it".

Then, "Everything that touches me becomes bad, because I am evil".

And, finally, this series of statements, which unfolded according to how they were expressed in the clinical work of the analysis.

"What I receive is right and 'good', but it is worthless (it's 'bad') because…" (for one or other of the following reasons):

- "I didn't receive it at the proper time (when I was a child, when I had so much need of it)". The analysand feels herself to be 'foreclosed' in Lacan's conception of the word. This is the opposite of the well-known saying 'better late than never'.
- "I didn't receive it from the right person (from my mother or my father, from whom I was expecting it; only what I receive from them can be good and valuable, but I received nothing from them…)". The object is unique, irreplaceable; even if it is defective, no transference or exchange is possible.
- "I didn't receive it in the proper way, as I should have done, exactly as I was expecting it… therefore, I can't make use of it".

It is not difficult to imagine that this kind of procedure is an obstacle to the clinical work of processing and integrating the vagaries of the history of past failures and traumas. What is thought about and understood in the space of the session is ipso facto invalidated by the fact that it was not there, beforehand, in the past.

Indeed, the present revelation that things can be different only increases the pain of not having received earlier what now appears possible. In this kind of situation, the patient, feeling obliged to do so, initiated a process of mourning and, in despair, at long last gave something up – only to find out that what she thought she had to give up, as if it were something intrinsically impossible, was in fact possible and depended on the inter-subjective context of the time, on the responses that were made to what was transpiring, not to the actual events themselves.

The past deadlock experienced by the patient is transferred onto the psychoanalytical space so that it is the psychoanalyst who experiences it, because the more "relevant" he is in what he suggests, the less the patient can make use of it!

Transference here is not a kind of displacement, as it is traditionally described, but a form of turnaround in which the analysand inflicts on the analyst what he or she had been subjected to without being able to integrate it – it may operate, in fact, in both modalities simultaneously, displacement and reversal, but these are split off from each other and set up a kind of double deadlock.

Hope, and the risk of suffering linked to the possibility of disap-pointment that every hope carries with it, are therefore actively counter-cathected: "Better the disappointment that we know about, than hope and its succession of unknown factors and potential suffering". What is bad is more "sure", more predictable than good; evil is better than good, which is more uncertain, and therefore evil is cathected and reproduced to a greater extent.

The individual thus puts him- or herself into a position of "existential foreclosure": what did not take place in childhood and with the parents is now too late; it can never be produced, never take place. Transference and the necessary "illusion" that lies at the root of its analyzable manifesta-tions are thus paralyzed from the very outset; nothing can be expected of analysis because what ought to have taken place at the proper time simply did not occur – and there is no possible way it can be replaced, no trans-ference can even be envisaged…

That kind of reasoning does, of course, bring to mind what Klein said about envy and the forms that it may take, as well as Rosenfeld's idea of the negative therapeutic reaction. However, when we go beyond the processual manifestations that I have described, the analysis reveals a subjective position that lies at the heart of the problem, one that per-sists thanks to ensuring that all therapeutic efforts are doomed to fail-ure. "If I didn't receive what was 'owed' to me as a child, it is because I am in essence bad; it's all my fault… Those in my early family circle, the context – none of that has anything to do with it". If what occurred in the past is due to the inevitability of fate, if it is linked to the "evil" that inhabits the individual, then he or she cannot bear a grudge against those past objects – and is therefore protected against experiencing any violent affect toward them.

Those violent affects are then turned back upon the self and contribute to reinforcing the feeling of a "bad self". The person concerned is thereby protected against experiencing feelings of infantile helplessness when faced with the limitations, inadequacies or failures of the primary objects.

Better to be guilty, better to be 'bad', than helpless and constrained.

"A piece of ego-analysis" and binding of the drives

These, then, are some of the processual modalities that are the outcome of the impact of the kind of destructiveness and negativity which, when they are activated, take over the workings of the mind. In Analysis terminable and interminable, Freud (1937c)[7] emphasizes the necessity of alternating between "a piece of id-analysis" and "a piece of ego-analysis". It would probably be quite useful to follow that advice and to examine whether some ego experiences may contribute to reinforcing the impact of destructiveness. This could be an alternative hypothesis to the one according to which innate destructiveness is particularly important in some people, who, for example, have "a temperament intolerant of frustration" (Bion 1970, p. 14).[8]

This is the point at which I must return to the first level of articulation that I mentioned earlier, relating to the issue of binding of the drives and primary amalgamating.

Binding of the drives is often looked upon – and perhaps even by Freud himself as going without saying; only their unbinding constitutes a problem. I would now like to discuss the relevance of a different hypothesis, according to which certain primary subjective experiences can either contribute to making binding of the drives possible – a primary amalgamating, a pre-form of ambivalence – or, on the other hand, be an obstacle to its structuring. According to that hypothesis, the binding of the drives is not a "given"; it is a product of certain primary and very early experiences. Conversely, failure to set up this primary binding is also due to experiences – of a primary traumatic nature – that result in the person being overwhelmed by primary erotogenic masochism. Thanks to the processes of libidinal and sexual co-excitation, that form of masochism is appropriate for binding; when it is overwhelmed, binding also becomes unable to cope.

I shall now present four clinical patterns or problem situations that will enable me to explore these initial ideas more deeply. Some of these patterns are directly related to the clinical work of psychoanalysis and can be identified through what Winnicott referred to as the kind of treatment that amounts to psychoanalytical exploration; others, however, have nothing to do with psychoanalytical treatment as such, but with mythology and with the institutional treatment of certain kinds of violence for which the traditional form of psychoanalysis is not appropriate. It is nonetheless possible to treat these situations while maintaining a psychoanalytical conception of the process; in this way, some highly significant clinical data can be discovered. I would argue that, for our thinking, we ought not to miss out on that kind of experience when it is possible to devise an appropriate analyzing setting; "extreme" situations can throw light on certain aspects of "borderline" situations – which can be treated in the traditional psychoanalytical manner, and which in turn throw light on the more ordinary situations encountered in our psychoanalytical practice.

Clinical work with extremely violent children

I shall therefore begin with an example of a non-traditional setting. This has to do with clinical work with extremely violent children; my collaboration with Dr M Berger and his staff in the St Etienne day hospital in Lyon enabled me to discover and explore this kind of situation.

I shall not go into any great detail as regards this clinical work and the overall setting in which the therapy was undertaken; I shall simply mention the main results of the clinical support given in terms of "exploration and research".

An 11 year-old pre-adolescent boy (who weighed all the same almost 80 kg [12 stone]) was always "breaking everything"; he had already caused several attempts at therapy, individual and institution-based, to fail. When he was admitted to Dr Berger's unit, we could say that all the "traditional" assortment of therapies had failed. After coming to the conclusion that, in the day center too, all the traditional forms of therapy had failed, the staff, who were being pushed to breaking point by him, asked me to supervise the care procedure that they were offering the boy.

After examining the clinical problem and coming to the conclusion that the staff were just about at their wits' end, I suggested that the boy could be given some support through "enveloping" him in a sheet at normal room temperature. After some trial and error, we managed to set up a procedure with three therapists (all of whom had had training in psychoanalysis) participating in each session. One of the psychologists would lie down beside the boy; she too would be more or less wrapped up so that she would be a "double" for the boy and be "with him", "by his side". Two other clinicians were present during each session; there were three or four sessions per week, each lasting for about an hour and a half. Whenever the staff had the impression that they were starting to feel overwhelmed again, I would be called upon to help, but it was usually Dr Berger, the consultant practitioner in the day hospital, who would give them support.

That part of the treatment lasted six months. After two months, it was the boy himself who asked for sessions whenever he felt panicky: these "on request" sessions were in addition to those already programmed. At the end of that six-month period, psychoanalytical psychotherapy at last became possible. This was done via the "alternating stories" technique that Dr Berger has devised; these could be seen as resembling a kind of "Squiggle" game in which parts of stories replace the lines that are drawn.

The two main results of this clinical work with an "extreme situation" could be expressed as follows:

In the first place, manifest destructiveness served as a screen behind which lay anxiety about being fragmented and the terror of exploding and disintegrating. The boy "exploded" with anger, with rage, in order not to be shattered or exploded; he "broke everything" because he felt that he was threatened with being broken up and did what he could to avoid this. That is an important point: destructiveness is not simply the direct expression of a "destructive drive"; there are underlying issues and it is at that level that some kind of help has to be offered.

Secondly, there is what can be reconstructed, through and thanks to this setting, of the primary narcissistic deprivation experienced by children such as that young patient. One of the things that did a lot to calm down the anxiety that he felt was the fact of being with somebody acting as a "double". The psychologist was lying down side-by-side with the boy; she acted as a kind of "double", experiencing and putting into words the feelings and affects that the boy seemed to be manifesting.

Functioning as a "double" like that enabled some degree of psychical containment and a bringing together of the boy's fragmented experiences; it was as though accompanying him in that way enabled some integration and binding of the subjective amorphousness in which he found himself, into which fragmentation plunged him.

Primary physical/bodily rejection

I shall now discuss the second clinical pattern dating from early childhood. This involves babies and infants who have experienced a kind of primary rejection, in particular the kind of primary rejection that is physical or corporeal. Ferenczi (1929)[9] was the first to explore this pattern of primary rejection in "unwelcome" children. Later, in a clinical study of children who were particularly aggressive and violent, Hopkins (1987)[10] emphasized the importance of primary bodily rejection in the way in which such an intensification of destructiveness comes about. A child who is physically rejected, or one whose mother develops a phobia about touching her infant, constructs an initial representation of him- or herself as "rubbish" – or "a turd", to put it even more precisely; violence then develops as a reaction to that basic representation.

In adding to that, I argue (Roussillon 1995 op cit) that the sense of self which is then constructed is organized not around the process which, for Freud, was the baby's first subjective position ("I am the breast" [Freud 1941[1938], p. 299])[11] but around one that has more to do with "I am (the) evil". I went on to study several clinical patterns that sometimes come into being in an attempt to survive such a subjective position, evocative of "some character-types met with in psychoanalytic work" as described in Freud's famous 1916 paper that I mentioned earlier:

- A negative exceptional position, such as that of Richard III, whom I have already mentioned: 'Let evil be my good'.
- Criminals because of their guilt feelings, in which violence and crimes are committed in order to localize unconscious feelings of guilt that are impossible to fence in.
- Failure neurosis and fate neurosis expressed as a compulsion to reproduce failures; these reinforce the individual's feeling of being 'damned'. Anything 'good' about success becomes 'bad' as a result of a kind of primary guilt.

These patterns, set up early in life, are an obstacle to the binding of the drives. They prevent any structuring of conflict involving ambivalence thanks to which violence could be bound and thereby lose its destructive quality. They are all the same difficult to distinguish as isolated phenomena since later in life other issues cloud them over somewhat.

The myth of Narcissus and Echo is to some extent an illustration of that process. As we know, Echo was punished by Hera for having distracted her attention by endlessly chattering, thus enabling the nymphs to flirt with her husband. Echo was punished by making it impossible for her to do anything other than repeat the final syllables spoken by other people. She did, however, learn to make use of that constraint in order to try to make known what she desired. That is what happened in Ovid's myth when Echo met the beautiful young Narcissus. She fell in love with him and followed him, hidden in the forest, waiting for a favorable opportunity to approach him and try her luck. She thought that she had found that opportunity when Narcissus left the group and found himself alone. In a very clever way, by skillfully repeating the final fragments of Narcissus's sentences, she succeeded in intriguing him to the extent that he asked her to join him.

When Narcissus said: "Let us come together here", Echo replied: "Come together here". She then came out of her hiding place, let herself be carried away by her love and came up to Narcissus. He shook her off roughly, saying: "I will die before you ever lie with me". Her momentum stopped, Echo was dumb-founded; full of shame, she withdrew and again hid away in the depths of the forest. She stopped eating, became anorexic, her flesh melted away little by little, and her bones became as hard as the stones which they ended up resembling. In that part of the myth, Ovid, in a remarkable way, figured out the cause-and-effect relationship between Echo's reactive anorexia, the fact that she turned into something resembling a pile of hardened faeces and the violent physical rejection she suffered at the hands of Narcissus.

The infant's eagerness is broken by a physical, bodily rejection imply-ing, for the child, that his or her surge of affection is bad. Fairbairn (1940)[12] emphasized the fact that physical rejection implies for the child that his or her love is "bad and destructive"; this creates a confusion in the child's mind as to what is good and what is bad, as I pointed out earlier. The child then feels that his or her skin-ego (Anzieu 1974)[13] is full of bad contents that are potentially dangerous for the object.

Clinical practice shows that two different kinds of control can be set up, sometimes coming into play alternately.

The first reaction is similar to Echo's: all drive-related impulses in the child are restricted, any surges felt to be unwelcome are frozen in their tracks; through internalizing the meaning that the object applies to them, the child also feels them to be bad and dangerous.

The second is quite the opposite. The child becomes horrible, similar to the mirror image that the object's reaction sends back, actively "bad" because there is no way of avoiding that outcome, in a last-ditch attempt at remaining in control; manifest destructiveness is then intensified.

Failures in primary satisfaction

A third pattern, which also dates from early childhood and tends to exac-erbate many kinds of destructiveness and violence, has to do with failures in primary satisfaction. For long, it had been thought that this level of satisfaction went without saying and that, in a way, it was a fundamen-tal "given" upon which metapsychology could be constructed. Clinical work with very early experiences in feeding and the structuring of auto-eroticism has shown that this is not the case; the satisfaction of needs, linked to self-preservation (the infant is indeed fed), should not be mis-taken for the experience of satisfaction as a whole and its value as a model.

This depends not only on self-preservation but also on the way in which the object expresses its affective presence and on what it mirrors of the infant's own feelings.

More precisely, the kind of affective presence shown by the object and the pleasure that it takes are necessary for the experience of primary sat-isfaction to be set up because the infant experiences them as a reflection of his or her own satisfaction, which, as a result, becomes an acceptable expe-rience. When the object shows no sign of satisfaction, the infant remains unaware of his or her own pleasure and satisfaction. This implies that some people have no knowledge at all of satisfaction, even though they may experience some kinds of pleasure: the affect of satisfaction, which cannot be mentally set up, remains unconscious.

One of the consequences of failure in the experience of satisfaction and of the exacerbation of primary disappointment (what Winnicott [1974][14] refers to as "tantalizing") is the great difficulty that the individual is in as regards producing the conditions under which a positive primary amalgam of drive-related experiences – a good "binding of the drives" – becomes possible.

Here too, envy in particular is exacerbated and the individual settles into the subjective position of the "eternally dissatisfied", criticizing or attacking what occurs in the name of that dissatisfaction. The experience of satisfaction is vital if the fervor of the drives and the ruthless object relation (Winnicott 1974) – the primary form of drive impulses – can bring together and bind both creativeness and destructiveness. The fervor that is typical of the drives must be able to express itself and obtain satisfaction in order for a basic form of binding of the drives to occur (if this does not happen, erotogenic masochism will tend to replace it but this will lead satisfaction onto the slippery slopes of perverse solutions).

When amalgamating of the drives is unsuccessful, destructiveness tends to become unbound and remain outside any conflict situation – examples of which are violence against the self (for example, in somatic illnesses) or against other people (in some kinds of negativism and antisocial manifestations of violence).

Destructiveness is then exacerbated by the very fact of not being bound; it appears to take place quite openly. Here is an example of psychoanalytical treatment in which issues involving non-satisfaction lay at the very heart of the work.

Paul, 40 years old, was a senior executive, energetic and very impressive in his work. He undertook analysis because he was suffering from a kind of cold depression; he did not (or could no longer) have any "taste for things" and felt that everything he did was futile even though he was usually successful in carrying it out. Before reaching that stage, he would project into the future the time when everything would be better; he built up for himself an ideal picture of what he was going to be like in order, at long last, to feel that he had reached what was right for him. Over the past few years, however, he had begun to draw closer to the fulfillment of his ideals (he had obtained a very significant promotion in the international company for which he worked, he had courted and married a very beautiful woman resembling the one he had dreamt of since his teenage years), so that his feeling of pointlessness was getting stronger and stronger. "What's the use of all this, of all this effort just to get where I already am?" In place of the satisfaction he thought would be his, he felt very disappointed, with the impression that he had let himself be taken in, especially in his work environment, where he felt that he had been "exploited".

When I met him for some preliminary interviews before beginning the analysis, he was in despair, very negative about everything that was going on in his life;

"What's the use of it all?" "And so what?" were the dominant theme.

The beginning of his analysis (with the setting that is quite usual in France: three sessions per week) was marked by a whole series of extramarital adventures. With his wife, he had no feeling of pleasure: "When

I come, I don't feel a thing", he said. Pleasure was there, but he did not experience it as such; the sexual orgasm accompanying ejaculation gave him no feeling of pleasure – he did not feel a thing.

Paul then set off on a whole series of female conquests. With those women, whom he chose because of their sensuality, he did have pleasure during sexual intercourse.

He gave them pleasure and he himself experienced pleasure. But what was striking above all was the fact that, immediately after intercourse, he did not feel well.

Pleasure did not lead to satisfaction: on the contrary, it gave rise to a general feeling of ill-being. Since that feeling went hand in hand with self-reproach, my initial hypothesis was that he was experiencing guilt feelings that were more or less unconscious. That kind of interpretation did give him some relief from his discomfort: identificatory links with his skirt-chaser of a father, famous for his many sexual escapades, could gradually be made. Those too went some way to improving how Paul felt but did not completely resolve his distress. He did, however, begin to get closer to his internal world bereft of any perception of his affects.

In the transference, even though Paul acknowledged that I was "doing a good job" and that he was "feeling better", he experienced me as "cold, not emotionally focused, impervious to [his] suffering and despair". Processing that aspect of the transference led first of all to a link with the relationship between him and his wife.

That beautiful woman, in love with him, the one he had always seen in his dreams as absolutely ideal, began to take on a somewhat different allure. As he gradually got back in contact with his emotions and feelings, Paul tried to talk things over with her and to set up a new kind of dialogue with her in their relationship as man and wife. But things did not turn out as he had expected; his wife, emotionally speaking, was quite a cold person and had little appetite for intimate emotional conversation. As long as he was searching for an ideal, focused on his attempt at narcissistic fulfillment, everything was fine between them but when he began to move toward a more "object" relationship and engage more with his emotions, things took a turn for the worse. Paul had the impression that he was coming up against "a wall of ice", with nothing to get to grips with, "with no feelings", and which "never gave [him] any feedback". The destabilization of their relationship led his wife to request analysis – proof, perhaps, that she was not as cold and unfeeling as Paul made her out to be.

In the analysis, it then became possible to go back in time from the criticisms he made of his wife to those that he had never allowed himself to express concerning his mother. She too had always been for him a "perfect" woman, always true to form; but then he began to see her as suffering from a kind of cold depression, never satisfied, never really happy, unable to experience pleasure and perhaps even to have any real feelings.

He came to the conclusion that she had remained a prisoner of her relationship with her own mother. A certain kind of narcissistic identification with her could then begin to be analyzed. His father's adventures also began to take on another dimension, that of the economy of survival within the atmosphere of cold depression that dominated their life together as a family.

At that point, Paul went through phases of deep depression. His feeling that it was all pointless, which had improved significantly in the first part of the analysis, reappeared; I could perceive the melancholia that underlay his condition, and for several months I was very worried by it. He resisted to have recourse to antidepressants as a solution: he had already taken that kind of medication in the past, but without much improvement. His despair was expressed through a series of important attacks: on the analysis, on his wife, on his mother, on the company he worked for and, in general, on anything that might happen in his life. I mentioned that I was worried because at times I was afraid that he might commit suicide. This was, all the same, always mitigated by the feeling that he preferred the emotional authenticity that he had managed to acquire to the kinds of false-self situations that had so often presided over his life. I felt confident in the way the analysis was progressing and in my own capacity to "survive" those attacks. Paul went through some very painful psychical phases, often fueled by what he felt was the "inhuman" way in which his colleagues were treated at work and by the conflicts he had with his wife. I made use of the various situations of which he spoke during the analysis in order to continue processing the history of his early relationship with his mother. A certain number of elements belonging to what I thought of as his primary relationship with her were still very much part of Paul's situation at that time. The very early aspects of that relationship seemed to have come down through the years, leaving a whole series of marks on Paul's childhood and adolescent years.

To conclude this overview of Paul's clinical trajectory, I must say that he did manage gradually to break free of his agonizing despair as we succeeded in reconstructing the specific features of his early relationship with his mother; this helped him to move on from his need to reproduce these in his current life. What turned out to be decisive in this development was the work we did on the failure of the maternal function of being the "primary mirror" of his emotional life. It was when the despair of ever managing to satisfy his mother came more and more to the fore and when Paul was able to connect that, not with any of her own features in particular, but with the vicissitudes of the relationship between his mother and her own parents that the improvement in his condition became more stable.

Moreover, Paul was a very gifted analysand and very satisfying from my point of view. This was the case even when he was going through some very intense negativistic phases – he remained very stimulating with respect to my analyzing function. I think he sensed the intense cathexis that I made of our work together; he was able to find in that cathexis the wherewithal to enable him to have a new kind of experience. I should point out, too, that his relationship with his wife improved significantly thanks to the combined action of the two analyses; in that domain too, he gradually came to have experiences that were more and more satisfying.

The "survival" of the object and the failure to survive

I shall now discuss briefly the fourth and final clinical problem situation that has its roots in the individual's past history. It is paradigmatic and central to this kind of situation, which is why I have used it in the title of this chapter. We have in fact already come across it in the various other clinical situations that I have described, because it is involved in all kinds of problems that have to do with destructiveness.

I am referring to the failure of what Winnicott called the "survival" of the object, which is necessary for the capacity to make "use of an object".

Once primary drive manifestations have been sufficiently bound through experiences of satisfaction, the question of a secondary differentiation of drive impulses arises – that between love and hate (I am not convinced that this is the best way to express it). According to Winnicott, the decisive experience is that of the encounter with the object's capacity for "surviving" the primary fervor of the drives, the ruthless nature of their primitive forms, and the earliest manifestations of destructiveness and anger. In a perhaps more "Freudian" terminology, we could say that all of this has to do with cruelty (Cupa 2007)[15] and perhaps even with a fundamental kind of violence (Bergeret 1984 op cit). According to Winnicott, it is the object's response, i.e. its capacity not to retaliate in the face of what it might be tempted to see as a destructive attack, which is decisive for the individual's subsequent ability to distinguish between the internal and the external object. The internal object is the one that is "destroyed" by the fervor of the drives; it withdraws or takes reprisals. The external object is the one that "survives", remaining sufficiently steadfast in its emotional stance.

The experience of "survival of the object" thus enables a distinction to be drawn between the two ways in which the object is present – the object of hallucination and the object of perception – given that the experience of the found–created object merges them together. This in turn means that a psychical topography can be set up in which the world of fantasy, in which the object is destroyed, can be distinguished from that of objective objects, which "survive" destruction. The possibility of destroying the object in and through fantasy goes some way toward pacifying destructiveness or offering it non-destructive means of expression. That is the fundamental paradox of destructiveness and its exacerbation: it is exacerbated when it does not reach its goal in fantasy and it is exacerbated when it is confused with actual destruction. Here again, it is the failure to satisfy the drive impulses in a "psychical" way that leads to the actual carrying out of something: the failure to set up a destructive fantasy is an incitement to actual destruction.

Conversely, topographical confusion between the world of psychical representations and fantasy on the one hand (Donnet & Green 1973[16]; Janin 1989[17]) and, on the other, that of objective objects (which are no longer "objective", given that topographical confusion) has a traumatic effect and tends to exacerbate the manifestation of destructiveness and forms of violence against the self or against the other person.

The experience of the survival of the object makes it possible to move from the "relationship with the object", in which the "external" object and the object of the drives – the "internal" object, as it is called – are merged together, toward the "use of the object", in which the external object is seen "objectively", i.e. without any infantile omnipotence, so that it can be put to use like a truly external object, distinct from that of the drives.

Another way of putting it would be to say that there is a movement from the object "perceived" as external to the object "conceived of" as such, i.e. conceived of as an other-subject. The use of the object thus represents the paradoxical prototype of the intersubjective relation.

Conversely, if that topographical differentiation fails, so that the capacity to be alone in the presence of the object becomes more difficult, this could well play an objective part in manifestations of relation-based violence. When the object survives, the topographical distribution – "Object, I love you because you survive" and "I destroy you all the time in my unconscious fantasy" (I can do without you, in the sense of an alienating form of dependence) – makes it possible to set up a conflict of ambivalence, which is the strongest of all barriers against expressions of violence. I shall now describe the vagaries of an analysis in which the issue of the analyst's "survival" contributed to the patient's capacity to move beyond the "non-survival" in the past of her primary objects.

Noire was a 35-year-old woman who requested an appointment with me to discuss her overall state of distress. In our first meeting, I felt her to be somewhat strange.

Although she was a high-ranking member of the legal profession, married with two children, and therefore appeared to be socially well adapted, I felt that she had a kind of psychotic contact that went beyond that of a false self. In fact, my impression was that I could not make any real contact with her at all. In the initial interviews, she did not look at other than via very brief glances, when her face would light up with a "little-girl" kind of smile, in stark contrast to the very stern attitude that she usually adopted. I therefore began seeing her three times a week in a face-to-face setting; about a year later, the three weekly sessions were of the traditional kind, with the patient lying on the couch.

From the very beginning, one feature of the sessions was the somewhat strange "associativity" that she presented. With her eyes closed, she would plunge into some kind of "vision" that became a daydream – in reporting these, she would always begin by saying: "I see...". I found it very difficult to remain in contact with her; I was obliged to enter into her daydreaming in an attempt to preserve at least a minimal link with her. Those daydreams led us in the end to a grave, beside which a young girl (no doubt the patient herself) was handcuffed, with the handcuffs going all the way down into the grave. Tied to the dead person? The corpse turned out to be that of a woman, who little by little took on the features of the patient's grandmother, no doubt the first representation of a transference link.

The daydreaming became almost delusional: Noire said that she was convinced that her grandmother had been killed by her mother and her family. Gradually, thanks to these "visions" and to my elucidating many details of them, part of her past history began to become clearer.

Noire was the younger of two girls, and her family was of noble origin, living in the Paris region. Her maternal grandmother ruled over the entire family in a despotic way; it was only with her paternal grandmother (the grandmother in the grave) that Noire received any degree of warmth and tenderness – but this lasted only until she was seven or eight years old, when a quarrel broke out and that grandmother never visited them again. Noire remained very attached to her, all the same, and, since she did not live very far away, she saw her once or twice a year.

As a daughter of the lord of the manor in that region, Noire did not adapt well to school; most of the time she was on her own, sad and rejected by the other children, with whom she quarreled a lot. Her family was never really well liked, and that had an impact on the kind of relationship with the other children that she had as a girl – they made her "pay" for her family. It was very difficult to reconstruct those few elements of her past. Noire was not only very embarrassed when she talked about it, but also full of shame and reticence. As our work was progressing and the contact between us improved, I invited her to lie down on the couch, in conformity with the traditional psychoanalytical setting. Although the analyzing situation was still threatened by derealization because of the pressure of her "visions" and daydreams, some "real" dreams did begin to appear. In one of these, Noire was in a mountainous region, with snow all around. In the distance, she saw her family going away, leaving her behind, all alone. The footprints in the snow were gradually erased. She woke up, feeling very anxious. I tried to make a connection with the analyzing situation – now that she was lying on the couch, she could not see me any more – but she did not react to that. It was another dream that gave rise to a kind of delusional transference.

In that dream, Noire was in a trench, being "bombarded" with pieces of bricks. The fireplace in my waiting room is made of large stones, and I suggested that there might be a link between this and her dream – perhaps she felt that she was going to be "bombarded" during the sessions. She remained silent for the rest of the session, then left without looking at me or shaking my hand, contrary to what usually took place between us at the end of each session.

As soon as I went to fetch her in the waiting room for her next session, I sensed that something had changed. She walked in front of me, a determined look on her face, without looking at me or saying hello. As she lay down on the couch, she said that she "was going to show me how [she] really was, because [she] was fed up being kind, [she] was not at all a kindly person". That was the beginning of a series of sessions in which she treated me in a tyrannical way, forbidding me in a very confrontational manner to say anything at all. I was at times amazed by the vigor with which she would yell: "Be quiet!" at me – or, occasionally: "Say something!" She explained that she liked records: "You switch the player on and it talks or sings, you switch it off and it falls silent". I understood that that was how I was supposed to be in her sessions – speaking or keeping quiet, depending on the "order" I was given. At that time, I felt that this had something to do with a "malleable medium" (Roussillon 1991), and I agreed to go along with it without any interpretative retaliation.

Noire went through some very painful phases that were also marked by a great deal of destructiveness. Then she refused to go on lying on the couch; she wanted to sit on the chair again but without my seeing her – she therefore demanded that I turn the chair round so that her back would be toward me. She felt more protected by the back of the chair, less exposed to my gaze or to what I might say – which she felt to be extremely intrusive. She was, however, unable to turn the chair round by herself because it was too heavy for her. I thought that it would be a good idea to come to some arrangement, so I offered her an armchair on castors that would be easy to turn round. That made her fly into a terrible rage, the reason for which I discovered only later, when I was able to make a connection between the armchair on castors and the wheelchair that her maternal grandmother used. It was sitting in that wheelchair that her grandmother, who was disabled, tyrannized the whole mansion, forcing everybody – and in particular Noire's father– to do what she wanted, ruling over them with an iron fist.

Without meaning to and without even realizing it, by suggesting that Noire sit in the armchair with castors, I had in fact "interpreted" a transference that was underpinned by Noire's narcissistic identification with that tyrannical grandmother.

Once I began to understand that the work of the analysis became easier. I still had to talk or keep quiet depending on the orders that I was given, but the overall atmosphere of the sessions was less violent and the terror which she made me feel and which she experienced in relation to me – began to diminish significantly.

When Noire agreed to lie down on the couch again, another phase of the analysis could begin. What became the key to our work together was made clear when she began to speak about her early childhood. According to her mother, she had been a frail baby, sickly, difficult and quick-tempered. Her older sister, however, was apparently from the very beginning much more satisfactory and warmly cathected by her mother. Noire's birth was a disappointment – she was a girl, not a boy.

This was confirmed later when her little brother was born. When she was about 18 months old, both girls fell seriously ill; her sister died, and as a result her mother became severely depressed. It was at that point that the paternal grandmother became so important to Noire and she quickly became very attached to her. Later, her mother said to Noire that she would have preferred her to die and her sister to survive.

It gradually became possible to interpret her fantasy of having killed her sister and made her mother depressed and dead-like; neither of them had "survived" Noire's destructive attacks. That interpretation took a lot of processing because on several occasions Noire's mother did not "survive" her drive impulses; it did nonetheless bring about a fundamental shift in Noire's relationship to the outside world, with a quite remarkable drop in her violence and destructiveness. Conversely, the important factor in that analysis seemed to me to lie in the lengthy test of survival to which Noire subjected me. During her tyrannical phase, and in addition to what she was putting me through in a kind of repetition of what the maternal grandmother had done to all the family, Noire was attempting to test my ability to preserve a psychoanalytical attitude in the face of her repeated attacks – she was trying to see if I could "survive" her destructiveness. I think that it was only when she came to realize that my creativeness had not been destroyed, that I was not going to retaliate nor become depressed, and that, even if I continued most of the time to obey her instructions, I still remained free and able from time to time to ignore them, that Noire began to reveal material from her past that made the ongoing process meaningful. It is indeed worth pointing out that it was when I obeyed her instructions, while at the same time remaining alive and creative, that Noire seemed to discover me as existing independently from her; she then became able to perceive my otherness, to see me as an other-subject, which, in the initial stages of that analysis, I most certainly was not.

Conclusion

What is interesting in borderline and extreme situations of subjectivity is that they force us, in our attempt to account for them metapsychologically, to go back to the very fundamentals of our theory and take a closer look at it. That is when what appears to be a primary "given" has to be examined again to see whether what looks as though it has always been there is perhaps in fact the product of an early phase of intersubjective history – and maybe even "prehistory". What seems to be due to the particular individual alone has to be looked at afresh since it may perhaps be the result of the internalization of what was initially an intersubjective pattern – or "inter- psychical", if that term is preferred.

Clinical practice teaches us also that what causes our thinking and mental processing to break down is the occurrence of the "identical to itself" phenomenon.

Whenever a process, a drive impulse or a psychical structure appears to be "identical to itself", to "go without saying", it can no longer be worked through; it loses its capacity for mentalization and symbolization. This is what, in thinking processes, is referred to as perceptual identity. I tend to think that the "death drive" is manifested in and by that identity equivalence between a thing and itself. The unconscious no longer exists, there is no longer a gap between a thing and its representation in the mind – and therefore there is no more interplay, no more space for work. Such are the threats that "silent" forms of violence impose on the mind.

That kind of violence need not be "raucous", it does not have to be expressed as violence; it is a kind of violence that belongs to what is presented as being "real in itself", a Real against which the mind is shattered and shatters all hope of making something meaningful. That is why also, in my view, as clinicians we have to be aware of the threat that treating a thing and the way in which it is expressed as identical represents for our clinical thinking. Violence comes from processes that abrade differences and present identity as being intangible. It is on that basis that I have tried to develop a concept of destructiveness that becomes meaningful in a dialectical context between an individual and his or her environment, giving to the responses of the environment their rightful place in the exacerbation and eventual outcome of destructiveness.

In this chapter, I have explored four kinds of traumatic situations in which certain particular features of the responses and reactions of the environment to the individual's drive impulses have impeded the integration and processing of these.

As a result, either directly or in response to this, destructiveness is manifested to an even greater degree. In clinical situations like these, binding of the drives becomes difficult to set up, and ambivalence, rather than being expressed as a conflict, tends to generate paradoxical patterns that imprison the individual in various kinds of existential deadlock.

One of the peculiarities of Paul's analysis concerns the use that he could make of his sexuality, a defensive use, masking his narcissistic difficulty. This remark opens the way to a wider reflection on the place of sexuality in the clinic of narcissistic-identity suffering and, beyond that, in psychoanalytic thought itself, which is the focus of the next chapter.

Notes

1 Roussillon, R. (1995). "Violence subjective et paradoxalité". *Journal de la Psychanalyse de L Enfant*, 18: 69–82, Paris: PUF.
2 Roussillon, R. (1991). *Paradoxes et situations limites de la psychanalyse*. Paris: PUF.
3 Anzieu, D. (1975a). *La résistance paradoxale: L'inconscient et le groupe*. Paris: Dunod; Anzieu, D. (1975b). "Le transfert paradoxal". *Nouvelle Revue de Psychanalyse*, 12: 49–72, Paris: NRF.
4 Roussillon, R. (1991). *Paradoxes et situations limites de la psychanalyse*. Paris: PUF. Roussillon, R. (1995). "Violence subjective et paradoxalité". *Journal de la Psychanalyse de L Enfant*, 18: 69–82.
5 Freud, S. (1916). "Some character-types met with in psycho-analytic work". *SE*, 14: 311.
6 Bergeret, J. (1984). *La violence fondamentale*. Paris: Dunod.
7 Freud, S. (1937). "Analysis terminable and interminable". *SE*, 23: 209.
8 Bion, W.R. (1970). *Attention and interpretation*. London: Tavistock. [(1984). London: Karnac.]
9 Ferenczi, S. (1929). "The unwelcome child and his death instinct". In: *Final contributions to the problems and methods of psycho-analysis*. London: Karnac.
10 Hopkins, J. (1987). "Failure of the holding relationship: Some effects of physical rejection on the child's attachment and on his inner experience". *Journal of Child Psychotherapy*, 13: 5–17.
11 Freud, S. (1941[1938]). "Findings, ideas, problems". *SE*, 23: 299.
12 Fairbairn, W.R.D. (1940). "Schizoid factors in the personality". In: *Psychoanalytic studies of the personality*. London: Tavistock, 1952.
13 Anzieu, D. (1974). Le moi-peau. *Nouvelle Revue de Psychanalyse*, 8:195–209.
14 Winnicott, D.W. (1974). "Fear of breakdown". In C. Winnicott et al. (Eds), *Psycho-analytic explorations*. Cambridge, MA: Harvard University Press, 1989.
15 Cupa, D. (2007). *La tendresse et la cruauté*. Paris: Dunod.
16 Donnet, J.-L., & Green, A. (1973). *L'enfant de Ça*. Paris: Minuit.
17 Janin, C. (1989). "L'empiétement psychique: un problème de clinique et de technique psychanalytiques". In: *Psychanalyse: questions pour demain*, 151–160. Paris: PUF.

3 Sexualization and desexualization in psychoanalysis

The sexual remains one of the crucial themes in contemporary psycho-analysis; it also remains one of the "shibboleths" of Freudian psycho-analysis. But its central importance is in fact under threat from certain developments in Anglophone psychoanalysis that, especially under the banner of narcissism and "self" analysis, are strangely diminishing its impact and scope of reference. It is also a theme that has returned to "fash-ion" through the centenary of the writing of the *Three Essays* (1905)[1] and more generally in the psychoanalytic literature, in all the discussions con-cerning the necessity and pertinence of the concept of the drive as it has been developing in the international literature.

Despite these debates, yet perhaps even more so revealed by them, in Francophone psychoanalysis, the sexual remains a major reference-point, even a defining one.

But is this reference necessarily clear and unambiguous?

Although all psychoanalysts acknowledge its central position in meta-psychology, do they agree about what precisely it covers or does the appar-ent consensus (in France) that seems to unite them under its emblem in fact conceal some divergences as to the essence of what the concept involves?

Often, and the same probably applies to many concepts that have this same defining quality, the sexual and what it covers seems self-evident and to need no definition, as if its mere utterance sufficed to describe it and subdivide its issues.

My reflection starts from the opposite assertion, which is that this is a highly problematic concept that probably still needs to be refined in con-temporary psychoanalytic theory and thought, and that there is a real dif-ficulty in the use and reference that can be made of it by psychoanalysts in practical terms.

The problem

First of all, it seems to me important to remember that psychoanalysis is not and could never be a "sexology", that is a knowledge of the sexual and sexuality, nor a "psychology" of the sexual or sexuality.

DOI: 10.4324/9781003198710-3

What it means instead is thinking about the role of the sexual in the psychic process and even more specifically in psychic functioning during the session while taking account of its specific characteristics.

It also seems to me, although of course I will return to this essential point, that the evolutionary trend in the theorization of the sexual in psychoanalytic metapsychology emphasizes sufficiently the effort to adjust the theorization to the needs of the metapsychology "of the psychic course of events", as Freud wrote in 1911, that is to say of the psychic process, and specifically the psychic process during the session.

In other words, it seems to me that one of the lines of development in the psychoanalytic theorization of the sexual is increasingly directed at inscribing it in what I call a "metapsychology of processes".

This means, more specifically, that the position of the sexual and sexuality in psychoanalytic thought increasingly seems to have to be evaluated by the yardstick of the issues of symbolization and subjective appropriation that vectorize psychoanalytic practice and the psychic work of the session. It is according to and starting from the position and the role of the sexual in symbolization and subjectivation that psychoanalysis makes its contribution to an understanding of human sexuality.

This problematic and these difficulties underlie the detours, even bifurcations, that the concept has undergone throughout the history of psychoanalytic thought and its various applications, which seem to me to tend increasingly to separate sexuality as a behavior from the sexual as a specific psychic process of cathexis.

At the outset, and this is the first aspect of the evolution and therefore also the difficulty, the sexual and sexuality do not overlap, no longer overlap, even if they are not totally disconnected either. There is some sexual beyond sexuality, some sexuality apprehended as "sexual behavior" and, moreover, there is some non-sexual in sexuality itself, as the sexualization of certain psychic functions or functioning found in clinical practice sufficiently emphasizes.

The same applies to the connection between the sexual and the drive.

Here too there is no exact overlap between terms. Freud was able to define the self-preservative drives that are "drive-based" but can oppose the "sexual" drives, in which he was able to describe some forms of transformation of the sexual drives that can themselves "be desexualized" in their progress and their transposition.

The mere statement of these formulations is enough to convey at the outset the complexity of the issues involved and the subtleties of how they are treated.

I cannot claim to encompass all this complexity in the present framework of reflection and I would be satisfied for my part with pointing out certain aspects.

I will start with the assertion, presented as my first line of reflection, that *the sexual is not and could never be similar to itself in psychoanalysis*, that it is necessarily the site of a diversion that determines it less "in itself" than as a form of process that is specifically characterized by its metaphorizing capacity, its generative capacity.

In other words, it seems to me that the evolution of psychoanalytic thought leads us to place increasing emphasis on a processual dimension of the sexual, on the sexualization or desexualization processes that psychic material is likely to encounter "in the course of psychic events".

But before reaching that stage and to be well placed to do so, it is necessary to recall certain points that are essential here.

The identical and the different: toward the primal scene

Although the drive is born in/of difference, and born of what is nonidentical to itself, it tends to restore identity: at its origin, it is pleasure in the same, pleasure in discovering the same, the identical, whether this is "identity of perception" according to the primary-process model, or "identity of thought" according to the more relative and moderate secondary-process model.

The sexual is engendered by difference but its primary meaning consists in the desire to reduce difference, the attempt to find the identical in the other, to produce the identical from the other.

It is only in its historical and then intrapsychic course that the drive integrates the need to recognize and accept its own origin, that it can be constituted as a pleasure taken in/by difference, that it "discovers" difference and its organizing role, that it discovers that it is the "product" of this difference, that it discovers and recognizes that it is the "sexual" outcome of a *sexion*.

We know that in this process, the encounter with the question of the father's position – the paternal value and the models it conveys – is essential. It is the father's symbolic function that makes it possible to recognize the value of the pleasure of difference, the pleasure taken in and by difference. It is the paternal metaphor that makes it possible to transcend the mastery of the pleasure in the same; it is this that blocks the return to origins, to the identical, and opens the way to a pleasure taken in and by difference.

From then, the sexual has to combine and dialectize three forms of difference to be organized, to allow it to unfold and assume its full meaning.

To state it quickly, and in a concise formula, sexual difference engenders a generational difference that itself then engenders a difference in the sexual, and it is based on the play of this three-fold difference that the question of identity then has to be tackled.

It is in the first encounter with the object that the sexual is born within a relationship in which the "primal separation" of birth is constantly "reduced" by a relationship "in duplicate" or "in the mirror", and, therefore, "primary homosexual" relationship.

An initial component of the sexual is thus produced in the object's presence, as Freud broadly anticipates when he writes: "No one who has seen a baby sinking back satiated from the breast and falling asleep with flushed cheeks and a blissful smile can escape the reflection that this picture persists as a prototype of the expression of sexual satisfaction in later life" (1905, p. 182). In this scene, the object is present and takes place in the first form of sexual satisfaction.

However, this first form encounters some obstacles that also contribute to structuring it.

There are some periods of the absence of the object, with the discontinuity they introduce into the bond and the subject's need to confront them; we know that this need is the source of the autoerotisms.

There is also the inevitable encounter in the maternal mode of presence with some heterogeneous aspects that are alien to the baby's psyche, broadly enigmatic to him, and connected with the impact of the mother's adult sexual organization. It is this heterogeneous element that introduces the question of the father and thus at the same time a difference of sex and the sexual.

But it is only later, in the shaping of the "primal scene", that these various forms of difference can be represented and organized around the presentation of generational difference.

This is why the "primal scene", considered not as a fantasy but as an organizing "concept" of the psyche, is so essential to our approach to the sexual, is foundational for it.

The "primal scene" not only structures sexual difference and generational difference in a unified metaphor, but it also integrates at its core the question of the child's mode of presence, that of the difference between infantile and adult sexuality.

It integrates in an organized form all the facts relating to the problem posed to the psyche by the sexual; it also integrates the question of the identical, one parent at least being of the same sex, as well as that of difference.

With the concept of the "primal scene", the sexual is thus forged from the differences it organizes; it both results from these and produces them, the sexual is then what makes difference "generative", what allows the generative value of difference to be released.

As has often been observed, the primal scene thus seeks to shape the question of identity based on the presentation of the question of origin.

Origin of the sexual

But the question of the origin of the self is intensified by that of the "origin of the sexual" itself, which also then has to be reflected in the symbolization process.

The question of the origin of the sexual is at the heart of the debate that divides proponents of "source-object" theory (such as Laplanche, in his theory of the enigmatic signifier) from adherents of a theory of the drive that is internal and "biological" from the outset (as Green argued in the debate between these two authors a few years ago).

Does the sexual come "from within", from the somatic foundation of the psyche, or does it come "from outside", from the object or from the relationship with it, with its otherness?

It seems to me that this opposition is interesting insofar as it discovers one of the oppositions revealed by clinical practice in connection with various forms of "sexual theories". But to assume its entire interest, this opposition must be interpreted or even transcended within a "metapsychology of processes" that simultaneously posits the origin as undecidable and the sexual as emerging from the meeting-point between inside and outside, their chiasmus and the work of their differentiation.

It seems to me that the origin of the sexual can only be well conceived metapsychologically as a process of *différance*, a differentiation process that is carried out starting from an initial amalgam in which self and object are mingled and enmeshed.

The sexual arises when outside and inside, the subject and its object, meet, collide and fuse, "amalgamate", to produce this "primary material" of the psyche mentioned by Freud various times in his work from 1900, which is later cathected by the drive impulses.

Although the sexual is initially produced in the encounter between the subject and the other-subject object, it is only manifested as such, understood as such in the resumption and incorporative internalization, as indicated by the theory of anaclitic (leaning on) and autoerotism, or conversely in an evacuation and an excorporation, a subjective discharge.

The internalization process manifests the drive cathexis of experience, it manifests its sexualization and it makes it perceptible by separating it out from self-preservation.

The oscillation we have just described, the oscillation of an experience between inside and outside of an internal, internalized experience, characterizes a primary level of subjective appropriation of the experience of the sexual.

This in its turn will have to be newly understood, reflected and secondarized. It seems to me that it is the role of the primal seduction fantasy to produce the vagaries of this second resumption.

The seduction fantasy will tend to rock from one side or another the terms of this basic dual polarity; it tends to resolve the undecidability of the origin by assigning a precise origin to the birth of the drive.

A "sexual" seduction therefore occurs every time one or other of the two amalgamated terms tends to be ousted, whether the sexual is represented only as a biological effect and therefore a kind of "biological seduction", by the biological, or is conceived only as an effect of the encounter with the object, a seduction by the object.

The sexual "seduces", just as it must be able to be conceived as seduced; it is perhaps that which is defined only by its overflowing of dichotomous categories, beyond "simple" oppositions, precisely that which can only be bound with difficulty by bipolar representational systems.

The difficulty I have just indicated also encourages us not to seek a "positivized" definition of the sexual, not to tackle directly the question of its definition, but rather to seek to define it from the way in which it functions in the psyche of specific subjects, or from the way in which it has "functioned" in the history of psychoanalytic thought, the second seeking to eliminate the impact of the first.

This encourages us to reconsider some milestones that are particularly centered around the question of the impact of the sexual in the treatment.

The injured sexual and the diverted sexual

Schematically at the origin of psychoanalytic thought, the sexual is that from which or by which "we suffer through reminiscence".

The sexual appears at the outset as an injured sexual, as a traumatized, injured sex, as a suffering sex, even, we will return to this point later, as a sex in suffering.

The 1895–1896 etiological theory of the neuroses presents the cause of neurosis as the result of an inadequate or incomplete sexuality. It is traumatic precisely to the extent that it has lost its naturalness.

Either its discharge is hindered, as in the theory of hysteria, in which affect remains "jammed", or, to the extent that the discharge is inadequate, the malfunctionings of sexuality in current neuroses are presented by Freud as the effect of sexuality in which discharge does not occur in the "right" place or is carried out "without an object" beyond the object. In the 1895 theory, Freud presents psychasthenia as the effect either of onanism or of various forms of incomplete sexuality – "coitus interruptus" or restricted coitus.

Although the connection with "genital" sexuality is still very much present, and as we can see this is the lived experience that underlies the symptoms, by contrast the symptomatology already "metaphorizes" sexuality, only evoking it symbolically.

The disconnection of the sexual from sexuality, considered a genital sexual behavior, then enters the theorization with increasing emphasis, without ever becoming completely detached from it.

As the introduction of an infantile "oral" or "anal" sexuality confirms still further, anality or orality is only "sexual", in the sense of sexuality, as a result of their offshoots in the "preliminary pleasures" of adult sexuality or its forms of perversion; they very quickly overflow the field of sexuality as such to designate relational models.

The idea of a "phallic" sexuality thus forms the pivotal bridge between "infantile" and "genital" sexuality.

In the term "infantile sexuality", its "sexual" quality is initially defined only as a result of its future evolution into sexuality.

Oral or anal infantile sexuality is only said to be sexual because its traces are later found in adult sexuality or its perversions.

It is indeed always, at least at the outset, adult sexuality that serves as a referent to the sexual, and then in a second derivation that which relates to orality or anality is retroactively defined as "infantile sexual" on this initial foundation.

The sexual and the drive: primary sexualization

It is this diversion from the sexual that also introduces the idea of "drive", and which makes it theoretically necessary. The concept of the drive indicates a disparity between the sexual and sexuality itself, a disparity between "adult" and infantile sexuality.

Sexuality from this point is nothing more than a specific instance of drive activity, a specific case of the "sexual" that will instead then be better defined by the drive.

But the theory of the drives, the first drive theory, introduces in its turn a disparity between the drive and the sexual and sexuality. There are the sexual drives and the so-called self-preservative drives, which are not yet "sexual".

However, the analysis of conflicts such as the hysterical blindness analyzed in 1910 demonstrates that self-preservation can be "sexualized".

In summary, we still suffer from the sexual, but this time it is the sexualization of a field that is not essentially sexual.

Thus, the first drive theory simultaneously restricts the field of the sexual – not everything is sexual – and conceives its possible extension. Although everything is not "sexual", by contrast everything can be sexualized and thus become sexual through this metaphorizing diversion.

Thus, we begin to move gradually from a sexual considered "in itself" to a sexual that appears to have issued from a process of "sexual" cathexis, a mode of functioning or a function that is "sexualized" as a result of this cathexis.

Although everything is not sexual, everything can begin to be "sexualized" and the model of a conflict that has emerged from this sexualization can begin to be developed.

The phallic model of sexualization and integration

As I began to indicate above, the pivot of this "sexualization" is so-called phallic sexuality.

One of the key characteristics of the "phallic" organization is to generalize sexualization, to apprehend everything, in a concern for integration and completeness, in terms of the binary phallic/castrated opposition, that is to say to interpret and "sexualize" everything according to this model.

In the infantile economy, this need corresponds to the need to inscribe everything in the orbit of the pleasure-unpleasure principle but also in that of a sexual identity, that is one characterized by difference, thus to enmesh the question of pleasure with that of difference, to transfer gradually from the pleasure of the same, the pleasure of the double, to that of the pleasure of difference, taken in difference.

What matters to us here relates to the fact that this conception of the phallic impulse introduces the concept of a sexualization process that transcends the sexual/non-sexual opposition, thus considered to oppose to each other "in itself" categories, to define a process of inscription in e sexual domain as a basic modality of binding and integration, in particular, from a metaphorizing process based on sex and the sexual.

Although not everything is sexual, everything will have to be inscribed primarily in the coordinates of the sexual to be libidinized and thus cathected and integrated.

The scope of the shift thus described is enough indication that it contains some fundamental narcissistic issues. It is also probably based on their understanding that the concept of narcissism will be elucidated.

Before being fully elucidated as such, narcissism needed to be recognized as phallic-narcissistic.

However, from the point that the sexualization process is conceived, the first drive theory proves untenable. There can no longer be any opposition between the sexual drives and the self-preservative drives, to the extent that the self-preservative functions must also be "sexualized" in the process of integration.

As a result, the opposition tends to oscillate within the sexual that then covers the entire field, between the sexual drives of the ego – ego libido – and sexual drives directed at objects – object libido. This becomes the second drive theory, the second because, contrary to what is sometimes asserted, there are in fact three in Freud's work.

The drive is either "sexual", narcissistic-sexual, taking the ego or its attributes as an object, or it is "objectal-sexual", taking the object as a drive goal.

There is no more specificity of the sexual, there is no longer a field reserved to the sexual, at least as concerns the primary cathexis and the functioning of the primary processes.

And the potential question becomes that of desexualization, then that of non-sexualization, of the failure of that primary sexualization.

Without this always being very clear to him or his successors, the evolution of Freud's thinking toward the third drive theory will be carried out in the direction imposed by this implicit theoretical "constraint".

To conceive the secondary "desexualization" process is to conceive the organization of secondarity and the problem of the super-ego, and specifically the post-phallic super-ego; we will return to this question later.

To consider the problem of non-sexualization, the failure of the primary sexualization process, is to consider one of the aspects of the death drive, the problem of the failure of drive fusion. The experiences "beyond the pleasure principle" are ones in which the primary libidinization process has failed at least in part. The nature of the trauma changes; it is no longer connected only to an overflowing of the drives, it can also be connected with an effraction and a failure of primary binding by the sexual.

The third drive theory, that is to say the life drive/death drive opposition, entails a "processual" theory of the drives; with this, the picture of the problematic of the sexual in Freudian psychoanalysis is now fully on view. It also involves, and we will return to this point, an analysis of the organizational modalities of the drive.

This is what I must now develop to continue to present my questions.

The model of sexualization by libidinal co-excitation

In this conception, the sexual is no longer only a first and "constitutional" "order"; psychic integration rests on the binding capacity of Eros, the life drive, which is revealed particularly in the concept of libidinal co-excitation.

The model of libidinal co-excitation provides a different model for the sexualization of psychic processes; it extends and amplifies the model of phallic sexualization.

Libidinal co-excitation refers to the process by which a psychic experience is "sexualized" to be bound at a primary stage, particularly when it does not directly entail satisfaction, or not sufficiently.

The libidinal co-excitation described in relation to masochism only appears then as a particular case of a much more general process, which can be defined as that of the necessity of a primary binding or a primary libidinization of psychic experiences.

Its description in relation to masochism results from the especially paradoxical shift that it then makes, in which it has the task of converting an experience of initial unpleasure into an experience of pleasure.

But it works progressively on all psychic experiences, and this is an essential characteristic of infantile sexuality; it "must" be able to work to bind these.

It represents the imperative to inscribe psychic experiences within the pleasure-unpleasure principle, an inscription necessary for integrating and binding these psychically within subjectivity; it represents the fundamental vector of subjective appropriation, its categorical imperative.

From this point, the characteristics of infantile sexuality must be conceived in terms of this fundamental appropriative task, in the direction of the phallic-narcissistic organization that represents the culmination of this "entirely sexual" process.

Everything has to go through the sexual to be assimilable, which is why although not everything is sexual, there must be some sexual in everything, such is the constraint of the primary process. But it is also an imperative of subjective appropriation, an imperative of the subjectivation process.

To be able to be subjective, the subject's experience must first be inscribed in the sphere of the pleasure principle, and this is carried out by means of its sexualization.

What eludes this process of integration and binding then appears threatened by the mastery of the repetition compulsion, by what are said to be forms of the death drive, beyond the pleasure principle, those which concern what is failing subjective appropriation. We will have cause to return to this point.

Secondary desexualization

It is then clear that such a process can only be maintained if, in another psychic system, a secondary desexualization process simultaneously operates, to which we must return.

Desexualization does not consist in withdrawing the primary sexual cathexis; it is only "secondary", concerns only one psychic system, that of the secondary process; it is a partial, relative desexualization, which concerns only the mode of drive fulfillment, not the foundations of the cathexis.

Classically, the work of desexualization is carried out under the aegis of the super-ego, which differentiates its modes of drive fulfillments.

The post-phallic super-ego has to differentiate between what can be realized in representation, that which must be realized only in thought or in words, and that which can also be realized in the act.

It raises the possibility of other modes of realization than those of the act (the hallucinatory fulfillment of desire or its interactive equivalents), that is to say the possibility of a "desexualizing", even sublimatory, work of metaphorization.

Sublimation is then conceived as a mode of realization that takes the representation, the mere representation, as a new and only drive goal. Representation then ceases to be the means or medium by which the drive represents its object; it becomes the very object in which the drive is satisfied.

This process is absolutely fundamental to the organization of symbolization; this is what makes the symbolization work so necessary to the drive economy. From this point of view, the sexuality appears as a language, a kind of body language, speaking of love and kind of desire.

To desexualize is to make do, in the name of the reality principle, with symbolically representing the drive fulfillment; it is diverting the realization with the aid of successive displacements that provide "distance" from the first source of the drive, which metaphorize it, change it beyond recognition and repress it. To desexualize is to emerge from the hallucinatory realization of the desire or its equivalents; it is to emerge from the necessity of the identity of perception to adapt to the identity of thought.

Desexualization and defusion

We must not, therefore, confuse this process, which "secondarizes" the drive, with the mode of "desexualization" that is only what results from the operation of the death drive, for which the term drive "defusion" has instead traditionally been used.

This "desexualization" is only a form of unbinding, of primary drive defusion. It thus only demonstrates the "poor quality" of the primary binding by the libidinal co-excitation, a poor quality that prohibits its later secondarization and therefore threatens its integration.

The question of this "poor quality" raises, as we know, the entire question of excess, abuse and trauma; it raises the question of an excitation that does not achieve its organization into a true drive – presupposing a minimal organization and, in particular, an object/source differentiation – or its binding into a representable drive form.

This has led to the prevailing idea that the drive is also no longer to be considered an entity "in itself" but rather something that results from an organizational mode of excitation. It then becomes theoretically necessary, to differentiate various levels of organization of excitation in the drive and in desire.

In the light of this evolution in the paradigms of the theorization, we can observe how the first conception of the sexual has evolved.

Although we still suffer from the sexual, this is now a sexual that cannot be organized as such, in its process, in its beating, its pulsation.

We still suffer from the sexual but, although we can always suffer from the excess of the sexual, from sexual abuse, we also now suffer from the lack of being sexualized.

The processual sexual and the object

It can easily be observed that the understanding of the sexual in terms of the process dynamics of sexualization/desexualization "transcends" a certain number of difficulties connected with a "naturalistic" definition of sexuality and the sexual; it also transcends, by framing it differently, the genital/pregenital opposition, leading to a conception of sexuality connected with the work of binding and symbolization and with its boundaries.

It allows the sexual and sexuality to be connected, but without being trapped in the alternative of a sexual considered proceeding solely from biology or the object-relationship. To the contrary, it is inscribed in a conception that takes the drive/object pair as the fundamental organizer of metapsychology. For such a process implies that the question of the object is posed; it makes it unavoidable.

In fact, whatever the "achievement" of the binding and symbolization capacities of the psyche, it cannot by itself alone bind the drive impulse in its entirety. Whatever the quality of the sexualization/desexualization process, it cannot process the whole of the sexual "force". Whatever the quality of the autoerotisms and "sublimations", they cannot exhaust the internal tensions.

There is a need for the object, for objects; we need the difference that they alone are capable of introducing. This is where we encounter difference.

This also begins to open up the question of sexuality, of the drive exchanges with a different object. Sexuality opens up where the "binding" sexual is lacking, where intrapsychic erotism is necessarily, inevitably, lacking.

Infantile sexuality, a point on which Freud becomes increasingly assertive, remains fundamentally unsatisfying; it is even in the final analysis what shatters the Oedipus complex. Sexualization by the primary process leaves an unbindable residue, a lack that engenders a difference in the sexual, *the* difference in the sexual.

The desexualization operated by the secondary process comes up against this residue that paradoxically "endrivens" the secondary system, penetrates it and "claims" the discharge, demands an object "for" the discharge, another modality for processing the sexual.

It is the non-event of infantile sexuality, its failure to occur, and therefore what is left unbound by it, that claims its place in secondarity, forcing it to reconsider the question of the sexual and to integrate it differently.

It is what could not occur in childhood sexuality that seeks to make its way into secondarity, seeks to be fulfilled in the secondary system and instigates adult sexuality.

This is why it cannot be definable without reference to the negative of childhood sexuality. We repeat, but in the sexual we do not repeat only what might have taken place; it is above all that which has not taken place that we repeat in and through sexuality, we repeat the non-occurrence of ourselves. We try to talk about, in a body language, what had happens and what sould better had happens.

Let us move on to the generative process to conclude our next reflection.

No object, either, can in itself enable us to bind what is lacking and strives to be discharged; an object of the object is required, another object, that is to say another subject, a third subject. The unbindable residue engenders an objectalizing generativity that is simultaneously a socializing generativity. We know that this can only be maintained and developed if it too can be adequately desexualized at a secondary stage.

Is this pulsation of sexualization and desexualization not the essence of what psychoanalysis can bring to a reflection on the sexual in contemporary clinical thought?

The adolescent sexual and the enigma

It is against this background that adolescence then introduces its specific "revolution" in the sexual. It is in the "orgasmic potentiality" that it seems to me the revolution specific to adolescence must be understood most fully, but it is also that the sexual will have to find conditions of satisfaction in the reunion with bodily contact of the other-subject object, in conditions that evoke the first physical contact. I have previously (2000) tried to assess the importance and extent of the upheavals incurred by the introduction of sexual maturity into the relationship of adolescence to symbolization, and I would like to amplify these initial reflections here with some supplementary remarks on the trajectory from the baby's sexuality to that of the adolescent.

The orgasmic potentiality, as the quotation from Freud comparing the baby's satisfaction at the breast with the pleasure of adult sexuality implies, puts the psyche at the risk of a confusion between the first hallucinatory experience in created-found and the sexual experience of the orgasm, as if adolescent pleasure "rediscovered" the baby's first and lost satisfaction. The idea that adolescent and adult sexuality rediscovers the path of primal pleasure, rediscovers the maternal breast, even the very site of their origins, is a highly topical idea in psychoanalysis and it is probably subtended by the primal fantasy of the "return to the maternal womb". But the adolescent's orgasm is not the hallucinatory realization of the baby's desire and the amalgam that threatens to be carried out between the two subjective experiences is probably as necessary as threatening to the adolescent's psychic organization.

It is necessary because the amalgam is probably inevitable for psychic integration; it prefigures the work of establishing psychic continuity that is imposed by the crisis undergone at adolescence and the experience of rupture it contains. But at the same time, it is accompanied by the threat that the gains of the work of differentiation in childhood, those of the mourning process connected with the elaboration of the oedipal constellation, and those of the symbolic organization and the sublimations it makes possible, will be lost on the way, made obsolete by the new potentialities offered by the accession to adult pleasure. The threat is that a short-circuiting from the baby's pleasure to that of the adolescent may be instituted.

Once again, I do not think that a certain part of the short-circuit is entirely avoidable; what matters is that it should be moderated by the maintenance of an adequate cathexis of the factual realities of childhood, that the buffer and the work of differentiation produced by the elaboration of specifically infantile sexuality is interposed between the early sexual of the baby and that of the adolescent.

I should like to conclude these reflections with an observation concerning the adolescent evolution of the enigma incorporated in the object's pleasure for the baby and the child, the "enigmatic signifiers" described by Laplanche. The discovery of orgasm produces a "partial lifting" of the enigma of the object's pleasure; it produces a reorganizing retroactive operation of the relationship the subject has formed with it and probably, in the same shift, a reorganization of the concept of the primal scene. I propose the hypothesis that, furthermore, one of the remarkable revisions thus made possible is a modification in the subject's relationship with the unknown, a reopening of the "capacity for the negative" (Bion's "negative capability") that contains the concept of a cathexis and a potential pleasure found in what is unknown, imperceptible. The adolescent's capacity to solve equations with unknown elements, to explore the physical and chemical sciences based on hypotheses beyond the sensory and even perceptible universe (atom, bounds of the universe etc.), the cathexis of spiritualism common at that age, then for some the cathexis of "depth psychology", and therefore the acceptance of an unconscious psychic reality, seem to me to stem from and be made conceivable by this profound revision in the relationship to the enigma of pleasure.

There is, therefore, one final implication that particularly concerns clinicians and takes us back to intersubjectivity, which concerns the form of thought about the unknown and the imperceptible that is contained in the encounter with the concept of the unconscious and specifically that of the object's unconscious. The baby and the child encounter the unconscious of objects with which they have had to construct themselves; they undergo its effects and vagaries; they also organize their psychic life according to the impact of this unconscious. Proponents of "theory of mind" have rightly emphasized the importance for the socialization process of constructing a conception of the other's mind, which I would personally formulate as the capacity to imagine that the object is a subject-other, with his own desires, intentions, emotions and so on. But this "theory" does not engage with the question of the importance for psychic life of an unconscious dimension of the mind – that is to say, the question of the mind's reflexivity and its mode of relationship with itself. I think this capacity is only truly completely acquired at adolescence and in the wake of the above-mentioned revisions concerning the lifting of the enigma of the object's pleasure. The discovery of a pleasure in oneself unknown to oneself ("a pleasure unknown to itself" as Freud said in relation to the Rat man) opens up the question of a pleasure of the object that is unknown to the object itself; it engages the paradox of an unconscious affect. The accession to the true dimension of intersubjectivity cannot be gained without considering in intersubjectivity of this particular characteristic of the human subject: he is inhabited by a shadowy and unknown zone; his messages contain a dimension that eludes him, an unconscious dimension that nevertheless acts and interacts between one subject and another. And what is true of oneself is also true of the object, and the parental objects, which is one of the aspects of the "murder of the object" encountered in adolescence, with the acquisition of the concept and the right to explore the object's unconscious, a supreme site of psychic transgression.

Finally, I would like to emphasize a point that I only mentioned in brief remarks in my reflections. The development of the secondary system does not make the impulsive issues of the primary system disappear, but by rediscovering experiences of early childhood body relationships, it enables them to find a form of body language, which must certainly be interpreted but makes sexuality a form of language. Adults do not "make" love, they "speak" love with their body-language.

As discussed in this chapter, the three-fold difference between the sexes, between generations and between infant and adult sexuality has been at the heart of metapsychological developments concerning human sexuality. This triple difference, its organization and psychological "management", has an impact on the narcissistic economy of the subject, it contributes to the construction of his or her sense of identity, it refines it, but it does not control the basic sense of identity. This is not the case of the fourth difference that we will deal within the following chapter, the difference I/not I, which represents the foundation, the base of the sense of identity. We must first perceive ourselves as a subject, a subject differentiated from the other-subject, before being able to enter fruitfully into the refinements that characterize objectal sexuality.

Note

1 Freud, S. (1905). *Three essays on the theory of sexuality*. SE, 7.

4 Deconstructing primary narcissism

Freud's contribution focused particularly on the analysis of different mental states (neurotic, narcissistic, psychotic). This was based on his exploration of the effect on the vagaries of identity related to how the difference between the sexes and generations is structured in the mind, as well as the changes in the organization of the differences that both unite and separate infantile sexuality from the sexual sphere within their adult counterparts. Winnicott invites us to extend Freud's ideas by thinking about the impact of the primary construction of the me/not-me distinction in narcissistic states and their adjustments. His contribution is crucial to the analysis of narcissistic states of mind and of pathological forms of the ego's defense processes when the self has to contend with the risk of trauma in early childhood.

For Winnicott, primary narcissism cannot be conceived of in any solipsistic way.[1] How it develops should be thought of within the context of the primary psychic relationship that is set up with the specific features of any given environment. A kind of primitive illusion, however, tends to obliterate that particular aspect of its construction. Analyzing primary narcissism thus implies reintroducing what the primary narcissistic illusion has erased, i.e. the role played by the primary object in its foundation because narcissism involves two and perhaps three people.

In cases where narcissistic and self-identity issues are uppermost, the individual remains a prisoner of that primary illusion. The subject deludes her-self that she is exclusively formed. That is the impasse: the individual forgets that she is not self-generated, whether as a flesh-and-blood creature or as far as her mental apparatus is concerned. That is what Winnicott meant in his paper on the use of the object, where he states that narcissism cannot be thought of exclusively in terms of the self (Winnicott 1971 op cit). The self cannot be thought of without considering the object considered as "another-self", i.e. a distinct self that has its own mental life and wishes. That other self who may be present has now become an important element since there has been a definite attempt to acknowledge that the counter-transference reveals hidden aspects of the transference. Historically, it is the "other" with which the individual constructed herself

DOI: 10.4324/9781003198710-4

in the past. To understand fully the implications of Winnicott's ideas, we must first of all remind ourselves of Freud's original position.

In "Mourning and Melancholia", Freud[2] wrote that "the shadow of the object fell upon the ego" [1917e (1915) p. 249]. This is an essential element in thinking about the blending of ego and object, and it suggests a fundamental direction for analyzing narcissism. If suffering involves the shadow of the object that has fallen on the ego, the analyst will have to help the patient give that shadow back to the object, break free of the blend brought about by her narcissistic defenses and deconstruct the basic narcissistic postulate of the self-generation of the mind.

Freud went on to emphasize the fact that one of the characteristic features of narcissism is not simply that it brings everything back to the self – all cathexes are aimed at the ego – but also that it erases or attempts to erase anything that comes from another individual. In *The Ego and the Id* (1923)[3] – and even more so in *Inhibitions, Symptoms and Anxiety* (1926)[4] – Freud showed how the ego assimilates and takes as its own what it cannot remove. Narcissism assimilates the object and takes in the shadow of the object that has fallen on the ego. At the same time, it erases the fact that there is a shadow that has fallen on the ego and is henceforth mixed up with it. The "lost" object does not have to be mourned by the ego. In bringing the cathexis of the lost object back onto itself, the ego incorporates the traces left by that object. Later I shall come back to the meaning of the idea of "the shadow of the object" that has also become much clearer thanks to Winnicott.

The narcissistic process does not simply erase all trace of the object, it wipes out the process by which that erasing occurs; it erases for the individual that by which she developed and what she owes to the object thanks to which the self came into being. Moreover, it erases the process by which the self assimilated what came from the other person in its own organization. These processes go to make up the primary narcissistic illusion.

The primary mirror-object

We can now examine in more detail the ideas that Winnicott contributed to the above concepts. How do his hypotheses help us in the practice of psychoanalysis to locate and identify retroactively those traces that have since become mute, silenced, assimilated, i.e.: the traces of the object's primary responses, the first human mirror reflecting the self's drive-related impulses and primary needs?

When the clinical presentation seems to involve only the relationship between the individual and her own self, Winnicott recommends that we try to reintroduce the historical aspect of the primary object and reconstruct what must have occurred between the individual and the object that gives rise to the narcissistic pattern we see before us.

Winnicott's main hypothesis is that the individual expects the primary object to be an emotional mirror that offers a representation of the self. In the relationship between the individual and her self, Winnicott reintroduces the gap, the fork in the road as it were, generated by the primary mirror of the object. He restores the paradox of an identity that is constructed through internalizing the reflection sent out by another person. Identity is the precipitate of primary narcissistic identifications, those that incorporate an object that is a mirror and the self's double. Later, the theoretical model that this implies will be explored but for the moment the focus is on clinical matters.

One concrete clinical consequence of Winnicott's hypothesis is that when the individual is defined inherently as identical to herself, that identification and the identification of her internal states of mind include something of the other person, i.e.: some degree of otherness brought about by the "reflection" carried out by the other person, through identification with what those primary objects reflected.

Any attempt at psychoanalytically restoring that "otherness" aspect and deconstructing the solipsistic narcissistic postulate of self-identity means that the objectification function of the drives is made possible or perhaps restored. This implies the possibility of rediscovering traces of the lost object in the ego. These traces represent the shadow that has been assimilated.

The following clinical sequence, from the standard form of treatment with a female patient who had suffered from severe anorexia nervosa, will serve as an illustration of this problem and the kind of analytic clinical work that is required.

Echo was a woman patient of mine whose clinical anorexia nervosa gradually diminished as the analysis proceeded. Her social life, however, was still extremely limited in scope. She was economizing, convinced that she could slow down the passing of time or even bring it to a complete halt. She limited her social contacts to what was strictly necessary. She herself toned down whatever faint drive-related impulses she did have and repressed her affects. In her sessions, she was often immobile and silent. It was only very sparingly that she talked of some aspects of her inner thoughts and feelings. I had the impression that she was treating the work of the analysis as she did food in her anorexic states, as well as the rest of her life, including her mental functioning: she neutralized everything. That impression of mine was not particularly useful on a practical level. The idea that, in a kind of transference reversal which was an attempt to share her internal world, she evoked in me an experience – and therefore was communicating to me – what she herself had gone through. This was useful only insofar as it helped me to tolerate the specific features of the transference without retaliating too much.

It was in another aspect of the transference that we had to find the wherewithal to revive her drive-related processes. When Echo became able to break free of her "from self to self" defenses – in other words her narcissistic defenses – she brought those issues into the transference, so that the analytical process could start to become meaningful. I helped her to externalize the shadow of the object by drawing attention to the fact that she seemed to be treating herself and treating me in much the same way as her primary environment had treated her.

As the work of the analysis progressed, the following intersubjective pattern began to emerge in the transference. Echo gradually began to express in words what was going on inside her when she came to her sessions. Initially, she would feel pleased and want to explain something that she had been able to formulate and understand between sessions. But as soon as we were both together, as soon as she came into my consulting-room, the source of that pleasure and the wish to share something dried up immediately. She remained cold, with no vital spark to her. What she had intended to say suddenly seemed insipid to her, devoid of any interest whatsoever – and she felt this before she even opened her mouth. The vigor she had felt before finding herself in my presence just melted away. That transformation sometimes occurred as soon as I entered the waiting room to welcome her – as soon as I opened the door, in fact, as soon as she caught sight of me.

Gradually, the incidental thought that came into her mind at that point could begin to be put into words. When she looked at my consulting-room full of books and files, she thought that I must be a very busy person, and probably not particularly available, whereas she herself was just a tiny little thing of hardly any importance to me, the "great professor". Gradually, these transference elements could be linked to certain specific features of the patient's relationship with her mother. When her sister was born, Echo suddenly felt de-cathected, because her mother gave all her attention to the new baby. Mother's mind was elsewhere, and she was unable to think simultaneously about both of her children. As we worked through that time in her past, there was some warming-up of her drives, but basically her relationship to the outside world remained much as before.

It was necessary to work through the everyday aspects of her life as a child, over and beyond the specific event that was the birth of her sister, because what then appeared could be seen as running through the whole of her relationship with her mother. Day by day, in the ordinary life of the family, Echo's mother gradually showed herself to be a hyper-active woman, always running around; there was no way to make contact with her. At meal-times, for example, she would rush around, serving one person then another, eating while she was still on her feet or at the edge of the table without sitting down, without ever stopping for a rest. She would serve someone and then start to clear everything away before the meal was over; she was a kind of "household tornado". Whenever Echo tried to get close to her mother in an upsurge of emotion, it would all fall flat because her mother was already elsewhere – she had turned away, busying herself with something else. Echo would simply slide off a smooth-surfaced object that could never be reached, and whose attention could never be captured. The upsurge of emotion fell flat, disappeared; the drive broke down, withdrew and retracted. At the same time, life itself became more restricted. No "use" could be made of the object and Echo's drives could not keep up their momentum; she had to neutralize everything as much as she could. She had to repeat that kind of sequence very many times in her sessions – and I had to formulate, just as often, my trans-ference interpretations in terms of the "nullifying" effect of her mother's responses on her drive-related and emotional impulses – before any sig-nificant change in the way she related to her drives and her affects could be integrated.

No such clinical pattern can be understood in terms of solipsistic thinking because it implies an intersubjective conception of the life of the drives, as well as an intersubjective conception of their organization. The idea of a "messenger" drive – one that is addressed to another person and is dependent for its development on the response of that other person – is one that all clinicians must come to acknowledge as a key concept. It wid-ens the scope of what the psychoanalyst can take in and expands clinical thinking in psychoanalysis.

In my work with Echo, I was initially confronted with a "from herself to herself" kind of behavior as the focus of the clinical picture at that time. That behavior was solipsistic in nature, it was purely self-related. It partic-ipated in her narcissistic economy and did not appear to be aimed at any-one in particular. Even when she was not in her sessions, Echo behaved in much the same way. The shadow of the object had fallen on her ego, which had assimilated its impact and the problem then became an internal one, one that was self-related. However, since it was after all brought into the psychoanalytic sessions, it began to take on an interactive dimension and had an impact on the analyst within the analyzing space. Thus, it became a kind of enacted message, a transference communication. In the end, I acknowledged it to be (or endorsed it as) a particular form of the trans-ference, a transference *Agieren*. Insofar as it affects the analyst, insofar as another person feels involved and can think about such a behavior pat-tern in terms of an enacted message addressed to the other, then the idea that there is an intersubjective dimension to that behavior which has an impact on the other person can be explored.

By taking melancholia as the fundamental model of narcissistic impasse, Freud gave a certain direction to psychoanalysis. The vector he thus introduced was taken up and put to extremely good use by Winn-icott. Thanks to the latter's hypothesis of the object as the self's emotional mirror, Freud's intuition was made operational for the analysis of the psy-chopathological aspects of narcissistic and identity-related states of mind.

This question will be discussed more fully later, with reference to Lacan's "mirror stage" and to the change in emphasis that Winnicott brought to it. Before doing so, another aspect of Winnicott's hypotheses should be pointed out concerning the various complementary features that he introduced which makes it possible to deconstruct the theory of narcissism itself.

The narcissistic theory of the drives simply involves the tendency to discharge; the object is looked upon merely as being the instrument through which drive-related discharge can take place. The object in this position is not experienced as another person. If the object is present, the drive can be discharged, released. If the object is absent, the self is threatened with loss of some kind and has to set up palliative auto-erotic measures in order to deal with that threat and await the beneficial return of the object. Putting the emphasis on the object's function in the construction of the self and on the object's responses to the self's libidinal impulses introduces a new dimension into the life of the drives, one which implicitly contains the idea that drives also carry a message addressed to the object, a message that is waiting for some kind of response. Drives are constructed through the interplay that is set up between self and object. A brief example will help us to understand the issues that this kind of hypothesis raises in our clinical work.

In one of his sessions, a male patient said that he felt "empty" and that his mind had "gone blank". The classic interpretation of that state, the one that I was taught when, in supervision, I was learning my craft as a psychoanalyst, was to link that inner emptiness to the feeling that, given the drive-related avidity of the patient, something was experienced as missing. The analysis would then attempt to explore the all-or-nothing processes that are typical of primary avidity. Later, I learned that this feeling of inner emptiness could be linked also, in a complementary manner, to thought processes such as negative hallucination. The empty feeling could then perhaps be seen also as a hollow space, an awaiting, a potential space for receiving something. Thanks to Winnicott, another complementary interpretation became available, one which, without in any way nullifying the previous two, points them in a new direction. The feeling of emptiness can be looked upon as the effect on the ego of the shadow of an unresponsive object that remained silent in the face of the self's entreaties, indifferent to the self's urges, perhaps even turning away in hostility. As Albert Camus put it in his *Myth of Sisyphus*: "The absurd is born of this confrontation between the human need and the unreasonable silence of the world" [2006, p. 21].[5] The emptiness of the object's response is then incorporated, leaving in the ego a trace of the echo of that silence and of the way in which it may have shattered the self's drive-related urges. The previous patient Echo is a good example of that process.

When Winnicott said to his patient Margaret Little (1985) that her mother was chaotic, he was not attempting to designate the mother as "the bad object" – that would have been neither apposite nor psychoanalytically helpful. The notions of "good" and "bad" objects have to do with infantile definitions of the object and do not correspond to the kind of categories that are useful to psychoanalysts in their attempt to think about the patient's past. In describing the mother as "chaotic", Winnicott helped the patient to move away from the idea that her inner chaos was simply the outcome of an anarchic and disorganizing drive or the result of an avid and limitless libido. The patient was able to grasp the intelligibility of an inner impulse that came up against a chaotic and disorganizing response from the environment. The analytic space illuminates the relationship with the self and revives the impact and the form of the response made by the primary mirror-object in the past. This means that the initial impulse can also be rediscovered in the present analytic relationship, and the message addressed to the object via that drive-related impulse might have a better chance of meeting with a different kind of response. The following clinical example will serve as an illustration of these ideas.

This patient from time to time had breakdowns that were melancholic in nature: loss of all liveliness and probably a disintegration of his immunological defenses. His overall condition improved significantly during an initial period of analysis with a female analyst. However, when he asked me to help him carry on exploring psychoanalytically his inner mental states, he was still suffering from a generalized depressive state and major inhibition of his potential. He had attended some of my lectures on narcissistic states and felt that I might be able to help him in a different manner from that of his previous analyst.

I shall skip the initial part of the analytical process, devoted to his working through in the transference the relationship with his father who was a man showing little emotion, was unyielding and not very often present. Processing his intense hostility toward a paternal figure who disappointed the love that his son had for him and who showed little interest in his son did indeed impact on the patient's depressiveness, but not in any really decisive way. The transference relationship began to show signs of how the patient and his mother related. She suffered from manic-depressive psychosis with delusional aspects, and this had a significant effect on the patient. When the analysis of that relationship came to the fore, the patient had two severe depressive breakdowns with major melancholic features. On each occasion, a psychosomatic disorganization ensued, with the patient "falling apart" as his immunological defenses collapsed. The decisive phase in his processing of these depressive breakdowns occurred when it became possible to link the collapse of all liveliness in the patient, when he was falling apart, with the response made by the maternal object to the impulses of the child he had then been. Very slowly we had to reconstruct the characteristic features of the primitive conversation between the baby, i.e.: the infant the patient was at that time and a mother who oscillated between melancholic and manic phases.

From the perspective opened up by Winnicott extending Freud's comment on the shadow of the object, the work of analysis enables the reconstitution and processing of the effects of the chaotic and erratic aspects of the mother's emotional responses. From time to time, the patient's mother would accept her son's affection toward her, exaggerating it until it became too powerful to keep in check, then her attitude would suddenly change and she would reject it. Most of the time the mother's sole response to any affect-based impulse was to turn her face away, close in on herself or even reject it as though she felt she was under attack. Her son was left in complete confusion – confusion between love and hate, between affectionate and aggressive impulses. At that point, all forward movement came to a halt; his liveliness weakened and collapsed and at that point he fell apart. His affectionate impulses toward the object were experienced by the child he then was as highly destructive. The para-doxical position in which he found himself, that had been created by the confusion between his affectionate impulses and his experience of being destructive, tended to paralyze all mental activity on his part. If, in the baby, the good (love) and the bad (destructiveness, according to the moth-er's interpretation of the impulse) are no longer opposable – with each cre-ating the other – the pleasure-unpleasure principle and its transformation into the reality principle are paralyzed, to such an extent that all mental activity tends to stop.

In the various clinical situations that are described here, the really crucial part of the clinical work was to facilitate a return of the patients' mental dynamics through highlighting the specific nature of the primary object's responses and reactions to the infant's drive-related impulses and urges. When the clinical picture gave the impression that the patient was in an impasse and that her mental processes were repetitively going round in circles, I reintroduced the specific element that had been the object's response. I tried to reconstruct that response on the basis of the transference indications that the patient evoked in each session.

There are two phases to that process. The first has to do with the present and it takes place in the transference. It is initially perceived and worked on at that level. Since the process is insistent by nature, historical recon-struction becomes possible in the second phase that enables the process to be stabilized and means that change is sustainable.

Naturally enough, this leads us to delve deeper into Winnicott's ideas concerning the process of subjectifying identification on the one hand and, on the other, the hypothesis that he put forward concerning what he called the use of the object.

The process of subjectification: subjectifying identification

The reading of Winnicott with Freud that describes the context in which mother and baby first come into contact with each other leads to the suggestion of the concept of a primary homosensual relationship that is

"double" in nature. This context brings about the process of subjectifica-
tion that lies at the heart of the organization of the primary narcissistic/
self-identity pattern.

French-speaking psychoanalysts differentiate between the sexual
sphere and sexuality as such. The term "sexuality" is used to designate
behavior, while the "sexual sphere" refers to the pleasure-unpleasure
issues that infiltrate all mental processes. From that point of view, the
"sensual dimension" has to do with the sexual sphere. French-speaking
psychoanalysts would, therefore, argue that although everything is not
sexual, there is a sexual element in everything, insofar as drive-related
cathexes always accompany mental processes or intersubjective encounters. To describe that relationship as "primary homosensuality" or "primary homosexuality" emphasizes the fact that pleasure and unpleasure
have to do with the movement in which the other person is either encountered or lost as a "double" of oneself.

Three of Winnicott's ideas could be seen as making this point more
explicit: the found-created object, the mother's mirror function and the
experience of interaction in the early feeding situation (Winnicott 1953,
1967, 1969, 1971).[6]

The idea of the found-created object is that the maternal environment
that presents the breast at the proper time and in a manner suited to the
infant enables the latter to have the productive illusion of being able to "create", via hallucination, the breast that he or she actually "finds" through
apperception. Contrary to the usual metapsychological description of
mental functioning, which emphasizes the contrast between hallucination and perception, Winnicott describes a paradoxical – "transitional" –
metapsychological dimension in which that contrast no longer holds. The
apperceived breast meets up with the hallucinated one and is superimposed on it as a real substantive double. This process lies at the heart of
the infant's invention of the subjective illusion of being able to create the
satisfaction that he or she finds. Maternal adequacy transforms that primitive hallucination into a positive illusion that supports the infant's belief
in her capacity to produce a satisfactory world. Object-cathexis and narcissism are, therefore, not necessarily opposed to each other; they combine
their effects and produce a specific kind of subjective state – one that is
"transitional" – in which the hallucinated representation of the object
and the "objective" object come together in such a way that pleasure is
obtained. Self-preservation and drive-related cathexes thus go hand in
hand and auto-eroticism and object-cathexis converge. Pleasure comes
about from that merging together and is a signal of that encounter and
blending.

This conception of Winnicott's takes us beyond the metapsychological impasse that is caused by the opposition between drive theory and
object-relations theory. Here, due to space limitation, it is not possible
to discuss everything that follows on from a conception of the mental

apparatus which sees it as capable, under certain specific circumstances, of simultaneously hallucinating and perceiving, without becoming confused in the process. Rather, I shall focus on describing the kinds of double relationship to which Winnicott drew our attention.

A further aspect of Winnicott's theory concerns his conception of the mother's face as "mirroring" her infant's internal states. Winnicott argued that his hypothesis was a development of Lacan's intuition about the function of the mirror stage. It involves the point at which issues concerning identification are uppermost, and when narcissistic identification and the sense of self are joined together. The main thrust of Winnicott's hypothesis is that what infants see when they look at their mother's face is a reflection of their own internal and emotional state. Some comments and complementary ideas would be useful here.

The first point is that the idea of the "good-enough" mother is implicit in this hypothesis. The mother, together with her surrounding environment, which, in particular, includes the father, adapts her movements, facial expressions and physical posture to those of her infant. She attunes emotionally to her infant, with whom she identifies and whose internal states she shares in her own way (Winnicott 1958). The infant sees in the mother's face a reflection of this supportiveness as a double, which is aesthetic, sensory and emotional (Winnicott 1967 op cit). I would nevertheless argue that we have to go beyond Winnicott's hypothesis and see this first "mirror" as being not only the mother's face but also her entire body and her behavior.

This mirror, personified by the mother's body when she is sufficiently adapted to her infant's needs, sufficiently malleable [Roussillon 1991][7] and sensitive toward her infant's internal states, has the effect of producing a narcissistic double. A "double" is something that is both "the same" – similar to the self – and also "another". No double can ever be simply the same because that situation would create confusion, rather than a reflection of the self. The mother must, therefore, show that she is different, an-other, through the way in which she reflects to her infant her sharing of emotions. The emotions and internal states that she reflects are similar, but not identical, to those of her infant. They have the same basic components, the same matrix, but not the same form. The maternal reflections are identical to those of her infant, except as to their mode: they are homomorphic but not isomorphic. Maternal adjustment is intermodal. Gergeli [2003][8] has pointed out that, beside this intermodal accompanying "double", the mother indicates also that the emotional states she reflects back to her infant are not her own emotional states but rather those of the infant. The message or metacommunication that the mother receives means that she is able to take on the role of a simple "mirror" of her infant's internal states. She can think of herself as a reflecting mirror. It is obvious that if one is to be able to mirror the internal states of another person, one must be able to empathize with that person's emotional states, identify them, acknowledge them and, therefore, share them, at least to some extent.

The concept of the mother as the infant's primary mirror implies that a primary relationship is set up and cathected as a movement reaching out toward the other person in an attempt to construct a relationship with that person as a potential double of the self. Here too satisfaction and pleasure depend on the capacity of the two partners to come together and see the other as a double – as a separate person, yet the same as the self. It is that movement, that ballet as it were, which governs pleasure and unpleasure. That interplay between mother and infant initiates the construction of a rudimentary form of symbol, i.e. what represents their initial encounter and what is shared between them and the union for which it strives. If a manifestation of the infant's mind-set can be echoed by the mother, it is no longer simply a discharge: it begins to take its place in a primitive system of communication, taking the form of a "shared sign", i.e.: of a message that can be addressed to the object. Sharing is the first prerequisite for the emergence of symbols, conceived of as a sign that meeting and coming together is taking place. Both infant and mother acknowledge and recognize themselves in such symbols, and the symbols carry traces of their encounter and their coming together.

These comments on Winnicott's hypothesis must, if they are to be complete, mention another implicit element of that conception. If we say that the mother's face is her infant's mirror, this implies not only that the mother must behave in such a way that she offers herself as her infant's mirror, but also that, whatever transpires, the infant treats what is expressed in the mother's face and body as a reflection of herself. In other words, the infant identifies with what reverberates through the manner in which the mother and other significant persons in the environment are present for him. "Whatever transpires" means that the infant treats the substance of what the mother expresses as a message that, in effect, concerns her, as a kind of response to the infant's own impulses directed toward the mother. Whether the mother's response is an accurate reflection of the infant's emotions, the effect of her own internal state or the way in which she feels and interprets the signals addressed to her, her infant will receive these messages as reflections. This point is of particular relevance for our understanding of the pathology of narcissism, which can then be seen to involve the specific features of the way in which the primary mirror has carried out the role potentially allotted to it. Either the primary parental mirror may have reflected only very little material for the infant to be able to identify her internal states, which then may become blanked out in the absence of any "double" response, or the reflection may have distorted them to such an extent that they have become warped.

Thinking along these lines enables us to hypothesize how Freud's enigmatic formula "the shadow of the object" can be better understood. In *Mourning and Melancholia*, Freud argued that, in melancholia, the source of the feeling of loss of the object derives from a disappointment emanating from the object. The hypothesis suggested here is that the shadow of the object arises from that which the object did not reflect back to the self as regards the latter's emotions and internal states. In other words, the object failed to fulfill its role as a mirror, and the primary narcissistic expectations of the self were thus disappointed. To go beyond both Freud and Winnicott, I would say that the self then tries to incorporate the object and the part of the self-felt to be confiscated by the object when nothing is reflected back. The self sticks to the object in what some post-Kleinian analysts have called adhesive identification. Esther Bick's term "adhesive identification" more accurately describes it, and it lies at the root of an area of non-differentiation between self and object. This is a shared area that, in fantasy, holds self and object stuck to each other as if they were Siamese twins. The process of mourning the loss of the object is thus paralyzed from the outset and trapped within a paradox because giving up the object implies giving up also the part of the self that is sequestered inside the object. Yet, letting go of the object, for example in the process of mourning, is carried out in the name of preserving the self or the self's wholeness and consistency (as in castration anxiety, for example).

The third point I wish to make concerns something that appeared later in Winnicott's writings. The most explicit indication of it that I have been able to find dates from a paper he wrote in 1969 (and published in 1970), although it is quite possible that what was being formulated clearly at that point was already implicit in his earlier work. In that paper, Winnicott emphasizes the importance of the two-way movement, the mutuality that is typical of the early feeding situation and, over and beyond that, of the mother-infant relationship as a whole. He comments on the fact that infants try to put their fingers into their mother's mouth and so "feed" the mother. Here again is the idea of "double". Winnicott emphasizes the importance of this reciprocity for a positive integration of the experience of being fed. The maternal mirror is no longer simply an effect of the illusion derived from the found-created dimension, it is not simply an effect of an emotional or sensory reflection, rather it implies also a two-way process of reciprocity, a mutual feeding, and perhaps, also a mutual transformation. Once again, the maternal mirror contributes to the emergence of a form of symbolic dialogue.

The process of objectification and the discovery of the object's otherness

The concept of a primary "homosensual" relationship that is "double", which entails the gradual construction of an encounter with the object as a "double" of the self, is tenable only if it comprises a theory of the discovery of the object's otherness and maintains a dialectical relationship with that theory (Winnicott 1969). The process is two-fold: identify with the other person and through that other person; differentiate oneself from the other person and differentiate that other person from oneself. Differentiation is meaningful only insofar as it is based on the construction of the other person as the self's double. It is because the other person is initially conceived of as a double that the difference can be constructed in a manner that is not simply a form of splitting or repudiation. On that point, too, Winnicott was an innovator: he complemented Freud's hypotheses and in so doing compelled us to dig more deeply.

For Freud, reality is a primary "given" of perception. There exists from the outset a reality-ego that is in a dialectical and conflicting relationship with the pleasure-ego. Reality-testing makes use of perception and the perception-motor pairing in doing its work and in maintaining active, during wakefulness, i.e.: in consciousness. This is the difference between hallucination and perception. Nonetheless, at certain points in his theory, Freud did seem to hesitate as to where his ideas were leading him. The sense of reality is not just a matter of perception, it entails conception. Similarly, the relationship with the object is not just a matter of perception; it too entails conception. When Freud wrote in 1915 that, at the very beginning, "the external world, objects, and what is hated are identical", adding: "If later on an object turns out to be a source of pleasure, it is loved, but it is also incorporated into the ego; so that for the purified pleasure-ego once again objects coincide with what is extraneous and hated" [1915, p. 136],[9] this goes much further than a mere perception of the object. As we can imagine, what complicates the question is the fact that hallucinatory cathexis of the object becomes mixed with the simple perception of it. Hallucination and perception may be in a dialectical relationship, in conflict, one with the other, or threaten to merge together.

Winnicott suggested that hallucination and perception could be superimposed on each other, a hypothesis that Freud himself seemed about to accept in his paper "Constructions in Analysis" [1937][10] in order to solve the problem of psychosis. Although Winnicott opened up a new way of looking at this issue, he did add a further complication.

When perception is cathected and the hallucination of a previous trace becomes mixed in with it, the result is an experience of illusion that carries with it a potential threat of confusion. Freud emphasized that in *Inhibitions, Symptoms and Anxiety* (1926 [1925]) and discussed the topic again in his "Constructions" paper [op. cit]: there is no point in trying to "prove" anything concerning the unreality of an illusion or a hallucination. An illusion does not contradict the reality principle, rather it is part of the relationship with reality and expresses the wish that structures that relationship. Reality-testing cannot have, as its basis, perception or muscular activity when these are libidinally cathected; experiences of pleasure cannot provide such a basis either, because from the outset they have their source in the superposing of hallucination and perception, and in the "double" encounter between these.

Illusion may give rise to unpleasure and lead to a lack of satisfaction, but such an experience does not bring about disillusion that offers the possibility for some differentiation between internal and external reality. That is the essence of Winnicott's position. The experience of unpleasure gives rise to what the author has suggested should be called a "negative illusion" [Roussillon 1991]. This is not disillusion but a negative form of illusion based on the subjective impression that the individual has destroyed her capacity to produce satisfaction. It triggers wounds, anger and destructiveness which, eventually and in the face of the disorganizing character of these states, incite the individual to restrict her cathexis of the outside world, withdraw from all contact, shut everything down, move toward dis-objectification and away from any discovery of the otherness of the object.

Winnicott's hypothesis makes the problem more complex in that it introduces, between the experience of unpleasure and the discovery of the reality or of the otherness of the object, an additional phase, a structural level that includes the part played by the environment and its response to the individual's drive-related impulses.

The object is "encountered" in an atmosphere of hate, it is pre-conceived in the experience of unpleasure and in the individual's reaction to that unpleasure. The object is potentially perceived in an experience of unpleasure that triggers destructive impulses. Destructiveness does not bring about a disillusion directly; it gives rise to a negative illusion, the illusion that one is the source of all the evil that inhabits the world (Roussillon 1991). According to Winnicott, what then happens depends on the way in which the object responds to the infant's destructiveness. That is when the veil that surrounds the mirror of the object will darken, become cloudy and burst; it will harden or harden its reflection.

If the object retaliates, mirroring or doubling the infant's drive-related impulses, if it counter-attacks, if it withdraws from the relationship, these responses will give substance to the negative illusion and anchor feelings of badness in the individual, a deep malaise, a nucleus of primary guilt that is pre-ambivalent because it is not in a dialectical relationship with love. Destruction takes place – it is no longer a message of unpleasure, an internal signal, a potentiality for differentiation; it has turned into a fact, and the destruction is real. The result is that narcissism remains locked in solipsism.

Conversely, if the object survives the destructive impulses and impotent anger, if it appears to be wounded but does not retaliate, if it does not withdraw either perceptively or emotionally from the relationship, if it keeps alive the link with the self, then destructiveness does not break anything; it remains potential. Reality-testing then becomes possible, and differentiation between internal and external objects may begin to take place. The object is "discovered" in its externality; it is no longer simply "perceived" as external – as we now know, this is achieved very early on in life – but "conceived of" as being external, as an external object cathected libidinally, as another being, not simply as the self's double or reflection. The experience of differentiation between the internal object – the fantasy object destroyed by the self's destructiveness and impotent anger – and the external object, the other person, the object that survives can then start to become meaningful. At that point, the topography of the mind can begin to organize itself. It is when there are two or three participants that it becomes possible to move beyond primary narcissistic solipsism; it is when we think about the object's responses, the questions these raise and the forms they take, that we can break free of the primary narcissistic negative illusion and its existential impasses.

The object cathected as the self's "homosensual double", which is the present object in its function of reflecting the self, is cathected and loved. The absent object, i.e. the object that does not take on that role, the object that becomes different and is not present as the self's double, the non-narcissistic object, is hated because it is absent and because of the gap that it leaves in its wake. That gap takes the place of negative illusion such that the conflict of ambivalence can begin to be set up. The object is loved because it is present or hated because it is absent – i.e. its presence is elsewhere – and because it is opening up to some third party.

The object's response seals the fate of destructiveness and its role in psychical economy. On the one hand, it can withdraw into itself and turn away or turn its effects against the mind and its cathexes; on the other, it can enable differentiation between the internal world – that of mental representation and fantasy – and the external world of perception cathected but maintained outside of the self's omnipotent creativeness.

Conclusion

In his exploration of the construction of primary narcissism and the ordeal that is its deconstruction, Winnicott argued that there is a gap between the individual and her or himself. He widened the gap that makes narcissism and breaking free of narcissism analyzable and thus able to be symbolized. He introduced the element that demolishes self-identity and forces psychoanalysis into an impasse. By bringing in this additional phase, that of the object's reflection and its responses to the self's drive-related impulses, that of the specific role the object plays in the construction and deconstruction of narcissism, he "de-narcissized" psychoanalytic theory. With the help of a theory in which solipsism is analyzed and deconstructed, Winnicott explored – and made thinkable – how narcissism is organized or becomes disorganized, puts itself into an impasse or finds a way out through organizing what is lacking and through the discovery of the objects that go to make up narcissism.

The next chapter continues to explore D.W. Winnicott's contribution to the foundations of narcissistic-identity suffering. He focuses on describing his hypotheses about destructiveness and the conditions of its integration. But, beyond Winnicott's proposals, he proposes a generalization of the hypothesis of the "survival" of the object, to the complex forms of these, not only intersubjective but also intrasubjective (intrapsychic).

Notes

1 Winnicott, D.W. (1971). *Playing and reality*. London: Routledge, 1999
2 Freud, S. (1917b [1915]). "Mourning and melancholia". *Standard Edition*, 14: 239.
3 Freud, S. (1923). *The ego and the id*. Standard Edition, 19: 3.
4 Freud, S. (1926d [1925]). "Inhibitions, symptoms and anxiety". *Standard Edition*, 20: 77.
5 Camus. A. (1942). *Le Mythe de Sisyphe*. Paris: NRF.
6 Winnicott, D.W. (1953). "Transitional objects and transitional phenomena: A study of the first not-me possession". *The International Journal of Psychoanalysis*, 34: 89–97.
   IJP editor The International Psycho-Analytical Press. Winnicott, D.W. (1967). "Mirror-role of mother and family in child development". In *Playing and reality*. London: Routledge, 1999.
   Winnicott, D.W. (1970) [1969]. "The mother-infant experience of mutuality". In: E. James Anthony & Therese Benedek (Eds), *Parenthood: Its psychology and psychopathology*. Boston, MA: Little, Brown & Co.
   Winnicott, D.W. (1971b). *Playing and reality*. London: Routledge, 1999.
7 Roussillon, R. (1991). *Paradoxes et situations limites de la psychanalyse*. Paris: PUF.
8 Gergeli, G. (2003). "Naissance de la capacité de régulation des affects". *Prendre soin du jeune enfant [Looking After Infants]*. Érès.
9 Freud, S. (1915b). "Instincts and their Vicissitudes". *SE*, 14, 111–140.
10 Freud, S. (1937b). "Constructions in analysis". *Standard Edition*, 23: 257.

5 Destructiveness and complex forms of the "survival" of the object

In this chapter, I intend to develop some thoughts on what Winnicott's idea of the "survival of the object" has contributed to the analysis of destructiveness and its specific clinical manifestations. My hypothesis is that the question of the survival of the object implies a paradigmatic variation thanks to which some aspects of the destructiveness typical of issues involving narcissism and the sense of identity can be interpreted psychodynamically; indeed, the whole question of destructiveness, above and beyond the aspect that I shall focus on here, probably becomes more understandable thanks to Winnicott's contribution. I would argue that the idea of the survival of the object is a crucial one if we are to preserve, when the floodgates of its manifestations are open, a truly psychoanalytic stance as regards destructiveness.

In psychoanalytic circles, the survival of the object is undoubtedly one of the most widely known of Winnicott's ideas – another, for example, would be that of transitionality. This does not mean that the idea in itself, or the consequences that follow on from it, are easy to understand. As for myself, as early as 1978, I was convinced of the fact that Winnicott's hypothesis concerning the use of the object amounted to a kind of revolution in our conception of the genesis of the idea of the object's reality – not with regard to the perception of the object, but its conception and discovery in terms of its being an "other-subject". Winnicott went on to add another significant paradigmatic modification with the idea that what becomes of a mental process depends at least partly on the interpretation that the other-subject to whom it is addressed brings to bear on that process, that is, on the object's response.

In a series of articles on the use of the object, brought together under the heading Psychoanalytic Explorations (Winnicott 1989),[1] Winnicott discusses the survival of the object mainly in connection with destructiveness, focusing particularly on the survival of the primary object. It took me some time – and the mystery of the passionate transference of one of my female analysands – before I came to the conclusion that the process that Winnicott describes is not restricted to manifest destructiveness; it concerns the whole of drive-related experience and the

DOI: 10.4324/9781003198710-5

destructive potential of the drives. I then drew the further conclusion that Winnicott was describing an exemplary form of survival of the object, but that there were other aspects to this, some of which are primary and prototypal, while others intervene later in mental life. And I needed even more time before I realized that what Winnicott was saying about the primary object could quite easily be applied to the relationship with the father and linked to the murder of the father in the myth of the primal horde: in that myth, of course, the father does not survive (or, at least, not very well).

At that point, the notion of the survival of the object, together with the whole clinical and theoretical context that it implies, seemed to me to cut across many phases and problem situations in life and development, so that it becomes almost a structural concept. It describes a particular form of dialectic concerning the relationship between the self and the drives, as linked to the responses and reactions of significant objects (objects cathected as having significance) in childhood and, more generally, in the self's own history.

In order to convey to the reader some sense of that matrix, it would perhaps be best to recall the different stages through which the process that Winnicott describes emerges then describe the subsequent more complex forms that it can take on; this will enable me gradually to complexify the dialectical basis upon which it is structured.

Winnicott's model

Winnicott writes of the survival of the object in early childhood and with respect to the construction of the concept of external reality and the differentiation ego/object. For Winnicott, this does not occur in response to frustration (at least, not primarily), which at first can only produce a "negative illusion" (Roussillon 1991), that is, given the dominant narcissism of the young infant, the illusion of having produced something negative. It would perhaps be better to say that it arises more from the frustration of destructiveness: the object is destroyed, it has to survive the destructive act and will be "discovered" if it does survive. For Winnicott, "survive" means neither retaliating nor breaking off all contact.

I have suggested that these two features noted by Winnicott are experienced when the object has been affected but remains creative. The object must feel affected and show this, otherwise the subject will feel that the attack aimed at the object was simply brushed aside; this will lead to an increase in destructiveness.

In addition, survival cannot be defined simply by what it is not (no withdrawal, no reprisals, no retaliation); the positive aspects must also be highlighted, by remaining creative, the object proves that it is still alive.

The object is thus discovered in terms of something that can resist destructiveness, it is discovered as being an other-subject, that is, as having wishes and impulses that are its very own; it is conceived of as being an other-subject.

Therefore, it lies outside of the baby's omnipotence. From then on, its responses to the infant's impulses become important; the object can no longer be seen in terms of the logic of an object relation, in which the object is simply that which is cathected by a drive (in the sense that we speak of an object relation that is oral, anal, genital, etc.). It must also be seen as having its own specific responses and reactions to the self's drive-related impulses. It is discovered, says Winnicott, "in itself", that is, it is not absorbed into the "for the self" aspect of narcissism; it is also "for the object itself", to some extent independent of the subject.

The logic behind Winnicott's model could be described as follows.

The logic of that model is to add from found–created to destroyed–found.

The infant's primary illusion of self-gratification is, as we seen, made possible by the fact of a good-enough maternal adapting (thanks to the primary maternal preoccupation) and the mother's ability to place (offer) the breast where (when) her baby is able to create it: the hallucination encounters the perception, thus creating a mixed structure that is no longer a hallucination nor yet a simple perception – it is an illusion that is thereby created.

In that primary encounter, the created object is found, the found object is created, the object is found–created. Subjective appropriation is made possible thanks to the fact that this primary kind of link is set up; this is what makes possible the primary illusion of self-gratification. In this model, perception and hallucination are not in opposition to each other; they can coexist, as Freud indicated toward the end of his life in his paper "Constructions in analysis" (1937d).[2]

In addition, Winnicott's conception of the mother's face as a primary mirror, in which the baby sees him- or herself and his or her affects, is closely linked to the found–created process, and is, indeed, a particular instance of this. The "found" aspect (grosso modo, what the environment provides the infant with), as long as it is sufficiently well adapted, will be seen by the baby as a mirror reflection of what he or she is able to create. The primary "doubled" homosexual relationship (Roussillon 2004a)[3] contributes as much to the found–created process as the latter supplies to it.

For Winnicott, the found–created situation is a prerequisite for differentiation, and what follows on from it depends on its quality. The subjective experience of the primary illusion creates a mixed structure; Winnicott's model concerning the breast can also be applied to the various systems of communication and interchange (adjustment and attunement) that are set up between the infant and his or her environment.

It may be worthwhile outlining some links between Winnicott's ideas and those of later writers who have, to a considerable extent, followed the paths that he opened up (although not all of them acknowledge this). With regard to the primary experience of the encounter with the maternal object, Little (1981)[4] says that the situation provides the nucleus of an experience of "one-ness", which is necessary if subsequent experiences of separateness are to be lived through in as positive manner as possible. The state of one-ness has first to be created before it becomes possible to leave it behind. Anzieu (1974)[5] highlighted the importance of creating what he called a "common skin", the quality of which determines how subsequent unsticking will be experienced and prevents separation from producing feelings of being torn apart. McDougall (1978)[6] has explored what becomes of certain kinds of failure in the dialectic between unity and differentiation in shared experiences; she describes, in narcissistic- and identity-related disorders, the preservation of shared, non-differentiated zones, involving particular parts of the body that have remained in a "Siamese twin" relationship to the mother: a body (or part of the body) for two, or, to expand a little on what she says, a mind (or part of the mind) for two. The idea of shared affect, as suggested by Parat (1995),[7] seems to me to have the same implicit basis: "sharing an affect" produces an affect that is common to both protagonists.

I have suggested that Winnicott's ideas about the maternal presence being like a primary mirror for the self could be linked to what we know of melancholia, in particular to Freud's famous aphorism "the shadow of the object has fallen upon the ego" (1917e, p. 249).[8] In that paper, "Mourning and melancholia", Freud emphasizes in the process of melancholia the importance of the disappointment coming from the object. I would say that one of the earliest of disappointments – and, no doubt, one of the most crucial – is that of not finding in the object an appropriate echo of the infant's expectations and impulses. The shadow of the object at that point has to do with the failure of its mirror function, its blind spots; the shadow is what in the object sends nothing back to the infant about who he or she is. It is the absence of an echo that constitutes the shadow of the object, creating points at which there is no differentiation between subject and object.

Let us return to the different phases of Winnicott's model. The illusion is subsequently knocked down little by little by the experience of the mother's gradual dis-adaptation which, when she leaves the state of primary maternal preoccupation, introduces a series of gaps between what she actually offers to her baby and what her baby is expecting – that is, between the found and the created.

These gaps mobilize destructive impulses in the infant, who is furiously angry with everything, both with him- or herself and with the environment, under the impression of having lost – destroyed any capacity for satisfaction (for self-gratification).

The rest depends on how the mother's guilt feelings will be adjusted. If she feels too guilty because she is no longer perfectly adapted to her baby, she will react either by trying to compensate for or repair the damage she thinks that she has done, or by becoming depressed because of her baby's tyranny (or of that of the overall situation). These reactions modify the kind of contact and encounter that she has set up with her infant, who can no longer "find" the object as it once was – the object thus appears to the infant as having been destroyed. If the mother's guilt feelings are not too great, and if she can get back in contact with her baby in a way reasonably similar to what it usually is, her infant will have the experience of the object surviving the presumed destruction; the object is discovered to be relatively independent of the baby's drive-related impulses, the object is discovered as an other-subject with its own life and desires, and the infant's illusory omnipotence has, in fact, no hold over it. The baby can then leave behind the primary narcissism in which he or she is the source and agent of his or her own satisfaction.

Then, Winnicott says, the infant can begin to draw a distinction between the fantasy object, the one that he or she had the illusion of destroying, the one destroyed in the infant's fantasy, and the external object, that is, the other-subject.

The topography of the mind can then begin to be set up and differentiate between internal reality, in which the omnipotent destruction of the object can take place, and external reality, in which the object is not destroyed but survives. The difference between the representation of the object – what Winnicott calls the subjective object – and the external object can then begin to be constructed.

It should be pointed out that were the baby to find the mother exactly like the one he or she thought had been destroyed, that would be equivalent to invalidating the infant's subjective feeling of destruction. It is necessary for the object to have been affected, as I pointed out earlier; it is this that gives value to the experience of destruction and vouches for the psychic reality of that destruction.

The object also has to survive so that the sphere of destruction can have certain boundaries around it. My hypothesis would be that this dialectic is similar to that which underlies the experience of gradual transformation of the relationship with the mother and, more generally, with other objects. It could also be pointed out that the mother is indeed affected: she does come up against her infant's destructive fury, and she can perceive it as being directed at her and as having to do with the fact that she has taken some steps toward recovering her own freedom and independence; at the same time, that kind of experience is indicative of the fact that the earlier state of their relationship is drawing to a close. In some ways, for the mother, too, that relationship with her baby will have to "survive" the infant's fury; she, too, therefore, can see that their relationship is changing.

Winnicott emphasizes also the fact that as soon as the object is discovered, it can begin to be loved. A few words of comment might be useful here. The object begins to be loved not only because love presupposes an object that is an other-subject, but also because, in the strict sense of the word, there can be no true drive if the object is merely subjective. If drives are seen as being composed of four elements, as Freud suggests in his Three Essays (1905),[9] a dynamic pressure that has a source, an aim and an object, then it has to be acknowledged that this introduces a distinction between the source of the drive and the object. The object of the drive alternates between a definition given by the internal representation of the object (which has its own history, one that is already part of the encounter with the object) and one that depends also, given that the representation is transferred on to the object/other-subject, on the response of that object/other-subject.

It oscillates, in other words, between an internal auto-erotic representation and an external presentation. I shall come back later to these issues in my discussion of how secondary narcissism is "taken back" from the object.

In Winnicott's conception, then, what becomes of the drives depends both on the self's quasi-biological assemblages and impulses and on the responses that the object makes to the drive-related urges of the self based on those biological assemblages. It means that we have to imagine different ways in which the drives can be structured, and that we leave room for the organizing (or disorganizing) impact of the object. Whether through the experience of found–created or what I have called destroyed–found, how the drives make use of their latent qualities depends also on the object and on the responses that the object makes to the infant's drive-related impulses. That was also what made Winnicott think that an excess of clinical destructiveness was not attributable to a constitutional intolerance to frustration, and that, when primary envious attacks are significantly intensified, this has not to do with a given state of the self's own parameters but is an indication of the fact that the self has been through some early trauma: either the primary illusion of found–created was not properly set up, or the object did not adequately "survive" the infant's early fury.

The matrix of conflictuality and the question of survival

Another consequence has to do with how satisfaction is obtained. Before, the baby could attribute this to him- or herself. The discovery of the existence of the object/other-subject means that the origin of satisfaction will have to be attributed elsewhere – and the infant begins to see satisfaction as being brought by the object. The object is then idealized; on to the object is transferred the primary representation of an ideal based on the subjective experience of primary narcissism, a state in which everything is produced by the self, immediately and altogether, all in one. The self attributes the representation of the ideal of satisfaction to the object, which thus becomes the source of everything that is good and is loved for that reason. However, in so far as the object is the source of satisfaction, it is also the source of dependence, it can go missing/be missed, hated for that and destroyed in fantasy.

This, then, is a second element that concerns survival. Will love for the object survive the hatred of dependence that it arouses, a dependence that wounds the infant's ego? Can one feeling survive in the presence of another, contradictory, one that comes into conflict with the first? The structure of mental conflict will depend on that. If all else fails, the two feelings will have to be split off from each other; each is protected from the other by separating them.

Here the question of survival has to do with internal matters, with the manner in which processes are able to coexist within the mental apparatus. Some forms of attacks on linking, as described by Bion (1959),[10] have to do with this problem situation; they try to test the strength of the link and call into question its ability to survive destructiveness in a way that I would tend to call "internal reality check".

If love holds out against hate, then love will be experienced as solid and reliable; the conflict of ambivalence can then be set up. But if it cannot stand fast, then only bad things will prevail; love will have to be protected by every means at the self's disposal because keeping it alive is vital for mental life and for the link with the object.

Of course, the survival of love depends also on the force of the attack launched by hate, which, in turn, depends on the intensity of the wound linked to dependence.

Dependence is tolerable as long as it is not (too) all-embracing; the self will develop auto-eroticism in order to resist dependence or to relativize it as much as possible. Two erotic directions will then come into conflict.

- The first involves the object/other-subject. Acknowledging its dependence with respect to the object, the self attempts to lessen that dependence by developing means of action against it: control, systems of communication, etc.
- The second is to develop auto-erotic capacities. Here, it is the internal representation of the object that is called upon; an attempt is made to bring together the satisfactions obtained with the object within the "auto-" or self-related systems. Auto-eroticism tries to claw back from the object what the former phase of idealization had attributed to it. Again, the question is whether this conflict situation will be able to find a sufficiently harmonious way of resolving itself; the hetero-erotic direction will develop mainly while the object is present, whereas the auto-erotic one will be uppermost when the object is unavailable or absent.

The issue here is whether the hetero-erotic avenue will survive and be able to resist the increase in auto-eroticism or whether the infant, even in the object's presence, will attempt to preserve everything that asserts his or her independence – the converse position being that the infant hesitates to go down the auto-erotic path in case the relationship with the object becomes too heavily affected and, in the end, damaged.

Part of what then takes place will depend on the quality of the auto-eroticisms that have developed, that is, on the degree of guilt that may be attached to any manifestation of them. This has to do with the guilt linked to auto-eroticism and what this is experienced as having taken from the object. Secondary narcissism (in the present case, the development of auto-eroticisms), as Freud points out in one of those aphorisms of which he had the secret, is accomplished "through the drawing in of object cathexes" (1914c, p. 75).[11] And if it is taken from the object, we must ask ourselves if and how the object is affected by this – and also, of course, if it survives that particular onslaught.

This brings us to a third level with regard to the survival of the object. Will the object and the relationship set up with it survive the attempts at reappropriation typical of the auto-erotic tendency? Will the object take back what the self tries to take for itself, what has been received and experienced in the encounter with the object? Will the relationship with the object be destroyed by the tendency toward autonomy that is implicit in auto-eroticism? Working through these issues is an important element of the capacity to be alone in the presence of the object, which creates a relationship in which the object's response to the development of auto-eroticism and its accompanying fantasies can be experienced and explored. The experience of solitude in the presence of the object – or, to use the slight modification that I suggested could be applied to Winnicott's formulation in order to highlight the crucial point at issue, the experience of the capacity to be alone, when faced with one's drives, in the presence of the object – creates an intersubjective situation in which the object is sufficiently discreet so that the illusion of solitude and the recourse to auto-eroticism can be maintained while at the same time sufficiently present for its response to be explored.

Typically, and this is the situation that will tend to be reproduced in the psychoanalytic session, children play at their mother's feet, they "play at being the object", they play at becoming the object and they take over the object's capacities for themselves during their play. The question then becomes that of the object's reaction to that play and to the appropriation that is part of it. What then happens will depend on the response of the object/other-subject. If the mother de-cathexes her infant, if she withdraws completely from this paradoxical kind of link – that is, if she abandons her child – or, conversely, if she participates in one way or another in the game, the infant will experience these various reactions (watching the mother, glancing at her, exploring her reactions, observing her observing) as responses to what she feels about his or her attempts at appropriation;

they will be felt, not unjustifiably, indeed, with respect to the unconscious interchange, as a form of retaliation aimed at his or her play and the subjective appropriation contained within it. Conversely, the infant will also be seeking the mother's discreet approval, watching out for some kind of acknowledgement that reassures as to the object's ability to survive without too much damage being done.

From the mother's point of view, we can imagine a conflict between, on the one hand, the fact that she perceives her infant as beginning to separate from her thanks to the development of auto-eroticism and the learning that this makes possible – implying some degree of mourning and of renunciation – and, on the other, a substitute satisfaction as she sees her infant grow and develop. It is this correspondence between the experience of the two protagonists that means that the infant's play and the mother's responses are not chance events; they are authentic with respect to the underlying issues of that interchange.

This is a brief picture of a matrix of conflictuality in human beings, with its three main aspects: the conflict over ambivalence, the conflict between auto-eroticism and hetero-eroticism and the conflict within auto-eroticism. I have emphasized the close connection between these three aspects of basic conflictuality, and I have highlighted the importance of the question of survival in the way each of these is dealt with. The quality of auto-eroticism weakens the feeling of dependence and, therefore, alleviates, to some extent, the self's hatred of the object; this, in turn, influences the choice between the auto-erotic and hetero-erotic solutions. In different and increasingly complex ways that matrix structures conflictuality all through life; it creates a dialectic as to the survival of the object/other-subject and as to the consistency of psychic contents and tendencies. When the external object survives, it increases the capacity for internal survival of the various mental impulses, and this, in turn, makes it easier for the object to survive.

At adolescence, however, other modalities of the question of survival will come to the fore. Although these are generally similar to those that I have just described, they do have certain specific features, and it would be interesting to study these in more detail.

My overall hypothesis is that survival – of the self, of the object or even (and we shall see the importance of this later) of an affect-related impulse when faced with antagonism – is also one of the major processes of drive-related introjection in adolescence (and probably at any age), because of the crucial role it plays in reality check. In other words, that process, usually described in terms of the relationship with external reality, is, in my view, just as active in "mental" reality check.

It would thus seem to be one of the crucial elements of subjective appropriation and of self-appropriation, which is one of the main issues that have to be dealt with in adolescence.

Survival of the object in adolescence and subjective appropriation

For an accurate investigation of the issues relating to the survival of the object in adolescence, it will be useful to draw the reader's attention to certain main points of the theory of adolescence.

As I have pointed out elsewhere, the main issues that have to be dealt with in adolescence have to do with the subjective revolution brought about by the arrival of a new category of pleasure – that of the orgasm, of the potential for orgasm, that is, of the possibility of having access to that particular kind of affect-related pleasure that we call orgasm.

The crucial issue to be dealt with in adolescence involves the introjection of that experience and the affect that accompanies it, as well as the distinctive yet paradoxical relationship that experience has with the ego. This is indeed a distinctive relationship, because it assumes that introjection of the affect will be accompanied by the disappearance, at least in part, of the frontiers of the ego, since it implies a kind of obliteration of the ego – the vernacular expression "petite Mort" ("little death") shows this quite clearly. The question that then has to be dealt with – decisive for the introjection of the sexual drives – is whether the ego will survive that partial disappearance of its frontiers, that "little death", or whether, if the threat is felt to be too great, it will rise up against the drives and their emergence and try to kill them off so as not to risk having to yield to them.

The ascetic reactions that adolescents may then develop are well known; they often alternate between ascetic moments in which they struggle against their drives and others in which their ego lets itself be carried along by their flux.

In that process, it is obvious that their previous history and what has been integrated of it will be crucial factors in determining these reactions; this is particularly the case with respect to their relationship to seduction and to primary seduction, that is, that of the mother. The primary maternal role cannot be described simply – as too often is the case, when the issues involved are not looked at closely enough – as being that of a protective shield against stimuli: that would only bear witness to her phobia of drives and to her fear of being tempted to reintegrate the product of her conception. I do not, of course, wish to imply that mothers should adopt an attitude in which their infant could be overwhelmed by enigmatic drive-related impressions: that would be an abusive form of excitation, and the impressions would be impossible to integrate. Between those two positions, there is the function that in the end Freud acknowledged as being part of the mother's role, that of initiating her infant to sexuality; mothers are the very first seductresses.

Clinical explorations of early childhood show that mothers are able to teach their infant to integrate drive-related excitations and impressions that increase in intensity, and this thanks to the virtues of their seduction: take, for example, playing at tickle-tickle, "this little piggy went to market", etc., which increase drive-related excitation; when that seduction does not become passionate, but stays within the limits of what the infant can handle, it helps him or her to learn to put up with increasing quantities of drive-related excitation, to tolerate moments of forgetting the self and bear with phases in which the ego seems to vanish in a kind of orgasm. These early experiences lay the foundations upon which subsequent experiences of orgasmic sexuality will be dealt with in adolescence.

Confronted with these issues, adolescents find themselves dealing with another great temptation. In addition to the ascetic solution that I have mentioned, there may be an attempt to control their problems by means of behavior evocative of ordeals – these have to do with some form of destructiveness or other.

Adolescents, as I have said, are faced with issues such as the death of the self and its close connection with belonging to oneself. Sexual pleasure brings these two aspects together: taking pleasure in oneself implies belonging to oneself, but that belonging also implies the disappearance of the self and, therefore, the question of survival. That paradox of self-appropriation, with its echoes of the disappearance of the self, will also often be played out through the testing of the self that the kind of ordeals that adolescents set up for themselves implies. Risking one's life, putting it in play and to the test, also implies experiencing the fact that it is indeed one's own – more exactly, it is a way of trying to calculate to what extent it does belong to oneself, to what extent one has control over it. Killing or threatening to kill the object that is in the self, killing the marvelous infant of early childhood, killing the child belonging to his or her lineage, to his or her parents, and in that way attempting to be at the origin of one's own lineage, becoming a parent, killing the other's child, the child for the other in an attempt to belong to oneself, all of this gets mixed up and the various elements come into conflict with one another. Putting oneself through ordeals may well be an essential aspect of the attempt to conquer oneself, to reappropriate oneself; it is obvious, too, that surviving that test is just as crucial, because, if it were not the case, then the question might no longer arise.

It must also be acknowledged, none the less, that putting oneself through ordeals is not simply a way of experimenting with certain issues, it is also an attempt at mastering the peculiar relationship between death and pleasure. The threat of the death of the ego contained in the orgasmic affect is experienced passively; it is a fact, whether the adolescent wants it or not, it imposes its presence through the very fact of bodily sensations and feelings, of drive-related urges, and, therefore, of the id. Ordeal-related behavior is under the control of the subject, of the subject's ego or at least tries to be; it is the adolescent who plays out the relationship between that behavior and its ultimate limit, death, sexual pleasure, self-appropriation. Although that behavior offers the ego a sphere of experience, it is limited by attempts at mastering it – rejecting the passivity that is crucial to the orgasmic experience and its introjective significance. Examples of this ordeal-related behavior are binge-drinking until the adolescent loses consciousness and other kinds of drug-related behavior; adolescents are quite partial to this kind of thing. I would see these as attempts to create, quite deliberately, subjective states similar to orgasmic pleasure in order both to abandon themselves to those states, vanish inside them, and to try to control how they come about. I shall come back later to the idea that there is also an element of making the object absent, the object/other-subject, with its connection to desire.

With the adolescent process still in mind, I would like now to say a few words about what Winnicott calls the "doldrums" of adolescence. This obviously includes the depressive dimension often encountered in adolescence, but to equate the two would be a mistake, one that would lock adolescents into a kind of impasse. In the kind of boredom and emptiness that adolescents come up against, there is also the quest for a passive role, for a formless (sometimes called "amorphous") kind of internal state which, when it is not cultivated over-actively, may lay the foundations for the adolescent's feelings of freedom, self-freedom, self-belonging – in other words, it may set up an internal state from which the feeling of one's true self may emerge. Formlessness – Winnicott taught us this – is a prerequisite for every true shaping of the self, a precondition of free subjectivation.

The introjection of the orgasmic affect also threatens the internal relationship with objects. As Freud quite correctly pointed out on several occasions, a child's love is characterized by tenderness. Ferenczi went as far as to argue that that dimension was specific to the difference between adult sexuality, which for him was passionate, and infantile sexuality, in which tenderness, he argued, is the characteristic element. Without following him completely with regard to that distinction, I would, nonetheless, agree that introjection of the genital drives and the demand for orgasmic pleasure that this involves represent a threat to this quality of tenderness; another issue that has to be faced at adolescence is that of surviving this situation also. The need to distinguish between objects of desire and objects of tender love is something that always crops up in those for whom that survival does not take place in a positive way.

Another aspect of that question concerns onanism and the kind of guilt feelings that accompany it. Internal sexual intercourse with the representation of the object, which is a manifestation of the object relation specific to the kind of drive-related urges involved in it, comes up against the object as other-subject, the subject of its own desires. Will internal intercourse with the representation of the object, onanistic intercourse with that object representation, "affect" the object that underpins the fantasy? Will the relationship with the object/other-subject survive that internal control of its representation? How do the internal representation of the object and the object/other-subject adapt to each other? Can they coexist? As I mentioned earlier, for Winnicott the survival of the object is a prerequisite for the setting up of a mental topography in which the representation of the object and the external object can be differentiated from each other.

There is another test of survival, one which involves the impact of fantasy life on the relationship between the adolescent and reality-first, the reality of the world, then that of the other-subject.

Orgasmic potentiality, especially in the initial stages of adolescence, is experienced almost as the equivalent of hallucinatory fulfillment, the only dimension of subjective functioning through which fulfillment seems to come of its own accord and immediately; it is the only modality of true satisfaction in early childhood. We can see in this a typical feature of adolescence, with its mechanisms such as "all or nothing", its "absolutist" dimension, its "revolutionary" aspect. Adolescents will have to renounce the possibility of finding themselves again, via orgasmic sensations, in circumstances in which primary hallucination, and the illusion of self-sufficiency that accompanies it, were a possibility. They will have to differentiate between the fulfillment of the sexual drives – strictly sexual – with which the fact of adolescence confronts them and primary hallucinatory fulfillment; they will have to discover that adolescence, like adulthood, is not a particularly well-chosen moment for accomplishing at long last their primitive infantile desires.

To some extent, they will have to acknowledge that part of their infantile systems of consolation were illusory. Killing the "marvellous child" of primary narcissism, killing the father of the primal horde presumed to have fulfilled the ideal of complete and total satisfaction of early childhood amount to that: killing the illusion, renouncing the illusion of satisfaction conceived of in terms of identity of perception, denouncing the illusion of immediate perception belonging to primary appearance.

Of course, that illusion must also survive; in adolescence, it will also oscillate between different poles, with the to-and-fro movements that are necessary for its gradual and effective integration.

Becoming involved in that process marks the dawn of adult functioning, that of someone who has gone through the adolescent phase and become an adult.

The murders that are involved in that process will be of different kinds: adolescents enjoy shooting down their idols just as much as they like setting them up, they enjoy great speeches that once and for all say how the world should be, they like breaking off all contact with the world of their childhood, their beliefs try to be as radical as possible, yet a murder/criticism process lies at the heart of all of this.

Identity of perception, the belief in fulfillment based on the perceptual appearance of things, brings the economics of pleasure to an impasse. Orgasmic potentiality is not observed, it is experienced in the depths of subjectivity even when it is not objectively perceived; it is there and has consequences above and beyond what sensation is able to indicate. The world of appearances, the world in which childhood was largely based, is a world of illusion to which only simpletons and children can give credit: one has to lose one's innocence …

Adolescents put to the test the world of perceptual appearances – they have to do so, in fact. The world of the senses, of material objects, which seems to be full, in fact turns out to be a void swirling with imperceptible atoms (physics); things are transformed through an alchemy of reactions between invisible substances (chemistry); intangible forces secretly govern what seemed to be natural elements and the essence of things. Identity of perception assumes that objects are similar; the identity of thinking calls that into question; it takes a knife to what appears to be without a background, in all the innocence of its manifest appearance.

Adolescents will also have to put to the test the appearances of the adult world, those of the socius. They have their doubts about the adult world, about the world that adults would like them to believe that it is as they say – those adults who keep a tight hold of their secrets in order to preserve their privileges, their power.

Adolescents do not really believe that society is organized in the way it seems to be: globalization, international capitalism, Zionism, or, in another category, Freemasons, Rosicrucians, Knights Templar and other secret societies – these are the secret forces that govern the destiny of the world and deceive us as to the true reason behind things. In early adolescence, some youngsters become involved in parapsychology, spiritualism, table-turning and object displacement under the influence of spirits, hidden forces that only the initiated can come to know and share in their secrets. Latency children do not become involved in dept psychology, because their horizon is what is manifest; only adolescents can explore the world of unconscious motives and hidden desires.

There are many more examples of these primary beliefs being put to the test, those that structure the world of childhood. Probably, at least part of these interrogations and challenges were already being undertaken in the latency period, and perhaps even in early childhood, but, in addition to the fact that they are not as wide-ranging as in the adolescent version, they could not at that stage be fully appropriated in any structural manner.

Nevertheless, it should be pointed out that adolescents do not enter into such an undertaking waving their swords and full of innocent enthusiasm, because even if it is stimulating it can also be uncertain. What will survive when the world is put to the test in this way? What will we still be able to rely on, on what certainties will we be able to set up a minima the secure base without which the world becomes full of threatening strangeness and hostility? We must also ourselves survive the critical murder of the other person, survive our own subjective revolution. Hope has to survive the murder/criticism impulse; pleasure in living, the "naturalness" of the pleasure we take in living, must survive the generalized loss of innocence, survive the solving of the enigma of orgasmic pleasure.

That adolescent movement has to be carried out with much toing and froing, with many oscillations, without pausing, without any ascetic freezing; no lost bodies, no lost subjects even, no subjectivity under the dominance of the doldrums. It would be a mistake to see in these oscillations and different phases signs of regression, because that is not what they are. We never go back in time, except in science fiction or metapsychology fiction, or unless we believe that we can turn the clock back. All these movements are an integral part of the process and of the requirement that that process can only unfold bit by bit, detail by detail. Letting go of earlier beliefs, of the innocence and naïveté of childhood, of one's belief in the innocence and naïveté of childhood, giving things up in a way that can be subjectively appropriated, presuppose choice and freedom of choice.

This, in turn, implies that growth is not a constraint, that we can experience the capacity to preserve earlier moments of pleasure, and that we can verify our capacity to preserve these. All the same, letting go does imply that, at one point, we can feel that the cost of hanging on to earlier satisfactions is too high, so that it becomes more of a hindrance than a form of reassurance.

To conclude this overview of survival in its various shapes and forms, I would like to say a few brief words about the connection between this and the myth of the primal horde and the murder of the father of the primal horde as part of its structure. (I alluded earlier to this connection.) The murder of the father of the primal horde is a story of a father who did not survive; that non-survival brings about a group-based fetishistic structure: a totemic society (at least in Freud's version, in Totem and Taboo (1912–1913[12])), a society without a history, caught up in a temporal cycle of always coming back round to the same point in a kind of compulsion to repeat.

This, however, was not all that Freud had to say about that myth. In his Postscript to Group Psychology and the Analysis of the Ego (1921c),[13] he comes back to that issue. The epic poet, the dichter, is another way of breaking free of the impasse of the collective fetishism of the Totem. This other character in the myth represents another form of survival of the object – I have suggested that we call this "standing alone to face the father" because of how Freud describes the situation in that Postscript. The invention of that new outcome was perhaps in some way connected to the possibility that Freud had of reworking his metapsychological undertaking and perhaps even of building it up on newer foundations that lay beyond the pleasure principle.

Conclusion

In this conclusion, I would like to emphasize some of the outcomes of the issues that I have explored in this chapter. A failure in any form of the survival of the object creates an area of mental fragility, threatens to bring about a state of confusion between representation and acts (a topographical breakdown), accentuates destructiveness and de-potentializes it so that actual destruction may result. Conversely, every successful survival of the object deepens the topographical structure and lends support to the process of differentiating between internal and external reality, between the objects and impulses of the inner world and those of the outer world; every success alleviates feelings of guilt and diminishes the threat of being a criminal because of those guilty feelings.

There is a strengthening of reality check, based on survival, which ought, therefore, to be seen as the third major element in the process of reality check, in addition to the one involving motility and distance, and that based on actuality testing; both of these have to do with solipsistic processes. The topographical differentiation that this allows means that the subject can, in internal reality, carry out the murder of the object or the murder of the self and assuage his or her feelings of hatred, without their being expressed in external reality other than via a capacity to differentiate and an access to individual psychology (Freud 1921).

Processes that have to do with the survival of the object are in operation each time that the subject needs to put the object to the test, to put the world to the test or to put some aspect or other of these to the test. They are present also, but in a more subdued fashion, in the analysis of all the internal processes of the subject in so far as they involve, to a greater or lesser extent, the history of the encounters with significant objects in that person's past. The mind is not constructed "by itself"; it is structured through encounters and interchanges with objects that are also other-subjects, having their own modes of response, not simply those of the "object relation", and it has as its basis models derived from significant relationships.

When we speak of self-generating, not only in the context of a delusion, we are referring essentially to the idea that the subject is self-generated; we ought also to remember that mental processes are not self-generated or produced by the subject alone, even though they are his or her processes, in the ego's pockets and packets, even if they are internalized. Interiority can no longer be looked upon as proof of true subjectivation; there are kinds of subjective appropriation based on alienated subjective positions, with no real choice. These are more or less the result of post traumatic solutions, as it were, worked out in an emergency that threatened to put an end to psychic survival. Here, the subject had to survive because the survival of the object had failed.

I shall say only a few words about the far-reaching question of the survival of the object in the course of psychoanalytic treatment. From what I have already said, it is clear that this survival will depend, in the analysis, on maintaining a sufficiently coherent attitude; this is one level of survival. This is not simply – as we tend to say without giving it much thought – a matter of preserving the setting; it means maintaining in that setting a psychoanalytic stand-point, that is, one that implies sufficient consistency of affects and a manner of responding that, whatever the circumstances, remains focused on making what transpires meaningful.

It is not, of course, when the analysis is proceeding at cruising speed that this sort of question arises, but more often in those critical moments that I call borderline situations. It has often been said that the question of survival is at the center of an analysis whenever destructiveness explodes and the negative transference is very much to the fore. However – and it is here that the concept of the survival of the object that I am proposing goes beyond that classic position – the so-called positive transference also has to be "survived"; the same is true in cases of passionately amorous transference, idealizing transference, etc. The transference itself has to be survived, whatever form it may take; surviving the transference implies being able to clarify its historical roots.

We have to agree to being affected by the transference, shaken in our emotions and in our thinking by the acted penetration of the transference, yet survive – in other words, remain a psychoanalyst. That implies – perhaps not immediately, perhaps not without some difficulty – doing something creative with what is transpiring; that is what "benevolence" means to me when the word is used to describe how the analyst listens attentively to the patient. Listening to what might prove to be creative, even in the kind of transference we call negative (and that is a misnomer). Benevolence is and remains a prerequisite for analysis to be carried out. Surviving, then, depends on that basic benevolence (and on empathy, and perhaps even on sympathy) without which no analysis can take place.

Whether the object enables the baby and more generally the child to maintain the field of illusion necessary for the development of his primary creativity, or whether it "survives" the forms of its destructiveness, it occupies an important symbolizing function in his development process. This symbolic function, to which the next chapter is devoted, is essential in the process of integrating lived experience.

Notes

1 Winnicott, D.W. (1989). *Psycho-analytic explorations*. Cambridge, MA: Harvard University Press.
2 Freud, S. (1937b). "Constructions in analysis". *Standard Edition*, 23: 257.
3 Roussillon R (2004a). "La dépendance primitive et l'homosexualité primaire en double". *Revue Française de Psychanalyse*, 2: 421–441.
4 Little, M. (1981). *Transference neurosis and transference psychosis: Towards basic unity*. New York: Aronson.
5 Anzieu, D. (1974). "Le moi-peau". *Nouvelle Revue de Psychanalyse*, 8: 195–209. NRF.
6 McDougall, J. (1978). "Primitive communication and the use of the transference". *Contemporary Psychoanalysis*, 14: 173–209.
7 Parat, C. (1995). *L'affect partagé*. Paris: PUF.

8 Freud, S. (1917b [1915]). "Mourning and melancholia". *Standard Edition*, 14: 239.
9 Freud, S. (1905). "Three essays on the theory of sexuality". *Standard Edition*, VIII.
10 Bion, W.R. (1959). "Attack on linking". *IJP*, 40: 108–121.
11 Freud, S. (1941[1938]). "Findings, ideas, problems". *SE*, 23, 299.
12 Freud, S. (1913). "Totem and taboo". *SE*, 12.
13 Freud, S. (1921). "Group psychology and the analysis of the ego". *SE*, 18.

6   The symbolizing function of the object

Every theory is necessarily a theory of the self and for a given individual, but at the same time it cannot but be a theory of the object and of the manner in which the object subjectifies the self or enables the self to take on board the feeling of being a subject. That is the symbolizing function of the object, if we agree to superimpose the development of symbolization on the function of subjective and subjectifying appropriation.

That is no doubt why psychoanalysis is constantly attempting to develop its representation of the symbolizing function of the object and of the process of symbolization. It is also why psychoanalysis modifies or adjusts certain sections of its theory in order to fit them more closely to the ongoing progress it makes in understanding symbolization. Psychoanalysis had first to acknowledge that symbolization certainly does not go without saying, but that it is the outcome of an internal processing that demands more than simply putting a curb on discharge; it then had to admit that the quality and nature of intrapsychic binding are just as fundamental as its purely quantitative aspects. Our conception of the work of symbolization had to integrate these points, and in so doing was modified. Those aspects have had an impact also on our conception of the intersubjective function of the Oedipal objects and on the way in which we conceive of their symbolizing – or potentially symbolizing – function for the individual concerned.

The theory of anaclisis that Freud put forward (1905d)[1] meant that all the object had to do was to ensure self-preservation; it was up to the infant, following the model of the satisfaction of bodily needs, to work out his or her auto-eroticisms in order to provide a basis for sexuality, both present and future. That theory, however, can no longer satisfy the demands of how we are to represent the urgent needs of the object's primary function. Closer clinical investigation of narcissistic pathologies of the sense of identity bring into much sharper focus what could, in other circumstances, remain relatively well-hidden – I emphasize the word "relatively", because of course the problem existed already, for example, in the hysterical patient's rancor or in the obsessive-compulsive patient's magical thinking. In so doing, it made it absolutely vital to think again about the

DOI: 10.4324/9781003198710-6

question of the specific features and nature of how symbolization could gain support from the object and the Oedipal objects.

It might indeed be advisable to abandon the concept of anaclisis, because too often it bears the hallmark of its origins and is understood merely in terms of the "support" that it offers or the backing it finds in bodily needs, often to the detriment of ego needs (Winnicott 1986, 1987)[2] or to what could make symbolization and subjectivity possible. It is not only the support or backing of the environment that these require – unless we extend the definition of anaclisis to a considerable degree and see it as the metaphor for all the preconditions of the activity of representation.

The same is probably true of the increasingly obvious polysemous nature of the concept of "object" in psychoanalysis. This too is a source of misunderstandings and ambiguities, not all of which can be looked upon as the undecidable elements that are required for mental processing – especially as regards what that clinical concept reveals of the historically crucial nature of the subjectifying function of being acknowledged by an other-subject.

These two issues tend mutually to reinforce their ability to make certain aspects less well-defined – the idea of anaclisis and even that of taking support from the object, the transference relationship that does not seem to be set up in terms of what I would describe quite generally as the relationship to the object or to the other-subject, and the relationship both to symbolization itself and to the process and/or apparatus of symbolization.

That is one of the ideas that I intend to explore in this chapter: the characteristic features of the primary relationship to the object tend to be transferred onto the self's relationship with the activity of symbolization and with the symbolic "acknowledgement" that could be expected of this.

In their developments of Bion's theory of thinking, Green and Donnet (1973)[3] argue that in psychosis damage is done not simply to a given fantasy but, more generally, to the apparatus of symbolization itself: what Bion (1962)[4] liked to call the apparatus for thinking thoughts. What psychosis makes abundantly clear through its impact on the mind seems to me to be present – in a less well-defined or perhaps more hidden way – in all narcissistic pathologies of the sense of identity (and perhaps, even more widely, in the transference neuroses themselves, even though what is at stake here is not as crucial as in the psychoses).

Each specific mode of mental functioning has its own relationship to symbolization, its apparatus and its functions, one that differs from all the rest. These variations highlight the existence of a differential relationship to the activity of representation and open up the question of the historical meaning of these differences, thus enabling some possibility of interpreting that relationship.

Following in the footsteps of other psychoanalysts, I have personally emphasized this factor, particularly in the relationship between the self and that part of the apparatus of symbolization that we call language;

it applies also to the relationship between the self and the dimension of primary symbolization, i.e. the sphere in which thing-presentations are produced. This is shown quite clearly through the analysis of differences in how dream activity functions and how the individual relates to dream activity.

Writers, and more especially poets – I am thinking here particularly of those who have engaged with the substance of language itself: Mallarmé, stylists like Céline or Proust (see the following chapters), and, much more recently, Novarina (1998)[5] – are outstanding examples (and cultivated ones, to boot) of this particular differential relationship to language or to the actual substance of language. Nevertheless, often in a more muted way and with less emphasis, the words of our analysands, pronounced while they are lying on the couch, also bear witness to this. In such cases, the transference goes beyond the relationship that analysands set up with their analyst or with the psychoanalytic situation as such; it has also to do with the use they make generally of the analysis and its symbolizing setting, and with the manner in which they treat the whole apparatus of language.

When we try to understand what phase of history or prehistory is being brought into the transference, when we try to follow what is being transferred into the relationship with the setting and the apparatus of symbolization, that is when it may become possible to grasp more clearly the fact that what is being reproduced is the relationship with the symbolizing function of the Oedipal objects, displaced onto the relationship with symbolization itself.

Does this way of looking at the situation – it is slightly different from those that have become classic in psychoanalytic literature – help us to "dig more deeply" or to deploy other aspects of the symbolizing function of the object? That is the issue that I am at present attempting to think through.

The question of the symbolizing function of the Oedipal objects has focused particularly on two aspects – conditions or perhaps preconditions – of symbolization.

The first has to do with the environment functioning as a protective shield against excitation or against the quantum of excitation. In order to symbolize or to develop a capacity for representation, the quantum of excitation that has to be bound via symbolization must be relatively moderate so as not to overwhelm the infant's capacities. In this way, the movement from perception-hallucination to simple thing-presentations with the support of the object's protective shield against the quantum of excitation becomes possible. Another way of putting it would be to emphasize that what is at that point the main factor of excitation – the absence of or separation from the object – must not exceed the capacity of the individual to restore, via representation, the mental continuity that is necessary for the feeling of ongoing being to be maintained or recovered.

The second goes more deeply into the conditions under which this protective shield against excitation can be brought into play; the idea is to identify the main axis of the qualitative aspect of a triangular structure: the Oedipal attractor. Whether it is via a reference to the father in the mother's discourse and desire, the censorship of the woman-as-lover, to use Fain's term (it has really caught on!), or, with reference to Freud, through evoking the various metaphors of the threat of castration pronounced by the mother and expected from the father, we would all agree that when the maternal object manifests a reference to or desire for a third party, the infant can thereupon break free of a pre-symbolic and antisymbolizing mirroring relationship.

There cannot be any symbolization unless some Oedipal structure is established, unless there is a gap between two other individuals who set up a third-party function and a process of metaphorization from one to the other. The protective shield *par excellence* is the outcome of this third-party dimension that lies at the heart of the structuring quality of that two-fold difference: between the sexes and between generations.

Benchmarks like these make up the matrix of the symbolizing function of the Oedipal objects; they no longer, however, seem to me to be sufficient to account for the specific clinical situations on which my present thinking is based. The Oedipus complex, together with its function as attractor-binder for symbolization, emphasizes one of the general conditions under which symbolization can take place and the setting in which it can unfold; it designates what must be appropriated and bound – but it does not show in sufficient detail how that appropriation may come about nor how it may miss its mark. The Oedipal situation includes within itself what has to be symbolized and how symbolization can be carried out, but in such general terms that its implementation in practice leaves much to be desired; the conditions under which it can be subjectively appropriated are too vague, at least when it is first actualized.

There is another level that stands in a dialectical relationship to the first, and which attempts to give a fuller picture of the specific features of the implementation of that matrix or general framework. I am referring here to the mother's containing function (or that of the parental couple) and, beyond that, to the mother's reverie. Here, as in the mirroring function of the primary environment described by Winnicott, another step forward is taken toward setting up techniques of primary binding that make possible the energy retention necessary for symbolization to take place. In this general model, there is a reflective function in the object's response to the self's feelings, distress and impulses. Here, it is when the object is *present* that the self has to discover the wherewithal to work at representation, not simply when the object is absent, albeit to an acceptable degree.

This model appears to satisfy most psychoanalysts, especially when the "mother's capacity for reverie" is endowed with a general metaphorical function such that it designates the set of means employed by the object in helping the self, in enabling the individual to bind and contain any outbursts of primary sensations and affects. In a somewhat paradoxical manner, Bion's more abstract formulations concerning the transformation of beta elements into alpha elements have also acquired metaphorical significance in discussions between psychoanalysts.

The work of metaphorization is important: it brings together all the elements of a question and "contains" them before all of their particular ramifications, hidden conflictualities and blurred paradoxes can be displayed. Could we now make an attempt at de-metaphorization such that we are not left facing too many raw formulations nor imprisoned inside a model which, although important – the model of fantasy and dreams – is nonetheless limited in scope, in our approach to the complex nature of the question?

It must anyway be said that, in the various models that I have described, there are two issues that remain unresolved, two questions that make it absolutely necessary to have recourse to certain theoretical suggestions that we owe to Winnicott.

The first concerns the shift from the symbolization and primary binding proposed by the object, by the object's behavior and reverie, to a symbolization that is the fruit of the self's own mental endeavors. This, in other words, is the work of deconstruction/construction, of the subjective and creative appropriation, by the self, of symbolization. As far as I know, Bion had very little to say about this; indeed, it is often lost behind references to the process of identification. In this case, however, the identificatory response would do nothing more than hide an unsightly shabbiness, because what is really at stake is the need to explain and to account for the processes that lie behind symbolic or symbolizing identification.

The second point has to do with how to articulate the two facets of the symbolizing function of the object. Objects are simultaneously – this is the problem that I pointed out earlier with respect to the Oedipal situation – objects *to be* symbolized (their differences, their otherness, their absence) and objects *for* symbolizing. Here too, the Oedipal matrix offers us a convenient framework for developing these issues, but at the same time, in our clinical work with patients suffering from narcissistic disturbances of their sense of identity, we can see that that framework is too simplistic; we can probably all the same "symbolize" the otherness of one of the objects with the other, and vice-versa, as long as we disconnect the relationship to be symbolized from that for symbolizing. However, this form of "triangulation", to which the psychoanalyst, during a session, may well have recourse – the psychoanalyst is there to be symbolized and for symbolizing – can never be more than a first step, especially if the difficulty in articulating the two facets of the symbolizing function of the object is always treated in this way. Distributing between two ambivalent polarities obfuscates the real work of conflictuality, i.e. facing up to the otherness of which the object is the cause and processing it with that object.

That two-fold necessity – facing up to the object's otherness and symbolizing that otherness with the object – is precisely what I mean by the phrase I used earlier: the other-subject. Clinically speaking, that symbolization can never be complete, but if progress is made along these lines this will be highly significant for the self's capacity to symbolize with a third-party figure (cf. the way in which auto-eroticism functions) the incompleteness and non-fulfillment that is experienced in the relationship with the object.

When I began this presentation, I was careful not to use the "classic" term object relation; I quite deliberately preferred the apparently more vague idea of relationship with the object. In *Playing and Reality*,[6] Winnicott suggested a concept that has not met with the same success as that of transitionality, even though it does shed light on the problems that I have just evoked. In addition to the idea of an object relation – the relationship that is set up with an object separate from the self – Winnicott suggested that there were also different issues that involve the *use* of the object. What I call the relationship to the object has to do with the dialectics that are set up between an object relation and the use of the object.

I would suggest that the use of the object has specifically to do with what I call "the object for symbolizing". It involves the object that lends itself to attempts at symbolization by the self, agreeing to annul or attenuate any reminder of its otherness in order to facilitate symbolization. Use of the object, particularly in the field of ego needs, is an extension of the primary maternal preoccupation; it operates mainly during intersubjective phases that amount to symbolizing situations.

In order to understand the articulation between object relation and use of the object in terms of the object's symbolizing function, it is necessary to go back to Winnicott's conception of how the otherness of the object is discovered.

Following Freud and Ferenczi (1913),[7] psychoanalysts saw the discovery of "reality" – or, rather, the exteriority of the object – as having its roots in the frustration imposed on the infant by the absence of the object; the discovery of reality is a direct effect of that frustration, and thinking and symbolization have their origins in the hallucination that the absence of the object produces. For Winnicott, however, that sequence is more complex and has also to do with the use of the object and with how this combines with destructiveness.

The first fundamental modification is Winnicott's idea that the hallucinatory process takes place whenever any increase in drive-related tension occurs (although the use of the word "drive" in the strict sense of the term may be inappropriate here), and not simply when the object is absent. Hallucinations are a response to the increase in tension, not to the realization that the object is absent; they are independent of the reality of the object. Hallucination and perception are not alternatives; hallucinations may occur even when the object is present. Hence, the problem of how hallucination or drive-related excitation can be bound by the object: the problem of "primary" binding.

If the object is absent, drive-related excitation and hallucination will be dealt with either through evacuative discharge or through some form of binding *in statu nascendi* (here, it is primary masochistic binding that comes to mind).

If, however, the object is present and its response "attuned" to the hallu-cinatory process, it will give rise to the found-created dimension and the transformation of hallucination into illusion. Later, once the dimension of primary illusion is set up in a sufficiently solid manner, if the "censorship of the women-as-lover" or a decrease in the primary maternal preoccu-pation weakens this "made-to-measure" adaptation and jeopardizes both the primary illusion of self-creation of gratification (or of non-gratification, which is also found-created) and the kind of primary link set up thanks to the object and the care that it provides, the infant will then be able to try out a further developmental step.

The threat that hangs over the primary illusion triggers an increase in destructiveness, linked both to the distress and to the anger experienced as a result of the feeling of failure generated by inadequate maternal attunement.

At this point, Winnicott suggests a second modification to the theory of how the mind is structured. In the classical view, exteriority is discovered because "the external world [...] and what is hated are identical" (Freud 1915c, p. 136)[8] – it is, therefore, a direct result of frustration and destructive-ness, and almost a way of opposing these. Winnicott, however, argues that the birth of exteriority depends on the response of the object to the self's destructiveness. This is the point at which object relations and the use of the object begin. Winnicott's suggestions, therefore, introduce an additional stage, the effect – and perhaps the function – of which is to make room for the response of the object within the infant's process of symbolization.

In order to be discovered, the object has to "survive" destructiveness, and this implies three aspects in the object's response to that destructive-ness. The first two are: no withdrawal – the object has to be psychologi-cally present; no reprisals or retaliation – the object must not enter into a power struggle with the self. However, these two very important aspects – they are often the only ones to be mentioned – are not in themselves suffi-cient; in addition, the object must break free of the orbit of destructiveness and re-establish contact with the self, showing itself to be creative and alive. It is in this way that the object bears witness to its existence in terms of an other-subject. It is re-establishing contact that is the decisive element in the discovery of the object's exteriority; basically, the other two factors are simply the necessary preconditions under which that contact can be re-established.

Strictly speaking, the work of symbolization can only begin once it encounters that boundary which holds back destructiveness: the link with the object survives the attack – or, more precisely, it is revealed in and through that attack insofar as it serves to bind the destructiveness that is part of it.

What Bion (1959)[9] called "attacks on linking" in narcissistic pathology is a way of trying to get back in touch – or to get at last in touch – with that experience, one which I would describe as the destroyed-found object. There is no need, then, to resort to concepts such as a constitutional incapacity to tolerate frustration in an attempt to explain certain problems encountered in setting up the apparatus for symbolization; as Winnicott implicitly argues, the inadequacy of the object's response in the attempt to bind primary destructiveness is a much clearer explanation.

Once the object is discovered in all of its exteriority, an object relation – which of course will be ambivalent – then takes root. The object "survives", it is "discovered" as the object of the drives and it is loved. At the same time, the self is dependent on that object; since it may be absent, missed by the self, it will also be hated.

The beginnings of primary symbolization arise from the "retroactive" restructuring that has to be carried out on the world of primary illusion, in order to take into account this new aspect of subjective experience.

The gap introduced by the object against the backcloth of its primary adaptation to the self's needs – the bulwark that is thus created – opens up a field of experience thanks to which the complex process that will lead to symbolization can begin. The object's response to the destructiveness that is thereby mobilized sets up the preconditions for that work of symbolization to become a possibility. Here, the object is just as much the barrier that primary illusion comes up against as the element that enables destructiveness to be the occasion for a structuring discovery. It operates just as much through its own limitations as in terms of those it imposes on the infant's destructiveness. Development and gradual integration are not automatic or dependent solely on the self's internal processes; they become structured only when they are accompanied by an appropriate response from the Oedipal objects, when the infant is not left on his or her own to face up to these destructive impasse situations. The intervention of the object is required if illusion and destructiveness are to be transformed into the mainsprings of the work of representation.

The next phase is that of the presentation of the object. As the primary maternal preoccupation diminishes, the need to compensate for that decrease means that the object must offer the infant some kind of substitute for what is felt to be lacking. The object offers other objects, suggesting to the infant that he or she adapts by transferring the feeling of something lacking on to these other objects, which will then become primary symbols. The "objects for symbolizing" will take over from what the object no longer provides or at least will help to narrow the gap that is always opening up between "found" and "created". A dialectic is set up between what the infant can continue to take directly from the relationship with the object and what will have to be obtained with the help of symbolization. What appears to be a pre-requisite for these beginnings of representation is that the infant must not feel over-dependent on the object nor feel hurt by his or her own immaturity and relative helplessness. The work of symbolization enables the object's efforts at adaptation to be finished off, so that they can gradually be reduced and lead to a "good enough" response with respect to the infant's narcissism.

Part of the object's symbolizing function is to offer the infant the wherewithal to compensate sufficiently for the feeling of loss that is part of the relationship with the object. Thus, it is that the limitations perceived in that relationship with the object open on to the need to use other objects to symbolize and make up for the inadequacies of the Object itself. The object, therefore, proposes that the feeling of loss that it generates be transferred onto and dealt with by the work of symbolization and the objects that make this possible. That "proposition" is essential if the infant is to use these objects in order to symbolize the feeling of loss that he or she experiences with the object. Once again, it is only metaphorically that such a "proposition" can be identified with the emergence of the paternal function. That function will indeed be found somewhere along that same dimension, but it represents only one specific instance of it, its processing horizon as it were, even though it does have a significant structuring aspect to it. I indeed have the impression that it can have a truly structuring effect only if it has been preceded by a significant degree of "use" of objects for symbolizing.

Let us now examine the nature and function of these objects and explore how they are bound up with the relationship to the object of which they are the *locus* of transference/transformation.

My first comment follows on directly from what I have just indicated. These "symbolizing objects" must be proposed by the object itself, which must acquiesce in and perhaps even encourage the way in which they are used.

By proposing other objects, the Object starts to open up the possibility of differentiating between the relationship to an object and the use of an object. The subjective appropriation of the work of symbolization assumes that this transference is carried out and that it is being encouraged by the primary environment – in other words that the primary environment agrees to some of its features being displaced onto other objects; this displacement will enable the secret of symbolization to be gradually revealed. This is particularly true of what is involved in the use of the object.

The object's agreement is vital also for another reason, this time linked to the auto-eroticisms that are mobilized by the work of representation and by the subjective appropriation that this makes possible. The ability to play with objects that are primary symbols goes hand in hand with the development of auto-eroticisms – these are quite different from auto-sensualities which do not possess any activity of representation other than hallucination – and comes up against the same basic problem complex as these, i.e. that of secondary narcissistic activities. These are "taken from the object" as Freud (1915c)[10] put it. This implies that the appropriation of the *objeu* and of all self-related activities (especially auto-erotic ones) is experienced as being taken away from the objects that are either directly involved or represented; that feeling goes hand in hand with the fear of and/or wish to dispossess these objects of the typical features of the work of representation. This activity and the work of autonomization and mourning which it implies always call *de facto* into question the object's ability to survive the subjective appropriation that is part and parcel of this situation.

The pleasure that these movements entail means that there is a fear of dispossessing the object of its own pleasure, but at the same time the wish to do just that; the new capacities that they offer the infant come up against the question whether or not they have been acquired in opposition to and to the detriment of the object.

Do the activity of symbolization and the auto-eroticisms that support it impact on the object and/or on the quality of the relationship that the self has with it?

If the quality of that relationship is not in any way threatened by the object's responses, this implies that it is of little value – it has not affected the object because it is more or less worthless.

If it is threatened too powerfully, according to the intersubjective testimony of the object's modes of response, this leads to a dilemma: a choice has to be made between a relationship with the object and symbolization, i.e. between a relationship with the object and the use of the object. That dilemma runs deep and knows of no solution.

The object's symbolizing response ought to be able to diffract those fears and wishes: the object is affected by the wish and survives in refutation of the fear. It shows itself to be affected, thereby substantiating the reality of the ongoing attempt at separation/differentiation, acknowledging the value of and the issues involved in that attempt, and at the same time bears witness to the changes thus brought about in the relationship with the object. It survives, with its capacity for pleasure, and thereby enables a difference to be made between actual reality and the psychical reality involved in the process of appropriation.

Ideally, the dialectic between the two components thereby differentiated with the help of the object's response will produce some modification in the relationship with the object; that modification will bear witness to what has recently been integrated thanks to the work of symbolization that has taken place. It then also becomes apparent that any continuation of the work of symbolization is dependent on the object's "accompaniment", on its mirror-role within the relationship and on how the object accepts and tolerates its representatives/representations being used and displaced in the interaction. The object can always impose a veto on the work in progress – which, therefore, remains subordinate to the object's acceptance.

Proposing objects for symbolizing, surviving the work of symbolization that is carried out on those objects, surviving the unfolding of auto-eroticisms and the way in which they affect and transform the relationship then reflect it back – these are the fundamental aspects of the object's symbolizing function and of the way in which that function vectorizes and makes possible the work of subjective and differentiating appropriation. The object's response to this displacement and the way in which it encourages and substantiates these responses fall within the scope of the deflecting function of the object.

This leads me to the third comment that I would make as regards the function of the object in the initial stages of the work of symbolization. Retroactively, the use of symbolizing objects will enable certain primary features of the relationship to the object to be diffracted and analyzed, given that it has now become possible to define them. Play is an analyzer of the relationship to the object. It enables, retroactively, what made the experience of the initial encounter with the object worth revealing through and in the work of symbolization; in addition, it is a fundamental aspect of the subjective appropriation of the experience itself. The transference and other ways of taking stock of that experience, including that with other objects, are crucial; they are of the same essence as the revelation of the value of the work of representation itself.

Even better, it is in and through this kind of play that it becomes possible, retroactively, to distinguish between what belongs to the object relation and what involves the use of the object. It is when this takes place that differences are deepened and are revealed; they become perceptible and can be represented. The object relation has to do with issues concerning the confrontation in the primary relationship with the object's otherness, with the non-pliable part of the object; the use of the object, and therefore symbolization, has to do with the way in which the object annuls its otherness in order to lend support to the self's efforts at symbolization and make itself appropriate for that use.

It is, therefore, retroactively and thanks to play that the gap between object relation and use of the object can be properly estimated; the relationship to the object is freed of the burden of the use of the object, with the latter being put to use in symbolizing that relationship. That gap depends on the ongoing work being done through play and changes as symbolization progresses – which thereby modifies the relationship to the object. This takes us far from a conception of object relations that are set up only with respect to the primacy of a given drive-related activation – it is rather the development of the capacity for symbolization that determines which drive-related impulses are activated and therefore the kind of object relation that will be possible or predominant. Object relations and use of the object are, therefore, in a complementary and dialectical relationship that varies according to the progression of symbolization; they are both differ-ent from each other yet non-separable – the one cannot be thought about without some reference to the other.

Play and non-play cannot be considered independently from each other. Experience and symbolization call upon and give meaning to each other reciprocally and dialectically; also, they are in a dialectical relationship with the deflecting and reflecting functions of the object that acknowl-edges and, therefore, appropriates them (or does not acknowledge and, therefore, invalidates them, disqualifying them as to their capacity to process).

That is why a study of the properties of symbolizing objects, of the pli-able medium, has much to teach us about the "relational" conditions and preconditions for symbolization. That pliable medium is both the object of transference of these conditions and preconditions and the *locus* in which their diffraction and differentiation can be analyzed. The way in which it is used – the way in which its various properties can be used in the work of symbolization – tells us something about what it inherits from the primary relationship to the object. The relationship that the self has with it bears the imprint of the history of its relationship with the use of the primary object; its "usable" capacities tell us what has been used in the primary relationship with the object, while its non-usable capacities highlight what was not available for use with the primary object.

The relationship with the pliable medium of the process of symboliza-tion also bears witness to the way in which the activity of symbolization was acknowledged and substantiated in the relationship with the object. This opens up the possibility of access to the symbolizing function of the object, through its transference onto the symbolizing-object that symbol-izes the symbolization.

Once the symbolizing function has been transferred on to the symbol-izing objects, the specific features of the way in which the object mate-rializes its symbolizing function can be interpreted and analyzed; they can be reconstructed in terms of the use of the object. At the same time, this enables us to improve our representations of relation-based quali-ties, incipient ego needs that will be required for the future deployment of the capacity for symbolization; it enables us also to get a better grasp of the forerunners of the primary relationship, so that the use of the object then becomes possible. This in turn allows us to go more deeply into the relation-based characteristics that maternal reverie must make possible in order to prepare for the forthcoming subjective appropriation that is inherent in the work of primary symbolization. The concept of the "good enough" mother can, therefore, be described in more detail, as can its articulation with the pre-symbolizing function of the object.

In light of what the pliable medium diffracts, the initial attunement, which makes possible the organizing of the primary illusion in terms of found-created that is required if symbolization and the symbolization "thing" is to take root, must contain a certain number of characteristics that can be identified and listed.

In several of my earlier papers (e.g. Roussillon 1995), I began to draw up a list of the various characteristic features of the symbolizing-objects of the pliable medium type; these typical features are also the qualitative characteristics of the primary attunement relationship – those which give initial shape to the future properties of the symbolization apparatus within the primary relationship.

Their principal components are as follows: a specific consistency (the degree of hardness and malleability), indestructibility, ability to be taken hold of and transformed, sensitivity, availability, reversibility, reliability and constancy. Once these properties have been sufficiently tried out, with their limitations – these concern the otherness of the object, the boundary that has to be symbolized on the basis of the properties of the object – they can be transferred onto the apparatus for symbolization and the symbolizing objects so as to make them fit for use in the process of representing a given experience. Coming across them and appropriating them through representation will create a specific level of the experience of subjectivity that lies at the heart of the ability to take hold of and define internally the subjective experience of the activity that is symbolization. The embodiment of their specific features will imbue the experience of symbolizing with their particular effects and nuances, thus echoing the history of how they were built up and the limits of their intersubjective deployment.

Given these specific modalities of the relationship to symbolization – in a psychoanalytic session or in the course of everyday life – it becomes possible to make legible a particular feature or other of the primary experience of the encounter with objects, as well as the specific manner in which these objects are present for the self; they can be reconstructed, notwithstanding the disguises to which the passing of time and the application of the pleasure/unpleasure principle have subjected them. An experience of destruction of the capacity for symbolization should make us think of the existence of a possible primary trauma. Destruction of the object or of the link to it and the unavailability of the words or substance required for symbolization raise the issue of the availability of the object. Stereotyped and unchanging formulations or style evoke matters concerning the object's sensitivity or lack of sensitivity, etc.

Of course, no immediate equation can be made between a given symptom affecting the relationship to the apparatus for symbolization and the history of the individual's encounter with the object. That working hypothesis, all the same, does open up possibilities and it would be a pity simply to dismiss them immediately in the name of the complex nature of retroactive reorganizations dominated by the self's pleasure principle – especially when what is at the forefront of the clinical situation has to do with narcissistic and self-identity issues and with what remains imprisoned inside the primary compulsion to repeat.

In the clinical situations that lie behind my hypotheses, the transference of the specific features of the primary relationship with the object onto the apparatus for symbolization itself is like a violent attack: there is very little processing behind it, so that in a relatively simple way it can reveal the traumatic past.

This leads me quite naturally to the question of the clinical and technical effects of the use of the object. I have just stated that the work of reconstruction of the specific features of the primary relationship with the object can begin to become possible based on their transference onto the work of symbolization. The question that then arises is that of the "psychoanalytic" use of the object's symbolizing function and of the importance that we attach to the object's responses at each stage of the process whereby the self's symbolizing function is constructed.

Green (1990) gave some indication of this when he emphasized that, in a session, the analyst has to supply the response that the object, in the past, did not communicate with the analysand, a response that would probably have helped the analysand to integrate and metabolize his or her experience. Although that first indication is indeed essential, I do not think that it is in itself sufficient, because it is important also to analyze the historical effects of the object's inadequate response – in other words, the consequences of the fact that the object did not let itself be (or could not, for whatever reason, be) used. In my experience – and this is particularly the case in the analysis of narcissism and its distortions – we have to reconstruct the object's response and the impact of this on the structuring of the self. The work of reconstruction, as Winnicott observed, involves not only the processes specific to the self but also the dialectical relationship between these and those of the object – not simply the object-for-the-self but also the object as such. I realize that this gives rise to a number of problems, particularly as regards the status of the historical reality that finds itself *de facto* implicated; what must also be taken into consideration, however, is the structuring bulwark that this kind of investigation makes possible.

No human being has ever been self-conceived in his or her bodily existence, and the same is true of our psychological make-up. The organization of our mental apparatus does not depend solely on a series of events and on the meaning that we attach to them; it depends also on the dialectical relationship that is set up between our mental processes and the echoes that these have undoubtedly heard coming from the environment. We are no more self-generated psychologically than we are physically; the primal scene has a considerable number of relation-based and intersubjective aspects in addition to the sexual bodies that it displays. The analysis of narcissism cannot avoid following also the path that leads to a reconstruction of the dimension that we call the use of the object. It cannot ignore the history of the self's object relations nor can it overlook the relationship that the object had with the self or the function that the self had for the object's psychical economy. How to take up in the course of psychoanalytic treatment the dimension of the use of the object seems to me to be one of the crucial questions that contemporary psychoanalysis must address.

In the following chapters, I return to the question of psychoanalytical practice. The work of reconstructing the place of the object's responses in the psychic organization of the subject, the need, as regards early ages, for an active part of the analyst opens the question of suggestion in analysis, which will be the subject of the next chapter. But it also opens the question of listening to the first forms of human language, of their traces in the present of the subject and of consider them, which will be the object of the next chapter.

Notes

1 Freud, S. (1905a). *Three essays on the theory of sexuality.* SE, 7.
2 Winnicott, D.W. (1986). *Holding and interpretation.* London: Hogarth; New York: Grove Press, 1987 [reprinted London: Karnac, 1989].
  Winnicott, D.W. (1987). *The spontaneous gesture.* London & Cambridge, MA: Harvard University Press.
3 Donnet, J.-L., & Green, A. (1973). *L'enfant de Ça.* Paris: Ed Minuit.
4 Bion, W.R. (1962). *Learning from experience.* London: Heinemann Medical Book.
5 Novarina, V. (1988). *Le théâtre des paroles* [*The theatre of words*]. Paris: P.O.L.
6 Winnicott, D.W. (1971). *Playing and reality.* London: Routledge, 1999.
7 Ferenczi, S. (1913). *Le développement du sens de la réalité et ses stades,* OC TII, Payot, Paris.
8 Freud, S. (1915a [1914]). "Further recommendations on the technique of psychoanalysis, III". *Standard Edition,* 12: 159.
9 Bion, W.R. (1959). "Attack on linking". IJP, 40: 308.
10 Freud S. (1915 *c*). "Instincts and their Vicissitudes", SE, 14.

7 Transference and associativity. Psychoanalysis and its debate with suggestion

"On Beginning the Treatment" (Freud 1913c)[1] is one of three papers that Freud wrote on the technique of psychoanalysis between 1913 and 1915, the other two being "Observations on Transference Love" (1915a [1913])[2] and "Remembering, Repeating and Working-Through" (1914g).[3] Taken together, they are the most effective of Freud's attempts to define the essence of the psychoanalytic situation and the work of psychoanalysis.

By 1913, he already had sufficient experience of the practice of psychoanalysis to be able to take stock of its strategy and essential characteristics. He was refining his conception of narcissism in a way that would open up a new chapter in the exploration of the mind and its workings, laying the foundations for what, in 1921, would be the analysis of the ego without falling into the trap of mere self-reference. As he was working on his theory of narcissism and the way in which this would help to identify narcissistic patterns, he undertook a series of reflexive and reflective reappraisals not only of the history of psychoanalysis (Freud 1914d)[4] but also of its practical and theoretical aspects; this led him to envisage undertaking the colossal task of writing the 15 papers on metapsychology that would provide an overall view of psychoanalysis and of its underlying theory.

The years 1913 to 1915 thus represent the first turning point in the development of his thinking, probably indeed the first great reflexive/reflective moment of it. The three papers on psychoanalytic practice that I mentioned above are the technical side of this reappraisal; in them, Freud sums up the overall development of psychoanalysis and highlights the essential features of what that experience had taught him. The paper on remembering and that on transference love highlight some specific issues in psychoanalytic treatment and what the psychoanalyst must do when these particular problems arise in the course of an analysis. The issues raised in the paper on which I am at present focusing – that on beginning treatment – are different: the overall framework and central theme of that paper involve the general strategy that underlies the psychoanalytic method and the conditions under which it can be implemented.

The fundamental feature of the psychoanalytic method involves two closely linked aspects: the reference to the transference, a precondition for

DOI: 10.4324/9781003198710-7

any attempt at interpretation according to Freud, and the associativity of mental functioning as evidenced in the rule of free association.

Analysis of the transference and the conditions under which this becomes possible

The first fundamental concept is that of the transference. The work of psychoanalysis is based on transference. It is this and what it brings into the here-and-now situation of a given session that give weight to the process as a whole and ensure that the analysis will not be superficial – that it will not be an intellectual form of analysis, but will call upon affects and drive-related experiences, the necessary conditions for genuine change and transformation to take place thanks to the analysis.

"When are we to begin making our communications to the patient? [...] The answer to this can only be: Not until an effective transference has been established in the patient, a proper *rapport* with him" (Freud 1913c, op cité p. 139).

There is also Freud's famous remark according to which "it is impossible to destroy anyone *in absentia* or *in effigie*" (Freud 1912b, p. 108)[5]; this makes it plain that, for any genuine transformation to occur, a given problem situation must be brought into the here-and-now of the transference.

The transference is therefore a precondition for the work of analysis. Its presence, its manifestations and its subsequent analysis draw the line between medical psychotherapies based on suggestion and psychoanalytic psychotherapy based on the analysis of the effects of suggestion linked to the impact of the transference on the way in which the analyst's comments are received and integrated. That was also why Freud remained skeptical of any preliminary remark about what was going to take place in the course of an analysis – for example, what as yet inexperienced psychoanalysts may say about a transference love that is still to come. Freud did of course point out in his paper on transference love (1915a [1914]) that this is a product of the psychoanalytic situation – indeed, this is the very condition for its being interpreted. For it to be interpreted, as Freud himself pointed out, it must appear to be spontaneous. The psychoanalytic process takes place within this kind of paradoxical context; these paradoxes must be taken on board by both analyst and analysand if the persuasive effect of the work of the analysis is to be in any way convincing, thereby enabling the anticipated in-depth changes to take place.

This allows me to make a brief comment on Freud's famous idea according to which cure or recovery comes as a bonus, a remark which, in my opinion, has often been misunderstood. That declaration is sometimes – mistakenly – attributed to Lacan; Freud did not mean by it that psychoanalysis is not a kind of psychotherapy or that its aim has nothing to do with a therapeutic outcome – quite the contrary, in fact. He meant that going on with an analysis, without looking for any immediate relief from symptoms of the kind that suggestion aims to bring about, is the best way of treating the analysand's distress – it is the best kind of psychotherapy for this. Freud did not contrast psychotherapy with psychoanalysis, as is often the case nowadays; he drew a distinction between a flawed or superficial form of psychotherapy and a good-quality one which, through its in-depth work, can bring about lasting change. He explained that very appositely in his metaphor of the dog-race in which a sausage was thrown onto the track (1915a [1914], op. cit., p. 169) – with the result that the dogs threw themselves upon it so as to have immediate satisfaction rather than focus on the much more enlarged satisfaction awaiting the winner of the race: a whole garland of sausages. Nevertheless, as I shall make clear later, when treatment is being set up, there are aspects of the psychoanalytic situation that have to be imposed from the outset; these have the unavoidable effect of "fatherly suggestion", as Ferenczi put it.

In such situations, suggestion would seem to be unavoidable; one major aspect of the treatment will be to make it possible to go beyond that thanks to the work of the analysis. The initial suggestion will then be seen as an "advance" that enabled the analysis to take place, a necessary suggestion that facilitated the subsequent possibility to go beyond suggestion.

Transference, however, is not exclusive to the psychoanalytic situation. As Freud pointed out as early as 1912, it develops in the great majority of treatment situations. The capacity to set up a transference represents a general process of mental functioning and is one form of the "compulsion to repeat" (Freud 1914).[6] Nor is transference neurosis specific to psychoanalysis; each time that a transference is set up with respect to some institution or other (Freud spoke of the Church and the Army; we could probably add the family and any kind of treatment situation), a transference neurosis is or can be set up too.

What is specific to psychoanalysis is that it makes it possible to *analyze* the transference neurosis – it creates the conditions not only for that neurosis to be set up but also for it to be analyzed. That was Freud's most fundamental response to the threat of suggestion that hangs over – and will never stop hanging over – psychoanalysis. The transference represents a fundamental threat to the veracity of the psychoanalytic process insofar as it is a factor of influence and suggestion. To counteract influence and suggestion, it is not enough simply to avoid giving advice or to refrain from making use of the suggestion impact common to "medical" psychotherapies (to use Freud's term) – that would simply be a matter of intentional self-control and willpower. That alone, however, would not do away with unconscious influencing and suggesting, since it applies only to the deliberate and intentional aspect of these. Suggestion and influence can have an impact that has nothing to do with the analyst's intentional decisions – they involve the manner in which the analyst's comments and responses are understood by the analysand; in other words, they involve the unconscious transference. That kind of suggestion, influence or even seduction cannot be countered simply by deciding to abstain intentionally from so responding; in order to go beyond the effect that it may have, the unconscious motives that underlie it have to be explored. This is one of the crucial issues at stake in the analysis of the transference – and that is why analysis of the transference is such an essential part of the definition of psychoanalysis when compared to other forms of psychotherapy based on suggestion; it is the dividing line between psychoanalytic psychotherapy and medical psychotherapy. The fundamental issue is therefore that of the conditions that make analysis of the transference possible.

One set of conditions concerns what we might call the transference arena – the early manifestations of the transference, those which, in the preliminary interviews, tend to focus initially on the setting and on the concrete rules that govern the treatment. This led Freud to explore how, in setting up the psychoanalytic situation, these early manifestations of the transference could be overcome – those that focus on the situation itself and take the initial stages of the analysis as their chosen medium. Freud was always drawing attention to the question of how those elements that tended to take the psychoanalytic setting itself as a locus for the transference or its manifestation could be moved away from that particular dimension and brought, as far as possible, into the transference onto the analyst. However, when the treatment is being set up, it is with respect to the setting itself that the transference and resistances tend initially to be manifested. The strategy behind beginning the treatment – the "general plan of the game" (Freud 1913c, p. 123), as it were – consists in not allowing the transference to focus on that particular aspect. But how is this to be brought about, given that transference – and, more specifically, transference onto the analyst – is the very condition that determines the possibility of the analyst's interventions being in any way effective? Freud's idea was to combine two modes of intervention. On the one hand, certain specific aspects of the setting have quite simply to be imposed, the hope being that, with the evolution of the analytical process, that initial enforcement will be transformed into something more convincing, based on the analysand's ongoing experience of the analysis. Some things cannot be justified in advance (for example, matters concerning payment of the sessions: "My answer is: that's just the way it is"); they will become meaningful only through the treatment process itself and be felt to be valid thanks to an experience which, at that particular point, is still to come. This echoes what I said earlier about the "advance" that has to be granted initially to the analysis. At other times, Freud explained the essential reasons for such a setting, and the limitations placed on the analyst's prior knowledge. He did this, for example, with reference to Aesop's fable concerning the length of the Wayfarer's stride (1913c, p. 128) as an illustration of matters that have to do with the length of treatment in general. He did not, therefore, immediately interpret this kind of "resistance", because the necessary conditions for such an interpretation to be effective were not yet in place. He imposed what could not be explained and explained what at that point could be – he made use both of coercion and of meaningfulness.

It was also for the analysis of the transference that he recommended that the analysand lie on the couch. His argument – which he did not share with his analysands – seemed initially to be a matter of personal comfort: he could not bear being looked at all day long by his patients. However, when he did get round to explaining why, it became clear that the real reason had to do with the analysis of the transference: on his face, in his gestures and movements, the analysand could "read" his reactions to what he or she was saying, and therefore adapt what was being said to the visible "responses" of the analyst. Whole chapters of associativity and transference processes might therefore be buried and prevented from being expressed. Here too, the actual setting is an attempt to offset any threat of unconscious or involuntary influence or suggestion coming from the analyst.

It was also so that transference feelings could be brought to the fore that Freud limited as much possible what we now call lateral transference. This represents a source of potential loss to the analysis of a whole aspect of the transference which is attempting to find another stage on which it can be played out. It should all the same be pointed out that what Freud meant by lateral transference was much more restrictive than the manner in which some contemporary psychoanalysts use the concept. For Freud, lateral transference was not just anything; it applied only to situations in which the analysand spoke about his or her analysis to some other person, reporting the sessions or duplicating, as it were, the analytical sessions with other "sessions" carried out with someone in his or her emotional environment.

At this point, it may well be worthwhile reminding the reader that Freud's definition of the transference was not limited to what transpired with the analyst and the psychoanalytic situation. This also is too often forgotten by contemporary psychoanalysts for whom the concept of the transference applies only to what transpires with the analyst. In "Remembering, Repeating and Working-Through", Freud wrote: "[...] the transference is itself only a piece of repetition, and [....] the repetition is a transference of the forgotten past not only on to the doctor but also on to all the other aspects of the current situation" (1914, p. 151).

Summarizing the conditions under which the transference can be interpreted leads us naturally enough to evoke the rule of free association and, beyond that, associativity in general.

In the first place, the logic behind the fundamental rule is that of making it possible to interpret the transference; it therefore has to be expressed in words. How could we interpret what is *not* expressed (the transference and its historical sources) other than by means of what *is* expressed (its displacement and therefore its transference onto the present situation)? This implies the lifting of the various levels of censorship that apply to what can be expressed in words.

   In addition – and this element was present from the very beginning in Freud's conception of the situation – there is an intrinsic and fundamental link between transference and associativity. In *The Interpretation of Dreams* (1900),[7] Freud points out that transference can be inferred whenever associativity breaks down or when resistance brings displacement and shifts in it. In that book, for example, Freud has this to say:

> We learn [...] that an unconscious idea is as such quite incapable of entering the preconscious and that it can only exercise any effect there by establishing a connection with an idea which already belongs to the preconscious, by transferring its intensity on to it and by getting itself 'covered' by it. Here we have the fact of 'transference', which provides an explanation of so many striking phenomena in the mental life of neurotics. The preconscious idea, which thus acquires an undeserved degree of intensity, may either be left unaltered by the transference, or it may have a modification forced upon it, derived from the content of the idea which effects the transference.
>
> (op. cit., pp. 562–563)

In the papers that he wrote between 1913 and 1915, Freud added to this central premise; he commented on several occasions that every breakdown in free associations should be seen as the result of some censorship being applied to the chain of associations or to some thought involving the analyst or the psychoanalytic situation. Transference and associativity are therefore linked closely together; the rule concerning free association is also a necessary condition for the interpretation of the transference, one of the ways in which the potential influence of the analyst can be circumvented. The idea of associativity opens up many more avenues for thinking, avenues that are to a large extent ignored by contemporary analysts for whom associativity is so well-known that it need no longer be the subject of any exploration. Recalling the historical background to these issues may well be of some use, because, after all, that background is an essential feature of psychoanalysis – one that perhaps is not well enough known. It is essential in that it illustrates Freud's ongoing attempts to liberate psychoanalysis from the effects of suggestion that are part of the method itself. Free association and associativity are not prescribed by the analyst – or at least not only and not fundamentally by the analyst; they are above all modalities in which the mind itself functions. Their recommendation in psychoanalytic methodology aims simply to encourage free expression in the face of everything that in the past or in the present situation might obstruct its deployment; the objective is to free the analysand from the effect of past influences that might have had an impact on it.

The fundamental rule and associativity

When we examine in detail what Freud had to say about the origins, as he saw them, of the method that he invented, our attention is drawn to a short paper he wrote in 1920, "A Note on the Prehistory of the Technique of Analysis" (1920b).[8] In that paper, he mentions the fact that, as a teenager, he had read the works of Ludwig Börne, a German writer of the Romantic Movement, and that this brought the idea of free association to his attention. In an essay entitled "The Art of Becoming an Original Writer in Three Days", Börne says that the "free association" method of writing is the key to what he does. In fact that method was invented by the followers of Mesmer and early spiritists of the clinic of the Chevalier de Barberin situated on the Croix Rousse hill in Lyons. The method was invented by two "artificial somnambulists" (called G. Rochette and The Unknown Agent) of that clinic, then brought via Masonic lodges to Strasbourg (Roussillon 1992),[9] which at that time was the hub for everything that concerned Germany and the German Romantic Movement at the beginning of the 19th century.

As to the history of the link between associativity and clinical matters, it is in Freud's *On Aphasia* (1891b) that we first come across it. In that book, Freud's theory of psychical representation is based on his work on aphasia – a set of perceptual elements that are associated or connected together. The model that he presents is, it must be said, astonishingly modern and "neuroscientific" – it comes close, for example, to the model of interconnected networks of representation (Varela 1989), and to that of groupings of neurons (Hebb 1949; Braitenberg & Schüz 1998).

In his famous "Project for a Scientific Psychology", Freud (1950a [1895]) continued his attempt to devise a model of the associative workings of the mind. In that paper, he refers explicitly to conditioned reflexes as a way of conceiving of how symptoms are generated – the "false connections" that lie at the heart of reminiscences come about through association by simultaneity or contiguity. Here again his model is a very modern one when we compare it, for example, with that of LeDoux (1996), in which conditioned reflexes are a fundamentally important feature of brain functioning, especially with respect to the emotions.

In that same paper, in his attempt to show how the ego functions, Freud again made use of associative functioning: the ego is a set of associated connections, of groupings that are themselves associative. He went on to say that some associations may be inhibited or hampered when primary defenses ("fending off" [Freud 1950a (1895), p. 321]) are mobilized; this tends to block the associative movement between different parts of the ego. The ego is a set of complex inter-related elements, a set of associative groups or networks. It is important to realize that this model applies both to basic mental functioning and to pathological mental states: certain life events may fortuitously fixate a set of associated elements (by simultaneity or contiguity); some elements may be associated for reasons that are no more than circumstantial. The primary defense fixates the associative flow of life and prevents the recombining that is necessary for adapting to present circumstances, which are determined by that primary defense. That is why, when the free association method is indeed freed up, it improves that situation; it restores the free movement of the flow of associations, liberates the mind from its "fixation-points", its *idées fixes* (Janet), its harmful historical impact.

In *Studies on Hysteria* (1895d [1893–95]), Freud gave a more precise description of the first version of the psychoanalytic method both as to its technical aspects and as regards its implementation. Initially, this involved the pressure of the analyst's hand on the patient's forehead; when the hand was removed, an idea emerged – the first idea that came to mind was the best one, the one that was awaited expectantly. The technique was to be repeated as often as necessary. By 1900 and *The Interpretation of Dreams*, that technique had already undergone some development. Henceforth, it was not simply the first idea that was seen to be relevant for the analysis but also those that were associated with that idea; in other words, the method aimed at uncovering a whole sequence of ideas. As a leftover from the suggestion method, the psychoanalyst breaks the dream down into its separate elements, each of which is the starting-point of a sequence, a crop of associations that are focalized on a given element. The psychoanalyst, who thereby "keeps his hands on" the treatment, then brings together the associative groupings that emerge and puts forward an interpretation of the whole sequence – a synthesis, as it were. Freud's own dream of Irma's injection is analyzed following that model, as the step-by-step description makes clear; this is the case also of Dora's dreams (Freud 1905e [1901]). It was not until the "Rat Man" analysis that Freud (1909d) announced that the psychoanalytic method was henceforth to be based on the rule of free association, without any attempt at inducing associations.

The *Minutes of the Vienna Psycho-Analytic Society* (Nunberg & Federn 1962) report that, in one of the two scientific meetings devoted to that case in October-November 1907, Freud said: "The technique of psycho-analysis has changed to the extent that the psycho-analyst no longer seeks to elicit material in which he is interested, but permits the patient to follow his natural and spontaneous trains of thought".

The meaning of these technical developments is quite clear: any remaining elements of influence and suggestion that derive from hypnosis have to be removed. They must be deconstructed so that, as far as possible, the analysand can function in a free and spontaneous manner that lends itself to analysis. Psychoanalysis depends on the gradual deconstruction of the backcloth of suggestion that is part of all kinds of psychotherapy; it is possible – and tolerable – to do this only as a result of developing its theoretical foundations. After 1907, the analysand chooses the associative theme of the session and follows his or her natural and spontaneous trains of thought – and this because Freud had come to the conclusion that so-called "free" associations are in fact constrained by the existence of unconscious associative networks that determine what path these associations follow. There is no need to be afraid of losing one's way because some internal cohesion secretly governs the flow of associations; there is no need to regulate this from outside, because it has its own internal logic and it is on this that the psychoanalyst must concentrate.

The psychoanalyst's careful listening to associativity and the transference

The method and the technique by which it is implemented depended on how Freud conceived of the workings of the mind and on his firm belief in its fundamental cohesion. The fundamental rule was meaningful because Freud had by then developed an associative theory of mental functioning and was convinced of the cohesion of the mind over and beyond any apparently psychopathological aspects; in his view, associativity depended both on conscious and on unconscious networks.

In his chapter on "The Psychotherapy of Hysteria" (1895d [1893–95],[10] he pointed out that hysterical patients are perfectly capable of giving coherent associations; if these do not appear to be coherent, this implies that one link in the chain remains obscure, hidden or unconscious.

> For we may make the same demands for logical connection and sufficient motivation in a train of thought, even if it extends into the unconscious, from a hysterical patient as we should from a normal individual. It is not within the power of a neurosis to relax these relations.
>
> (p. 293)

He became more and more convinced of this as the years went by. He was then exploring in depth how associative links came secretly to be organized and combined together, and discovering the logic behind associative networks and other products of the unconscious.

This gradually led him to think that what was "fundamental" was not really the actual "rule", because this simply expressed how the natural associativity of the mind should be listened to and made that work easier. What is fundamental is that the psychoanalytic method enables the lifting of the censorship that surrounds the free expression of ideas. What is fundamental is the rule that applies to how the psychoanalyst attends to the material. Associations should be listened to with the idea that they are coherent; this implies that, if any two elements are brought together, there must be some kind of link between them. If that link is manifest, if it is obvious, conscious, expressed as such and coherent, there is no difficulty; the problem begins when the link is not manifest, not obvious, not expressed as such and not conscious. It is at that point that the specific nature of psychoanalytic attentiveness comes to the fore in the clinical sphere. The analyst must listen to those associations with the idea that there is some kind of implicit and unconscious link between them; hypotheses have to be made as regards that link, and the analyst must try to reconstruct it and reconstruct the logic that underpins the sequence of associations.

Two kinds of cohesion and unconscious logic emerge from Freud's perspective at that time. On the one hand, cohesion may be circumstantial and related to the specific events in the individual's ongoing history. In this case, links are set up according to the conditioned reflex pattern that I mentioned above; they are conditioned by elements that may be fortuitous, and they come into play only because of their proximity, contiguity or simultaneity with respect to the mentally significant event.

On the other hand, cohesion may be structural, as Freud came to understand only gradually. In this case, it is related to the important issues, conflicts and problems that occur in the life of human beings – especially with respect to emotions and sexuality (the father complex, followed by the Oedipus complex). Since most of the time these issues are in stark contrast to ordinary social life (which to a considerable degree is desexualized), they are often repressed. Freud would go on to show that they are "drawn" to the structures that organize the life of the unconscious; these unconscious concepts or "products of the unconscious" (Freud 1917c, op. cit., p. 128) took on an almost structural quality in his thinking.

It is on this minimal theory of mental functioning that Freud developed his view of psychoanalytic listening; it forms a latent part of this attentiveness and structures the forms that this will take. For a more detailed view of the relationship between transference and associativity, we must look again at Freud's paper on beginning the treatment (1913c) and consider another element concerning the fundamental rule and the interplay of transformations that it implies.

Freud stated that, in describing to his analysands the fundamental rule, he used the metaphor of a train journey: "Act as though, for instance, you were a traveller sitting next to the window of a railway carriage and describing to someone inside the carriage the changing views which you see outside" (1913, p. 135). That metaphor implies a double transfer, a twofold transformation: transferring something from the motor/sensorimotor sphere – the train must pass through the countryside – to the visual one; the idea is to describe the countryside, then transfer that visual impression into the apparatus for verbal language. It emphasizes the fact that the psychoanalytic method implies that the individual is able to carry out this twofold transfer/transformation. The transfer into speech and the transference tend therefore to become superimposed one on the other or at least linked together. In this method, both sensorimotor and visual spheres are transferred into speech and the apparatus for verbalization. Listening to what is said in the course of a session – the transference listening to its vocal vector – can be a good way of trying to identify not only the conditions required for listening attentively but also what is conveyed about both of these spheres, i.e. what is produced when something is transferred into vocal expression. The body lends support to the voice and to what is said, and at the same time, the voice conveys something of what is physically experienced – it carries with it the person's body as it conveys something of what he or she wants to say. The analysis of the transference is therefore not something "intellectual"; it is the analysis of what is actually taking place in the session, of what is expressed through the here-and-now act of speaking. This is all the more the case when the sensorimotor and visual spheres are effectively transferred into the verbal apparatus. That apparatus will take on board both the metaphorical aspect (a visual image transferred into words) and the pragmatic and rhetorical effects (the effect of motor acts on language, which becomes an action on the other person, a force for influence and suggestion). In psychoanalysis, words are not simply representations; they have an impact and they actualize something – they are a "represent-action". When this double transferring occurs, the analyst is the one who is subjected to the seductive aspect of the transference; it is on the analyst that the impact of suggestion and hypnosis falls. That is why the analysis of the transference and that of the counter-transference have to be brought into a dialectical relationship – more precisely, that part of the counter-transference which, in a *lapsus calami*, I once referred to as the "showing-transference".

What happens when this process fails or encounters significant resistance? When the individual cannot transfer his or her primary feelings into the apparatus for language? When sensorimotor experiences have not been organized in such a way as to enable them to be transferred into speech? It is not enough simply to listen attentively to what is actually expressed in words – Freud himself pointed this out on several occasions (1913c, and in his papers written in 1914 and 1915).

Listening to associativity is not restricted to what the analysand says; it pertains to the transference as a whole, which is not simply a way of enacting through or by means of words, as if it were some kind of verbal enactment or other. The transference can be manifested in all kinds of expressiveness and through non-verbal language (cf. next chapter). In order for it to play its full part in the analysis of the transference, listening to associativity must therefore be able to integrate pre-verbal and non-verbal language; it must integrate and consider not only sequences of verbal associations but also those pertaining to primary forms of expression that are conveyed through the body and through actions. These are to be seen as primary forms of language because they contain within themselves aspects that are of great importance for the analysis of the transference whenever it has more to do with enacting than with remembering.

That kind of careful listening to associativity was present from the very beginning of Freud's work. My feeling is that not enough attention has been paid to it; I would therefore like to add a few comments of my own.

In *Studies on Hysteria* (1895d [1893–95]), and in particular in the chapter on the psychotherapy of hysteria, Freud describes his understanding of how the associative method is employed. It is quite clear that he included in this various physical manifestations, in particular those that had to do with symptoms of conversion hysteria, which he saw as "joining in the conversation" (op. cit., p. 296). He brought into his own manner of attentive listening everything that had to do with facial expressions, gestures and postures – these too have something to say. It is important to note that, for Freud, symptoms and bodily manifestations were a means of expressing truth; he saw in them a kind of compass. This implies that he was already seeing the transference as an important feature of what was being actualized in the course of the session. If a patient stated that he or she had nothing more to say, yet the symptoms were still present, Freud followed the indications offered by those symptoms, sure in his own mind that something had been left unsaid. It was only once the physical symptom had been eliminated that Freud would consider the associative network linked to it as having been expressed in its entirety; the elimination of the symptom implied that what was being played out in the transference had found other means of expression, so that the patient was no longer under the unconscious influence of what he or she was expressing by means of enactment.

> Further, her painful legs began to 'join in the conversation' during our analyses. [...] As a rule the patient was free from pain when we started work. If, then, by a question or by pressure upon her head I called up a memory, a sensation of pain would make its first appearance [...] it would reach its climax when she was in the act of telling me the essential and decisive part of what she had to communicate [...] I came in time to use such pains as a compass to guide me; if she stopped talking but admitted that she still had a pain, I knew that she had not told me everything....
>
> (op. cit., p. 148)

In 1913, in a paper devoted to the scientific interest of psychoanalysis (1913j),[11] Freud makes it clear what "speech" means in psychoanalysis. He points out (p. 176) the fact that "'speech' must be understood not merely to mean the expression of thought in words but to include the speech of gesture and every other method [...] by which mental activity can be expressed". That comment is the culmination of a series of ideas that can be found in several papers in which he explored neurotic symptomatology.

In his paper on "Obsessive Actions and Religious Practices" (1907b),[12] he wrote of the girl who was under the compulsion to rinse round her wash-basin several times after washing. It was only then that she could throw out the water. Freud's analysis of that compulsive ritual shows that "obsessive actions are perfectly significant in every detail [and] they serve important interests of the personality" (p. 120). In addition, they are a representation, direct or symbolic, of something that has been experienced – they must therefore be interpreted either in terms of a given event in the individual's past or symbolically. In the example of the wash-basin, the analysis revealed that it was a warning addressed to the patient's sister who was thinking of leaving her husband – she should not throw away the dirty water of her present husband before finding the clean water of someone to replace him. It is important to note here that, for Freud, that ritual was meaningful not only as regards the relationship of the patient to her own self, the intra-psychic meaning; it involved also her relationship with her sister insofar as it was a message addressed to that person. Compulsive actions are meaningful; they tell a story – a history – which, in addition, is addressed to someone else. In that sense, they are transferred toward some other person in the form of a message – in this particular case, a "warning", as Freud put it, addressed to the patient's sister.

The action and the transference understood in terms of an action, an enacting, illustrate a thought or a fantasy; they tell of a particular moment in time. They are shown to or spoken to someone else who plays a mean-ingful role in the individual's life; they are addressed to that person, even though their actual content may not be taken fully on board or if the thought that underlies them is hidden behind the means of expression itself. An enactment "shows" something, it does not "speak" about it. It tells a story, but hidden behind a mask; it forgets its own primary histori-cal origin and displaces or reverses the original scene, which is transferred onto the here-and-now situation. In this way, it disguises the significance of what was originally experienced.

In 1909, Freud developed further his thoughts about hysteria and the show that this can put on, following what he had already set out in 1892 in his paper, written in collaboration with Breuer, "On the Theory of Hysterical Attacks" (1940d [1892]).[13] In "Some General Remarks on Hys-terical Attacks" (1909a [1908]), he emphasized the fact that in hysterical attacks, fantasies are "translated into the motor sphere" and "projected onto motility" (p. 229). Hysterical attacks and the "pantomimic portrayal" that they display are the outcome of the condensation of several fantasies (in particular relating to bisexuality) or of the acts of several characters in a traumatic scenario from the past. For example, what appeared to be an incoherent restlessness in one woman, as if she were playing out a mean-ingless pantomime, began to be meaningful once the overall movement could be broken down into its component parts – it could then be seen as a rape. One part of the scene, in which the woman tore off her clothes with one hand, represented the rapist's attack on her, while the second part of her movements, in which she pressed her clothes to her body, represented an attempt at protecting herself from being attacked.

In that example, an apparently meaningless pantomime which, on a manifest level, seemed to be uncoordinated restlessness could be shown to have meaning once it was analyzed and broken down into the various components that secretly structured the overall pattern. What initially seemed to be simply a "discharge" then revealed the complexity of meaning that was in fact part of it, although hidden away. Hysteria "speaks" through the body; it "shows" what the person cannot put into words and hides that aspect. In hysterical processes, actions can be interpreted in terms of affect representatives; they are a kind of language, more of an acting-language than an acting-out. They transfer language into the body and the modes of expression that are specific to it. They are also addressed to someone, to the self – a way of saying something to oneself – and to another person; there is perhaps the expectation that the other person may be able to understand the message and reflect back on the speaker what he or she said without realizing it, without actually putting it into words. In *An Outline of Psycho-Analysis*, Freud (1940a [1938],[14] p. 202) remarks on the importance, in all of the scenarios that are reported and played out, of the person whom he called the detached spectator. The scenario is addressed to that spectator, who is also an externalized representative of the self, a double; it tells something to that spectator and once again is a message addressed to someone else, who is required to bear witness to what, in the past, had not been witnessed. Here, then, new forms of the transference are implicitly at work.

All the examples that I have taken from Freud's writings concern the neuroses. They have to do with the anal or phallic economic dimension and are part of the universe marked by the apparatus of verbal language. Surrounded by verbal language, that universe is structured by metaphor. The body "speaks", plays out, what the individual cannot express in words – although the potentiality for this is present; the body metaphorizes the scene. The structure of the action and of its playing out is that of a narrative, as Freud makes clear. The scenes that are played out narrate a scenario, a story, the story of a chapter in the person's life that he or she cannot take on board. That narrative is part of the world of language and of its symbolization modalities, even though it is the body that actually talks and shows. Although there is an attempt to tell it to the person him- or herself, it is also – and perhaps above all – a narrative addressed to some other person in his or her own right.

In the section of his paper devoted to the psychological interest of psychoanalysis (Freud 1913j), Freud expressed his belief that actions – including the stereotyped gestures that can be observed in dementia praecox (schizophrenia) – are not meaningless. Even in that extreme case they are "the remains of perfectly significant mimetic actions" which belong to the person's past (p. 174). He adds that, into

> [the] craziest speeches and the queerest poses and attitudes [where] hitherto nothing but the most freakish capriciousness has seemed to prevail, psycho-analytic research has introduced law, order and con- nection, or has at least allowed us to suspect their presence where its work is still incomplete.
>
> (Ibid.)

These ideas would be added to all through his life; they are at their most complete in his writings of 1937–1938,[15] which put the finishing touches to these theoretical concepts.

It is clear, then, that although the fundamental rule of free associa- tion concerns verbal language as such and attempts to channel associa- tivity along that path, the psychoanalyst's attentive listening cannot be restricted to that domain alone. This is particularly true when the ana- lyst's attentiveness is dependent on the analysis of the transference and on what attempts to be enacted in that transference. In the psychoanalytic situation, suggesting and influencing are not confined to verbal speech; every kind of expression and all forms of language contribute to transfer- ring the forgotten situation onto the present one.

Freud took all these issues into account when – partly influenced by Ferenczi – he wrote his paper on "Lines of Advance in Psychoanalytic Therapy" (1919a [1918])[16] and when he explored compliant dreams in 1923. In such cases, the analyst is faced with an alternative. On the one hand, there is an attempt to force all other modes of expression to adopt verbal language and thus make interpretation possible. That was the attitude adopted by Ferenczi at the beginning of the 1920s: increase abstinence, prohibit any other means of expression – that's the way it's going to be – and have recourse to a "forceful" modality, the suggestion and influence effects of which cannot be ignored; indeed, these are potentially a para- doxical form of superego seduction. The other possibility – Ferenczi later tried this way of proceeding – is to adopt techniques that would increase the receptiveness of language and of the analysand to the sensorimotor sphere. This would develop the effects of cathartic trance (Ferenczi 1930) in the psychoanalytic situation. In order to do this, some kind of interven- tion based on psychodrama or with a psycho-dramatic aim to it could be adopted; here, all the same, the threat of another kind of influencing and suggesting appears – this time more narcissistic.

It was only after a slow process of development of psychoanalytic the- ory that lasted until 1936–1938 that Freud again took up the question. It could then be expressed in terms of other problem situations concern- ing psychoanalytic technique, and developed in his final papers on the subject: "Constructions in Analysis" (1937d) and "Analysis Terminable and Interminable" (1937c).

In this chapter, I raised the issue of listening to non-verbal language in listening to associativity. In current psychoanalysis, many psychoanalysts still restrict the listening of associativity to verbal language only (when they still listen to psychic associativity because this has disappeared from many analyst trainings!). It seems important to me to devote a deeper reflection to the place it occupies in Freud's thought and practice and, beyond that, in psychoanalytic listening.

Notes

1 Freud, S. (1913). *Beginning the treatment.* SE, 12.
2 Freud, S. (1915a). "Observations on transference-love (further recommendations on the technique of psycho-analysis, III)". *Standard Edition*, 12: 159.
3 Freud, S. (1914). "Remembering, repeating and working-through (further recommendations on the technique of psycho-analysis, II)". *Standard Edition*, 12: 147.
4 Freud, S. (1914a). "On the history of the psycho-analytic movement". *Standard Edition*, 14: 3.
5 Freud, S. (1912). "The dynamics of transference". *Standard Edition*, 12: 99.
6 Freud, S. (1914). "Remembering, repeating and working-through (further recommendations on the technique of psycho-analysis, II)". *Standard Edition*, 12: 147.
7 Freud, S. (1900). *The interpretation of dreams.* Standard Edition, 4 & 5.
8 Freud, S. (1920). "A note on the prehistory of the technique of analysis". *Standard Edition*, 18: 263.
9 Roussillon, R. (1992). *Du baquet de Mesmer au « baquet » de Freud.* Paris: PUF.
10 Freud, S. (1895). *Studies on hysteria.* Standard Edition, 2.
11 Freud, S. (1913). "The claims of psycho-analysis to scientific interest". *Standard Edition*, 13: 165.
12 Freud, S. (1907). "Obsessive actions and religious practices". *Standard Edition*, 9: 117.
13 Freud, S. (1909). "Some general remarks on hysterical attacks". *Standard Edition*, 9: 229.
14 Freud, S. (1940a [1938]). *An outline of psycho-analysis.* Standard Edition, 23: 141.
15 Freud, S. (1937a). "Analysis terminable and interminable". *Standard Edition*, 23: 209.
   Freud, S. (1937b). "Constructions in analysis". *Standard Edition*, 23: 257.
   Freud, S. (1938a). "Splitting of the ego in the process of defence". *SE*, 23.
   Freud, S. (1938b). *An outline of psychoanalysis.* SE, 23.
16 Freud, S. (1919 [1918]). "Lines of advance in psycho-analytic therapy". *Standard Edition*, 17: 159.

8 Associativity and non-verbal language

Situating the problem

One of the fundamental issues confronting the future of psychoanalysis seems to be to inquire into the direction of the possible extensions of the psychoanalytic method. This is centered on listening to psychic associativity directed at the analyst and the imperative of considering the narrativity resulting from this address.

If the rule of free association defines the fundamental rule of psychoanalysis, what distinguishes psychoanalysis even more critically concerns above all the way psychic associativity is listened to by the psychoanalyst. It appears in effect increasingly probable, in light of neuroscience, that the associativity regulated by inhibitory processes characterizes the very functioning of the brain and the ensemble of psychic life, and that it thus cannot by itself define the psychoanalytic method. In my view, we must now distinguish this method not only by the so-called fundamental rule, but additionally by the specificity of the psychoanalyst's listening, a specificity of the listening that I would define in the following way: the psychoanalyst listens to psychic associations with the hypothesis that what is associated possesses a link that is, at times, manifest – when, for instance, the association yields to the logic of the secondary processes – and, at others, unconscious – when, on the contrary, it does not appear to yield to such logic. This is the idea that, in all cases, an association reveals the existence of a link between the associated ideas, a link at times organized by an episode or a moment in the history and at others, produced by the impact of unconscious psychic organizers such as originary fantasies or large formations of unconscious psychic life.

I wish to take advantage of this to emphasize in passing that such a clarification enables us to draw a simple but relevant contrast concerning the action of psychoanalysis versus that of cognitive and behavioral therapies. The latter tend to regulate the basic associativity of psychic life by developing the inhibitory processes of associativity, whereas, on the contrary, psychoanalysis is predicated on the idea that the progressive freeing-up

DOI: 10.4324/9781003198710-8

of associative liberty will make regulation possible by means of becoming conscious and through psychic reflexivity.

Approaching the problem that has brought us together through this angle means situating it in these terms: the question with which the form of unconscious communication confronts the psychoanalyst is that of the homogeneity of the associations or that of their heteromorphism. Extending psychoanalysis to borderline and even psychotic patients, its exploration of the forms of the anti-social tendency or perversion, its developments in the direction of psychoanalytic work with the different forms of child psychopathology, indeed, of groups and human groupings, encounters head-on the question of the forms of associativity that may not only be confined to the verbal register. This is obvious when working with children but it is no less central in the other clinical pictures I referred to in which the body, and its train of sensations and perceptions, and the act, and how motility is put into work, "blends in" with the psychoanalytic "conversation", to use Freud's expression.

The problem posed by the heteromorphism of the thus-implicated psychic components may be summarized in the question of knowing how far the manifestations directly born of the body may be considered "forms of language", or still more of knowing what is necessary so that they appear as forms of language that may be used in psychoanalytic listening. The working hypothesis I am submitting for your reflection is precisely that corporal (and even somatic) manifestations and acts must be understood in psychoanalysis as forms of "narrations" born of body language or "incomplete" acts (Freud 1913),[1] or as forms of body language and of potential acts. "Potential" signifies here that they will become so only if they are understood and treated as such. This hypothesis rests on the complementary hypothesis, to which I shall return, that the drive is a "messenger" that is expressed with the help of three languages born of three forms of representance: the word presentation-representative for verbal language; the thing (and action) presentation-representative for the language of the act and of corporal expressiveness; and the affect-representative for the "language of affect" adumbrated early on by Charles Darwin. It is thus the attunement and adjustment between these three forms of expression and language that organizes psychoanalytic work.

Here then is a summary of the argument.

The act and the body as refuse of the psyche

One fundamental characteristic of the psychoanalytic approach is to consider that what is generally taken as waste or refuse of psychic or human activity, and thus non-sense, in fact bears a hidden meaning that is expecting to be revealed, discovered and, indeed, constructed. Psychoanalysis thus reconsiders what learned psychology tended to think of as irrelevant. It emphasizes what appears not to have meaning but which, in fact, possesses another meaning and complies with forms of logic differing from those that are typically considered as such. Thus, historically it has been a matter of the dream, Freudian slips and parapraxes as well as psychopathological symptoms and productions of human madness or, in other words, everything Lacan called the "formations of the unconscious" (1966).[2]

Even at the present time often enough the forms of bodily expression, those passing through psychosomatic symptoms in particular, are considered by most somaticians and even certain psychosomaticians as devoid of meaning. Some would even call them "stupid". In the same way, in the way given by the psychiatric notion of acting out, some see in the recourse to the act and to taking action that one may observe in certain forms of psychopathology, merely an inclination toward "discharge", merely an avoiding or emptying out of psychic contents. There again human activity, however complex at times, is considered insignificant, or rather signifying nothing other than the refusal of meaning, as only an attempt at emptying it out.

What comes from the body receives bad press and it often represents what must be accepted in order to exist, but which must remain mute, must remain silent since it is devoid of meaning. Those who claim, on the contrary, that the body and the act may conceal greater organization and meaning than it appears are thus thought of as romantics of the ineffable, as dreamers projecting a meaning on to what cannot inherently possess it, and are thus not scientific or even rational.

Certain psychoanalysts have sometimes been accommodating with regards to these positions, which, one finds, originate in certain medical thinking in the name of considering economic factors, in the name of an epistemological separation of the fields, in the name of a definition of the "psychic" that excludes the body, and of the "mental" without the soma. Others, on the contrary, working within a more strictly Freudian tradition, are convinced that nothing in mankind may be bereft of meaning, and they try to discern the logic and languages underlying what may then be thought of as forms of expression, not only of the drive, but also of the subject animating it.

My reflection proceeds precisely in this direction. It develops, concerning the act, the work of re-evaluation that I began to outline previously[1] with regards to symptoms known as "psychosomatic" (Roussillon 1995)[2] and to affects. It seeks to extend the Freudian position aiming at isolating a form of language of the act bearing a directed meaning. It is in line with a conception of drive life that recognizes a value of discharge in the drives with a view to satisfaction but also a value of mastery (Denis 1992)[3] in addition to a "messenger" value (Roussillon). We shall take this point up again later in our reflection.

Freud's position, on which I wish to base my thoughts, is widely misunderstood by the majority of today's theoreticians. It is thus useful to recall a few of his principal propositions as we set out on this reflection.

The language of the act in Freud

In 1913, in a text entitled "The claims of psychoanalysis to scientific interest",[4] we read, "in what follows 'speech' must be understood not merely to mean the expression of thought in words but to include the speech of gesture and every other method, such, for instance, as writing, by which mental activity can be expressed" (p. 176). What follows in the article indicates that Freud is considering the 'language of the dream', that is, that of thing-presentation, but also that of body language, which (Cf. in particular Roussillon (1995, op. cit.) for the somatic symptom and Roussillon (2003)[5] for the affect he will explore.

We will see later that he has already gone into the question of the non-verbal forms of language in hysteria and obsessive neurosis, that is, in the neurotic universe, but I should like to emphasize straight away that one may not summarize Freud's position by limiting it to the neurotic universe as he also mentions *dementia praecox* in the article. The attribution of the quality of language endowed with meaning is extended for Freud to acts, whatever the pathology or the psychic functioning of the subjects in question. It is a generic, structural and not a local statement, and it is one arising from a particular conjuncture of circumstances.

I wanted to insist on this point early on and now, having done so, we may go into the different milestones of this hypothesis in the course of Freud's thinking.

In 1907, in the article on "Obsessive actions and religious practices" Freud[6] mentions the ritual of a woman who is obliged to spin dirty water several times around a basin by her ablutions before draining it in a toilet. The analysis of this obsessive ritual not only showed that it is "found that the obsessive actions are perfectly significant in every detail [and] that they serve important interests of the personality ..." (p. 120), but that they are, further, the direct or symbolic representation of lived experiences and thus that they should be interpreted either in function of a given historical conjuncture or symbolically. Thus, concerning the basin ritual, in the course of the analysis it takes on the meaning of a warning directed at the patient's sister who plans on leaving her husband – of not separating herself from the "dirty water" of the first husband, before finding the "clean water" of a replacement. I would like to emphasize here that for Freud, the ritual does not only take on meaning in the relationship of the patient to herself, and thus intra-psychically, but that it is also in keeping with the relationship to her sister, as a "message" directed at her. The obsessive action has a meaning, it "tells" a story – the story – but, says Freud, it is moreover a story that is directed at, a message or a "warning" to her sister.

The act "shows" a thought, a fantasy. It "recounts" a moment of the story, but it shows or tells to a significant someone; it is addressed, and this is so even if it does not fully assume its contents and even if the thought is hidden behind its form of expression. The act "shows", it does not "say"; it tells, but it advances as though it were concealed.

In 1909, Freud draws out his reflection concerning hysterical attacks[7] and their mimics along the same lines he had begun to clear away in 1895 in *Studies on Hysteria*.[8] In "Some general remarks on hysterical attack", he then emphasizes that within them the fantasy is translated into "motor language" that it is projected on to "motility". The hysterical attack and the mimic it constructs appear to him as the result of the condensation of several fantasies (bisexual in particular) or of the action of several "characters" of a historical, traumatic scene. For instance, what was taken for the incoherent agitation of a woman, for a meaningless mimic, becomes meaningful if one is mindful to break down the overall movement in order to bring out a rape scene. The first half of the body and the woman's body language "figure", for instance, the attack of the rapist, who tries to tear the woman's clothing off her, whereas the second half of her corporal expression represents the woman attempting to protect herself from the attack.

Here again, an apparently meaningless mimic, which seems, on the manifest level, like wild excitation, is made comprehensible should one analyze and break down the different elements secretly organizing its scheme. What at first appears like "pure discharge" then betrays the signifying complexity that inhibits it and is masked. The hysteria "speaks" with the body, which shows what the subject cannot say. It thus hides it. Previously, regarding conversion, Freud had emphasized that the hysteric's body attempted to say the words that the subject could not accept saying and becoming fully conscious of. For instance, nausea would expresses the language fact of feeling "queasy" *(in French : mal au cœur),* and the ache of being "queasy" *(mal au cœur)* would echo the metaphoric form of feeling pain in the heart *(peine de cœur),* that is, of being disappointed in love. The act, in a hysterical process, may be interpreted as the affect-representative was; it is a language of the act, it is the passage of language through the act more than acting-out.

It is directed language – directed at oneself, in a manner of speaking – but also directed at the other, perhaps with the expectation that what it is said without awareness, without saying as much, might be understood by the other and reflected by him.

Beginning with *Studies on Hysteria*, Freud noted the place held by what he called in 1895 the "indifferent spectator" in the ensemble of the scenarios thus recounted and represented. The scene is directed at a particular spectator who, further, is an externalized representative of the ego, its double. It recounts "for" the spectator and is further present as a "directed message" to the other who "becomes witness" to what was not historically incorporated by it.

And so again in 1920 Freud[9] undertook the analysis of a suicide attempt of a young woman who had thrown herself from a bridge. When this case was entrusted to him, he did as he had in the earlier ones. He analyzed the meaning of the act – its language – and examined at whom it was directed, in this case the father under whose eyes the act was committed.

The examples that we have just noted in Freud's work belong to the neurotic universe. They exhibit the representatives of anal or phallic economy and they belong to a universe that is already distinguished by the language apparatus, that is, already organized by it and thus to a universe that is already structured by it. The body "says", it displays what the subject cannot say, but what it might potentially say. The body metaphorizes the scene. The act's structure and staging is narrative here – Freud is clear about this: the scenes recount a scenario, a history, the history of a part of the life that the subject cannot come to terms with. It thus belongs to the language universe and its modes of symbolization, even if it is the body that "speaks" and "shows". Further, if it attempts to recount to the subject itself, it is also and perhaps first a narration for an other-subject.

We recall that Joyce McDougall (1996),[10] in the texts she wrote on "neo-sexualities", or on what one most often terms "perversions", comes to a similar conclusion concerning these specific clinical pictures. The "indifferent spectator" of the *Studies on Hysteria*, to whom the neurotic symptom is directed, will become simply an "anonymous spectator", a variation, in the perverse scenarios now belonging to the narcissistic universe of the former.

In 1938, this time concerning the psychotic universe of delirious patients, and in the same breath as "Constructions in analysis" (1937),[11] in which he put forward the generalization of his statements of 1895 concerning the way the subject, even if he is psychotic, "suffers from reminiscences", Freud extends to psychotic states the remark according to which psychotic manifestations are also played out under the eyes of an "indifferent spectator", and thus also appear as a "message directed" to this spectator. But from 1913, in the section dedicated to the claims of psychoanalysis for psychiatry, Freud had affirmed his faith in the fact that acts, even stereotypes observed in *dementia praecox*, that is, in schizophrenia, were not bereft of meaning but appeared as "the remains of perfectly significant mimetic actions, which at one time gave expression to the subject's ruling wishes" (p. 174).

He then continues: "The craziest speeches and the queerest poses and attitudes adopted by these patients become intelligible and can be given a place in the chain of mental processes if they are approached on the basis of psychoanalytic hypotheses" (p. 174).

The incomplete state of 1913 is complemented by two hypotheses he put forward in and around 1937. First, in "Constructions in analysis" he underscored that the psychotic symptom "recounts" the history of "something that the child has seen or heard at a time when he could still hardly speak" (1937, p. 267), and thus before the age of 18–24 months. He then added, in one of the short notes written in London, that the episode is maintained as it was (the second hypothesis he put forward) due to the "weakness of the power of synthesis" (1938, p. 299)[12] of the period.

In a certain way, he thus implied that what was experienced during a time when verbal language was not yet able to give a form to subjective experience would tend to return in a non-verbal form – a form that is as archaic as the experience itself – and thus in the language of the time, that of babies and all small children, that is, a corporal language, a language of the act.

This intuition provides the starting-point for the main hypothesis I now wish to examine: through later acts – those of manifestations of anti-sociality, for instance, or, in a more general way, those accompanying the clinical pictures of narcissistic-identity issues – archaic experiences of a period preceding the mastery of verbal language attempt to express themselves and seek to communicate themselves, in other words, to make themselves known and shared.

Bodies and messenger acts in narcissistic-identity disorders

But before I can make this hypothesis fully clear, it will be necessary to focus on the specificities of primitive experiences in so far as their particularities are in part found in the language of the act and of the body that we find in the modes of later recurrences observed in clinical work involving narcissistic suffering.

The baby's subjectivity is not a unified subjectivity. It goes through different subjective states and the "weakness of the synthesizing capacity" Freud mentions does not at first enable these different experienced moments of subjectivity to be unified. The infant lives in a "nebulous subjectivity" (David 1997),[13] its ego is constituted by "agglutinated" cores (Bleger 1967)[14] before they may be brought together into unities constituting an "emerging ego-subject". The consequence of this is that early experiences may be without any links among them, which is not due to splitting but to a lack of an integration of the ensemble. They may be "partial" and filed away with this characteristic. I agree here with Winnicott, who emphasizes that the non-integrated state does not resemble the process of disintegration of an already integrated state. In the second case, the idea of splitting takes on meaning, but when the subjective states have not yet integrated, the notion of splitting is without subjective signification.

Primitive subjective experiences are closely related to body states and sensations originating in them. The corporal sensation is thus at the center, it is accompanied by motor movements into which it is closely blended, which makes the idea of sensorimotor processes pertinent. They may thus be of an erotic nature and subordinated to the principle organized by the pleasure-unpleasure affects couple. But the erotic element that they contain is not of an orgasmic kind; it is a matter of the difference between infantile sexuality, even early or "primordial" sexuality (Botella 2001),[15] and adult sexuality. They may be called "homosensual".

They are not experienced outside time, or in any case outside chronological time, which signifies that, whatever their real length, they tend to be without a beginning and without an end, in particular when they are charged with unpleasure. When they are charged with pleasure, they tend to be inscribed in elementary rhythmic forms (Roussillon[16]; Stern 1985[17]; Marcelli 1983[18]) organizing them into rudimentary forms of temporality.

Basing ourselves on this, we see that they are not subject to recollection and may not form themselves into memories. Thus, they are not included among the form of memory known as "declarative". On the other hand, they may contribute to the creation of memorial systems, or to memories known as "procedural", which create "internal working models" (Bowlby 1951, 1969) and systems for the treatment and organization of experience. They tend to give their shape to subsequent experiences. An important consequence is that they exist "throughout time": they tend to cross time and thus be reactivated and brought back up to date in a hallucinatory mode. They tend to be imparted and are presented as "actual", as always actual.

When they do become reactivated, it is not in a form that is imparted to subjectivity as a representation, but as a presentation (*Darstellung*), and this is so even if they attempt to "recount" themselves with the help of this reactivation. They are thus imparted as always present. What makes it difficult to locate their reactivations as such is that they blend in with actual perceptions and become confused with them. They further contribute to the present experience, whose feeling of a hallucinatory imprint they "bloat", but they may also be modified retroactively. They are thus expressed electively through the different forms of affect, "a traumatic perturbation of the entire being", according to Freud (1926, op. cit.), that of somatic expression and by means of the act. This, furthermore, may potentially occur at any age.

They seek to be communicated (McDougall 1996), acknowledged (Dornes 2002) and shared (Parat 1995) by the significant individuals of the most intimate circle. But their communication and sharing, or acknowledgement, pose a problem since they are always more or less charged with ambiguity and subject to interpretation.

On the one hand, because they are expressed in barely digitalized language, which remains distinguished by analogy and models of thing-presentation, the language of affect, that of the miming-gestural-postural register or that of acting. On the other, because a part of their meaning is incomplete and closely depends on the way it is interpreted by the other-subject to whom it is addressed.

In fact, it is the intimate circle's response, which, by acknowledging it as such, gives it its value as a message and which defines it as a signifying message. If this is not the case, it "degenerates" and loses its potential proto-symbolic value. It is threatened with becoming but an insignificant evacuation and its expressive and proto-narrative value is nullified.

My clinical hypothesis is that such experiences are attempts at communicating what, by dint of not being acknowledged as such and of not being qualified by the intimate circle's responses, will express itself in psychopathological pictures of the child, adolescent or adult, and in particular in the symptomatology of narcissistic-identity disorders having a corporal expression, that is, acting or psychosomatic. On the one hand, the ego is made globally fragile by the narcissistic harm implicating the disqualification or the non-qualification of corporal and affective communication; on the other, their un-signified forms represent a flood of enigmatic points for the ego, which sees itself as inhabited by meaningless movements.

The full intelligibility of these utterances presupposes the complementary hypothesis that the experiences thus preserved originate in subjective experiences having a traumatic nature and having thus mobilized, at the particular moment and afterward, modalities of primary defense that have thus shielded them and, along with them, entire sections of the ego's subjectivity and organization (cf. the ego's archaic functions Freud mentions in 1923[19] as being "sedimented" in the "severe and cruel superego" that one may observe in the negative therapeutic reaction) from a later evolution. The complement I am putting forward presupposes that the separating is made among archaic experiences or between those capable of being secondarily taken up and signified during later experiences, and those that have been kept separate from these forms of retroactive resumption and are then presented as *"fueros"*, to use the metaphor Freud suggested in 1896.[20] In other words, in the "natural", or at least sufficiently maturational, integrative future, the experiences preceding the appearance of the language apparatus are at least in part taken back up into the language universe. This occurs in three possible ways.

First, through the binding of memory traces and thing-presentations with word-presentations established afterward. Subjective experience is named retroactively, and sensations and affects comprising it are named, analyzed and thought about "detail by detail" due to their secondary binding in the linguistic forms. The verbal language apparatus, and the verbal binding that it makes possible, transforms the relationship that the subject entertains with his affects as with his mimicry, gestures, postures and acts, and so on. Verbal binding makes possible the containment and transformation of affective networks and those of the thing-presentations; it is then in the associative chain itself that one must seek its impact. The miming-gestural-postural expressions may then accompany verbal narrations; they give form or expressiveness where the subject fears they are inadequate, or where words do not succeed in transmitting the "entirety" of the thing experienced. Children and adolescents are used to the corporal expressiveness of accompanying, but it never entirely disappears from adult expression. In still more elaborate forms, the playing with language or words that comprises it takes up, buttresses and develops the former games with things, the miming-gestural-postural register and affects.

Next, through a transference into the non-verbal aspects of the language apparatus, that is, in prosody. The voice "says" the experienced breakdown by itself breaking down. The rhythm of its enunciation is broken up and its intensity attempts to express the variations in intensity of what is felt ... What is felt, by transferring itself into the verbal language apparatus, affects it in the most "economic" aspects of its functioning.

And lastly, after adolescence, through a transference into the very style of the language utilized and into the practice that it confers to the utterances, and which makes possible – between the words, in their very organization – what is to be transmitted and communicated. I have shown elsewhere (1994)[21] how Proust's style, and in particular his handling of punctuation, conveys an "asthmatic" shortness of breath to the reader without which nothing, or almost nothing, would betray this feeling in the contents of the text itself; in short, entirely unconsciously. It is thus that the reader must feel what the subject does not say but feels, but which he conveys "through" his verbal style. However, the capacity to transfer into the style of the enunciation the wealth of feelings is not attributed equally to everyone and, in any case, not before the reorganization of the adolescent's subjectivity. Children do not yet possess a veritable verbal style.

One may thus, by merely listening to the verbal associative chains, retrace the history of the way certain early subjective experiences were taken back into the language apparatus. When the integrative resumption is adequate, the three registers of the language apparatus that I have just mentioned conspire together in order to recapture the early subjective experiences and give them a certain secondary representative status in order to symbolize secondarily the primitive experience.

These different forms of the transference of the primitive subjective experience into the language apparatus do not impede the mimics, gestures and corporal postures from accompanying verbal expression. It is in these three registers of expression of drive life and psychic life that the subject expresses it. He speaks with the word-representatives and conveys the thing-presentations and "represent(action)" (in Vincent's apt expression, 1983, 2006) that move him through his gestures, mimicry, postures and acts, and he expresses with his entire body the presence of the affect-representatives accompanying the other forms of expressiveness.

The domination of verbal language in self-expression must not make us forget how much it is accompanied by corporal expressiveness – without which it can but perform its function poorly. Verbal expression cut off from any affect and any corporal expressiveness produces an effect of malaise in the interlocutor. It makes empathy difficult and reveals how the subject is split from the child he was, in addition to the depths of human affective experience.

The first forms of language – the language of affect and the language of miming-gestural-postural expression, which were witness to the first moments of psychic life and the first attempts at exchanging and communicating – are maintained throughout life and remain necessary for expressiveness, and this is so even when verbal language has secured its domination over the forms of expression.

The central clinical question – the one whose details in Freud's thought we have outlined and which we would now like to focus on – is what becomes of the early subjective experiences that have not been secondarily sufficiently recaptured in the verbal language apparatus. I specify "sufficiently" as one cannot exclude, even for those forms having a traumatic and disorganizing aspect, a certain form of recapture within the language apparatus, at least for what concerns a part of the narcissistic "states", indeed, even psychotic "states". But what I find of special interest here is what, having early on been removed from the process of language symbolization by repression, splitting or projection, will seek and find non-verbal forms of expressiveness.

In all the forms of narcissistic-identity suffering that I have focused on, a part of the displayed clinical picture surpasses single verbal associativity and is expressed by a pathology of the affect or of action that seems to attest and extend the hypothesis put forward by Freud concerning the "reminiscence" of subjective experiences preceding the emergence of verbal language.

The hypothesis I am advancing as a complement to Freud's is that these subjective experiences will tend to express themselves in forms of non-verbal language that borrow their privileged forms of expressiveness and associativity from the body, the soma, motility and the act. In the same way that the "preverbal" child uses affect, the soma, the body, motility, the miming-gestural-postural register, and so on, in order to communicate and make his states of being known, subjects who are prey to forms of narcissistic-identity suffering in connection with early traumatism will also use these different registers of expressiveness and associativity in an attempt at communicating them and making them known, and this occurs in a central way in their psychic economy.

Another way of expressing the essential point that I wish to consider is to say that the drive representation – and this is why I could advance the idea that the drive was necessarily also a "messenger" – is developed and conveyed according to three "languages" potentially related between them but nevertheless disjointed: verbal language and word-presentations, the language of affect and affect-representatives, and then the language of the body and the act and their different expressive capacities (mimicry, gestures, postures, acts, and so on) which correspond to thing-presentations[22] (and represent(actions)). Should we take psychic associativity into consideration we will not only hear the connections operating between the verbal signifiers but also how the language of affect and that of thing-presentations and represent(actions) blend in with the former. One may hear the polymorphism of psychic associativity.

The subjective traumatic experiences I am referring to in my hypothesis concerning narcissistic-identity suffering are subject to primitive forms of the drive, not only to primary anality (Green),[23] but also to primary orality, that is, un-reorganized under the primacy of genitality, even when it is that of "infantile genitality" (Freud). These are subjective experiences that reach the subject before the organization of the "no" (Spitz's third organizer, 1965),[24] before the first forms of the "mirror stage" (Wallon 1931[25]; Lacan 1966) and the emergence of reflexivity, before the organization of the continuous representation of the object and the organization of secondary anality (Roussillon), that is, so as to give an approximate idea, before the reorganization of the subjectivity that most of the time intervenes between 18 and 24 months of age.

I am emphasizing these different "analyzers", these different "markers" of subjectivity, since their lack of organization colors the kind of communication conveying the forms of non-verbal language I am treating here in a specific way. They often attest in effect to a "primary" and barely organized drive organization, to great difficulty in the expression of negation, to a failure in and a quest for reflexivity, and to a dependence on forms of perceptive presence of the object. One might say, to paraphrase Freud, that "the shadow of the object hangs over and falls on to non-verbal languages".

As such the languages of the act and body remain in effect fundamentally ambiguous. They bear a potential, virtual meaning, but one that depends on the meaning that the object, to which it is directed, gives to it. It is a language which, more than any other, must "be interpreted". It is but the potential for meaning, the bearer of potential: it is meaning that has not yet been finished (Freud would say that it is incomplete). It seeks a respondent, it does not exhaust its meaning in a single expression, and the reaction or the response of the object is necessary for its signifying integration. This is also why our clinical practice most often displays it in a "degenerate" form, that is, in a form in which, when the respondent has not been located or has not given an adequate subjectifying reply, the potential meaning loses its generative power.

Here is a first example that will help us grasp what I wish to say. We are familiar with a classic stereotype observed among certain autistic or psychotic subjects who are fascinated by a movement of their hands that appears to turn and return infinitely toward the subject. Authors of a post-Kleinian orientation would speak of a form of auto-sensuality. Undoubtedly, as far as I am concerned, I understand that such a gesture "recounts" the history of an encounter that has not taken place. The first part of the movement seems in effect to move toward the outside, toward the object. I then imagine an absent, or unavailable or ungraspable object, an indifferent object, an object upon which the gesture of the encounter "slides" without being able to grasp even a fragment of a reply. It then returns toward the subject as the bearer of what did not take place in the encounter. It spins in the emptiness and gestures toward a virtual other. It returns to itself and forgets in the return what it had extended itself to; but this emptying out, or forgetting, is full of what did not take place. The emptiness potentially "recounts" what did not occur in the encounter. The shadow of the un-encountered object falls upon the gesture, it falls upon the act "in the hollow", in the shadow. I wonder if certain formal signifiers described by Didier Anzieu[26] (1974, 1989) are not shaped in such a way, like the first motor "narrations" of the experiences of encounter and non-encounter with the object.

But the shadow of the object also falls upon the body and its gestures. I hypothesized (1995)[27] that listening to the forms of sensorial, sensorimotor manifestations present in psychosomatic affections that are considered traces of forms of communication of disqualified, primitive experiences, remains in part possible. Here is a brief clinical vignette in which this question emerges.

Marine undertook a psychoanalysis (with a "standard" French setting consisting of three weekly sessions on the couch) apropos an ensemble of pain in her sexual and affective life, which she only spoke about with difficulty and which were accompanied by important depressive and self-deprecating feelings. The first part of the cure centered on the analysis of a "paternal" transference – to put it briefly and in a hardly "conventional" way – and of the effect of the "paternal" demands on her psychic economy and, in particular, that of her sexuality. The analysis of a masochistic fantasy – in order to make love with pleasure, she had to imagine herself trapped in an impasse, "coerced" and raped anally by an older man at the same time that her real partner was sodomizing her – was one of the organizing axes of the work of this period during which the affect of intense shame, which this sexual practice marshalled in her, was integrated. The "pleasure theory" of her father – in order to take advantage of life's offerings, you had "to be coerced", the only "good" pleasure was that which was obtained when one was obliged – was thus elaborated beginning with its displacement on to a "masochistic" theory of the analysis by turning it into an intrusive coercion. Imperceptibly, beyond this "first" transferential layer, a maternal transferential backdrop began to become more perceptible and analyzable, which at first, and above all, was dominated by feelings of intrusion – first they were "anal" but little by little they would echo the initial "oral" inter-relations. Here again, I've put this very briefly.

At the time, a somatic symptom – a painful ulceration of the stomach with sharp burning sensations within a cortege of digestive dysfunctions – began to occupy a greater place in the analytic sessions. The somatic symptom had been present for a long time and it varied in intensity without disappearing when it became almost permanent one year before the

beginning of the analysis – at the time when she began a romantic relationship with her present partner, a man who was much older than her. It
rapidly regressed during the first part of the analysis only to reappear at
the time of the sequence I wish to mention.

The fragment of the session that I am going to relate thus appeared at
the end of a little more than three years of analysis and within this double
clinical context: a "primary" maternal transference of an intrusive kind
and an accentuation of the stomach ulceration.

For an instant at the beginning of the session, Marine was tense and
wincing in silence, as was often the case during this period of the cure.
Then she began to speak about a burning sensation that had assailed her
just as she had come to the session. She "hurt, it was burning" – she placed
her hands on her sternum as if this was the un-nameable location of her
pain. I waited for her next associations before intervening. However, the
pain continued and it was sharp. She was entirely taken up a paroxysm
of pain and it manifestly occupied what was available in the entire field
of her psyche. I was feeling physical and psychic tension as an echo of her
own, and I then thought it was necessary to intervene in an attempt at signifying the burning sensation. I thus ended up by venturing: "When you
were a baby the bottles your mother gave you were too warm, they burned
you". Marine fell quiet for a moment and then said: "I can't say, but when
you said that to me I thought about the coffee my mother always served,
it was burning, and she always insisted that it should be drunk like that.
She herself always drank it very hot". The pain disappeared when Marine
mentioned the burning coffee given by her mother.

The end of the session and the sessions of the weeks that followed worked
through the "burning" aspect of the mother, first by a series of memories
dominated by their "perceptive" aspects and then, in an increasingly metaphorical way, in order to evoke the stimulating and stimulated aspects of
the maternal attitude concerning her that her father could not really "cool
down" and which, on the contrary, he tended to augment. Simultaneously,
the digestive disorder attenuated and then disappeared, and the stomach
ulceration became "but a bad memory", in her expression.

This interesting outcome does not, by itself, illustrate the validity of
an interpretation or a construction. I only mention it in order to emphasize how a new psychic movement was thus mobilized, as if the suffering in the burning sensation could receive a representative outcome and
"enrich" the mother's object representation and its lack from the moment
it could be understood as a message and form of "narration" of a fragment
of her early history.

Marine's state of consciousness during the session was overwhelmed
by pain that presented itself as "actual" and whose intensity did not allow
her to interpret its sensation in relation to the maternal transference, nor
even to suggest the least association. Marine needed me to make this connection and the associations for her; I had to hear the mode of primitive

communication that her pain was potentially conveying. The fact that she indicated where the pain was emerging, but without naming it, made me think and then evoke an "experience preceding the organization of verbal language" – hence my reference to the bottle, the breast itself incapable of burning. I used this index as a kind of historic "marker", that is, as an index of the moment in her history that had been mobilized in the transference.

In Marine's case, her "body" could begin to speak and blend in with the conversation only when the working-through of the defenses produced a disintegration of the earlier splitting. But quite often the splitting leaves the expression of the modes of communication originating directly in the primitive experiences unhindered. Thus, for instance, another patient systematically "sniffed" every time I shook her hand and as she walked by me. She "sniffed me" and smelled me without any consciousness whatsoever of what she was doing, and as such she expressed her early universe. Another, whose work was carried out face-to-face, systematically placed her hand over her mouth with her palm turned toward me each time I gestured that I wished to speak. If what I said did not suit her, she drew her hand aside and half-opened her mouth. The expression on her face then became that of a very little girl. Still another patient tightly closed her mouth when she did not want to let what I had said seep into her. But once more I am going too quickly.

I now wish to go into the question of the more sophisticated forms of the presence of primitive experiences in body language and sexual language. I have in mind, in particular, the question of sexual fetishism. When Freud considered this question, he attributed the origins of the fetish to the traumatic character, in certain subjects, of the distinction between the sexes and especially of the sight of female genitals interpreted as a sign of castration. The fetishist then makes a choice in function of its proximity to the place of the discovery, which is often the last thing perceived before it: a stocking, a boot, a shoe and so on. Its interpretation thus refers to the infantile dimension of the symptom. But this hardly explains why the discovery is traumatic for certain subjects and not, or less so, for others.

In 1927, in his article on fetishism,[28] Freud went into the case of the fetish of the Wolf Man, a unique fetish since it had to do with the necessity of the presence on the face of the beloved woman, if he were to desire her, of a "shine on the nose" (p. 152). The text wavers from English to German and between a shine on the nose and a look that "shines" the nose, to put it rather concisely. The fetish is unique; it is on the face and a part of the body that is not particularly near the female genitals. In other words, Freud's hypothesis according to which the fetish is chosen due to its perceptive proximity to the female genitals may be applied but loosely. One may of course still suppose, like Freud, the hypothesis of a displacement from below to above, but one may also wonder why such a displacement would be made and if it does not mean something else. At about the same time (1922),[29] Freud was also working on fright when faced with Medusa's head. There again he interpreted the presence of hair in the form of snakes adorning the forehead of Caravaggio's Medusa, which he took for an exemplary figure in his analysis by introducing its pictorial representation into his text in connection with an undone representation of feminine "castration". However, the figuration that Caravaggio proposes is distinguished by the fact that Medusa's head is itself filled with fright. Medusa is supposed "to petrify" (in French, *méduser*) the other with fright and her face is itself that of fright, as a kind of mirror reflection.

In the two cases referred to by Freud, he interprets the contents in function of castration anxiety. We haven't any reason not to follow him along this path. But this interpretation can exhaust neither the question nor the signifying material that Freud suggests to us. It does not explain, in effect, that in each case it is on to the face that the question of castration seems to be displaced nor why the face is chosen if it is the last perception preceding the discovery of "the horror of castration" that ought to be used to determine the fetish, as Freud argued on several occasions. The hypothesis I am suggesting as complementary attempts to give meaning at once to the fact that it is a question of the face, and that it appears to function as a mirror – a mirror of the shining gaze that makes the nose shine, a mirror of the fright that Medusa is supposed to provoke.

Winnicott[30] emphasized that the primitive function of the mother's face, and thus the connection in his conception to the primary feminine, is to reflect her own states of being on to the child and, thus, to function as an initial form of the mirror of the soul. It is not so difficult to take a further step forward and consider that, in the experience of the discovery of the secondary feminine, represented by the female genitals, is blended the trace of an experience of the primary feminine – of what the mother's face reflects, then. That upon the discovery of the distinction between the sexes is also transferred a primitive experience in connection with the expression of the mother's face and the threat, for example, of an extinction of the "shine of her eyes", as the initial signifier of her desire and her pleasure at contemplating her son. The first forms of the child's encounter with the feminine are blended in with his secondary "conversation" with the figure of the female genitals.

I could very well add to these examples, but I should like to emphasize, as a conclusion and extension to what I have just evoked, that the idea of a language of the act has a value that goes well beyond the psychopathological register.

First, I will mention the sexual act in particular, which seems to me to be entirely interpretable along the lines I am proposing. The meeting of the bodies, the way they are encountered, how one penetrates the other, the rhythm of the "comings and goings", the gentleness, the brutality, the postures, the intensity bestowed in the self's engagement and so forth, "recount" the self's drive to the other, but also how, in the "preverbal" primitive body contact with its early objects, the bodies are encountered and penetrated, and how they may be taken back up, integrated, mediated and symbolized in adult sexuality. The bodies "speak" the sexuality, and the sexual act "recounts" the experience of the self and the history of the experience of the meeting with the object.

My final example is drawn from body language as it is observed in the animal kingdom. "Taming" dolphins conforms to an interesting ritual that, moreover, may also be found in certain forms of the sexual act or corporal encounter among humans. The trainer must begin by presenting a part of his own body – his arm, for instance, his limb, then – to the dolphin's mouth, which is full of sharp teeth. The dolphin may, in a bite, slice what has thus been given to him, but he is happy merely to apply some light pressure on to the given limb, the arm. He makes it "felt" however that he could cut or damage it, but he stops himself short of wounding the trusting "trainer". Then the latter withdraws his arm and the dolphin turns over and offers his abdomen, that is, the most vulnerable part of his anatomy. The trainer in turn places his hand on the abdomen and applies a slight pressure signifying that he can exercise his power over this vulnerable part, but that he does not. Here then is a corporal "dialogue", which seems to me to be the corporal prototype of the operations at the bottom of what one may call the "basic transference" that may be observed when a psychoanalytic cure is going well. Of course, such a dialog is polysemic; it may be interpreted in many different ways – from the viewpoint of the forms of engaged sexuality, from the viewpoint of the narcissistic stakes of vulnerability and security and so on. But it is likewise a fundamental characteristic of the language of the act and, more generally, of the body.

The ideas developed in this chapter introduce those that will be developed in the next chapter on "primary symbolization". Non-verbal languages show an effort to transmit primitive experiences in an attempt to integrate them. They open the way to listening to "formal signifiers" (Anzieu)[31] in analytical communication and to psychoanalytical work on forms of primary symbolization.

Notes

1 Freud, S. (1913). "The claims of psycho-analysis to scientific interest". *Standard Edition*, 13: 165.
2 Lacan, J. (1966). *Ecrits*. Paris: Seuil [(Trans. B. Fink). New York: Norton, 2006.]
3 Roussillon, R. (1995). "Perception, hallucination et solutions «bio-logiques» du traumatisme". *Rev franç psychosomatique*, n°8. Paris.
4 Denis, P. (1992). "Emprise et théorie des pulsions". *Revue Française de Psychanalyse*, 1992, 1297–1423, PUF.
5 Freud, S. (1913). "The claims of psycho-analysis to scientific interest". *Standard Edition*, 13: 165.
6 Roussillon, R. (2003). La séparation et la chorégraphie de la présence. In: *La séparation*. ÉRÉS.

7 Freud, S. (1907). "Obsessive actions and religious practices". *Standard Edition*, 9: 117.
8 Freud, S. (1909). "Some general remarks on hysterical attacks". *Standard Edition*, 9: 229.
9 Freud, S. (1895]). *Studies on hysteria*. Standard Edition, 2.
10 Freud, S. (1920). The psychogenesis of a case of homosexuality in a woman. *SE*, 18.
11 Mac Dougall, J. (1996). *Éros aux mille et un visages*. Paris: Gallimard.
12 Freud, S. (1937b). "Constructions in analysis". *Standard Edition*, 23: 257.
13 Freud S (1941[1938]). "Findings, ideas, problems". *SE*, 23: 299.
14 David, M. (1997). Activité spontanée et fonctionnement mental préverbal du nourrisson. In: *Que sont les bébés devenus*. Cahors.
15 Bleger, J. (1967). *Symbiose et ambiguïté*, trad franç. Paris: PUF, 1981.
16 Botella, C. et B Botella, S. (1984). L'homosexualité inconsciente et la dynamique du double en séance *in Revue Française de psychanalyse 2–1984*, PUF.
17 Roussillon. R (1984). "Construction de la scène primitive et co-construction du processus analytique, à propos de l'interprétation". *Bulletin de la Société Psychanalytique de Paris*, 1984: 27–44.
18 Stern, D. N. (1985). *The interpersonal world of the infant: A view from psychoanalysis and developmental psychology*. London: Karnac Books, 1998.
19 Marcelli, D. (1992). "Le rôle des microrythmes et des macrorythmes dans l'émergence de la pensée chez le nourrisson". *La Psychiatrie de l'enfant*, XXXV(1): 57–82.
20 Freud, S. (1923). *The ego and the id*. Standard Edition, 19: 3.
21 Freud, S. (1896)." Letter of 6th December 1896". In J. M. Masson (Ed), *The complete letters of Sigmund Freud to Wilhelm Fliess 1887–1904*. Cambridge, MA: Harvard University Press, 1985.
22 Roussillon, R. (1994). "La Rhétorique de l'influence". *Cliniques Méditerranéennes n° 43–44*, ÉRÉS.
23 Green, A. (2002). *La Pensée clinique*. Paris: Odile Jacob.
24 Spitz, R.A. (1965). *The first year of life*. New York: International Universities Press.
25 Wallon, H. (1983). *Les origines du caractère chez l'enfant. Les préludes du sentiment de personnalité*. Paris, PUF, coll. Quadrige Le psychologue.
26 Anzieu, D. (1974). "Le moi-peau". *Nouvelle Revue de Psychanalyse*, 8: 195–209. NRF.
     Anzieu, D. (1989). "Principe d'analyse transitionnelle en psychanalyse individuelle". In *Psychanalyse des limites*. Paris: Dunod, 2007.
27 Roussillon, R. (1995). Perception, hallucination et solutions «bio-logiques» du traumatisme. *Rev franç psychosomatique*, n°8. Paris.
28 Freud, S. (1927). Fetishism. *SE*, 21. PUF, 1969; *OCF.P*, XVIII.
29 Freud, S. (1922). Medusa's head. *SE*, 18.
30 Winnicott, D.W. (1967). "Mirror-role of mother and family in child development". In *Playing and reality*. London: Routledge, 1999.
31 Anzieu, D. (1987). *Les signifiants formels et le moi-peau, Les enveloppes psychiques*. Paris: Dunod, 1–22.

9 An introduction to the work on primary symbolization

One of the changes affecting psychoanalysis, and which seems to me amongst the most fecund, concerns the evolution of the conception and the model of the activity of symbolization, which for the most part controls the work of subjectivation that is, for me, at the heart of psychoanalytic practice.

Classically, symbolization, and, more generally, representational activity, is directed toward the question of the absent object. W.R. Bion, for example, takes the absence of the breast as his point of departure for thought activity, but all French psychoanalysis also roots the work of representation in the encounter with the absent or separated object. This conception has produced some of the most beautiful jewels of psychoanalytic thought, and it is not for me to call this into question; its relevance is beyond doubt. The absence of the object, its "perceptive" absence, compels the subject to widen the distinction between the object perceived in the present and the internal trace of previous perceptions of the object, from which construction of the internal object representation is made possible. When the object is present, the internal object representation is superimposed upon the perception of the object. Thus, it does not appear as a representation, it is not "reflected" like a representation, except of course if the subject perceives a gap between his or her object representation and what he or she perceives of it.

In this conception, the presence of the object and the link with the object in presence do not pose any problem; they are deemed "givens" through perception and its investment. Only absence, separation, differentiation and loss appear as potentially problematic.

Once again there is a great deal of cogency in this conception which remains very useful in understanding broad swathes of psychic functioning.

The difficulty comes from the fact that clinical practice, and in particular the clinical treatment of narcissistic pathologies, comes up against modes of psychic functioning which pose questions which this model can only address in a very incomplete way. The broadening of the scope of psychoanalytic metapsychology – to comprise clinical pictures and

DOI: 10.4324/9781003198710-9

problem complexes in which the construction of links and the investment of links is at the center of the subject's suffering and difficulties – calls for a more complete conception than that afforded by the classical one, and one that comprises a reflection upon other earlier or more archaic aspects of the symbolization process. These clinical problem complexes indeed show that the link, and in particular the construction of the primitive link, is not a "given" – always there at any human encounter. Indeed, these may exhibit failures or specific features in their construction such that the whole of psychic life may be lastingly affected by it.

These clinical pictures show that the construction of the primitive link is not automatic and is not necessarily a given. They demonstrate that it results from a process which, if it encounters too many difficulties, may struggle to organize itself or may present weaknesses rendering such a construction very vulnerable to the vicissitudes of social encounters. These then display certain "autistic", "melancholic" or "anti-social" traits when they come up against particular difficulties, the subject then resorting to forms of retreat or even de-subjectivation more akin to the splitting of subjectivity than the repression of a part of psychic life. It therefore seems necessary to make reference to the action of forms of destructivity – most often silent, but at time more violent – which requires us to reframe the problem of our representation and our theory of construction of early links and the basis of the link in a more wide-reaching way.

But when we come to consider the construction of the primitive link, and to support this, the work of specialists in very early childhood, we must then address the broader question of the emergence of early forms of symbol representation and to consider that these are produced within and from the mode of encounter and mode of presence of the object. Man is born with a system of preconceptions (Bion)[1] on the type of human environment that he will (must) encounter, but these preconceptions are nothing more than "potential" (Winnicott)[2] or "virtual"; their true appropriation presupposes that the human subject will encounter a certain number of responses from the early environment and that certain responses will be present at the early encounters with relational life. Otherwise, these remain "dead letters", they lose their generative potential or they take "degenerated" forms, hindering their integration into the psyche.

The failures of these early encounters produce an affect of "primary narcissistic disappointment" and mobilize a procession of primitive defense mechanisms (Fraiberg 1991)[3] in which, at one end we see the early forms of retreat in an autistic line and at the other, the attempts at healing by an intensified primary masochism. Between the two, the forms of psychotic, borderline, perverse or anti-social processes are situated.

I don't want here to enter into detail on the factors involved in the determination of the "choice" of these different psychopathological "outcomes", which interweave biological and personal factors and the characteristics of the early environment, preferring instead to attempt to elucidate certain forms of the work of analysis which psychoanalytic practice now offers up to us.

The question of primary symbolization

In the 1970s, a series of authors, primarily in France, grappling at times with the question of psychosis or that of the functions known as border-line, at times the treatment of infants, will offer concepts which, without necessarily concatenating directly and deliberately to the questions I have just touched upon, will allow us to draw out our exploration of the pri-mary forms of symbolization. Some of the best known amongst these are P. Aulagnier[4] and his concept of the "pictogram" and D. Anzieu[5] and his "formal signifiers".

I shall confine myself to first extracting certain characteristics which seem to me to be common to both.

My first point relates to the fact that by various designations, and by those which were current at the time of their formulation, the two authors are describing processes of transformation. This indeed inscribes their proposals within a metapsychology of the psychic processes. I think it is important to underscore that these are processes of transformation, as the processes described – very clearly in Aulagnier but also present in Anzieu – are processes which raise the question of early forms of subjec-tive appropriation: the processes described represent forms of transforma-tion necessary to allow subjective appropriation to occur, even though – at least in Anzieu, whose material I shall principally draw upon – this is not explicitly formulated.

Consequently, it seems to me that the processes described all exhibit a significant anchoring in sensory-motricity, they are underpinned by the body of sensoriality and the "staging" of a movement, and this is what confers them with the value of a process.

Finally, the various authors describe intrapsychic or intrasubjective processes, while underscoring how much these are contingent upon con-ditions of environment. But here again, the time in which they were for-mulated was not won over by the intersubjective approach (or interpsychic if one prefer) and the position of the responses of the other-subject objects, while noted, is not fundamentally integrated into the metapsychological description.

A clinical situation by way of example

To demonstrate the psychoanalytic cogency of these works, I shall draw upon fragments of the treatment of one patient.

Mr. M comes to see me following his disappointment upon noting that the symptom that had prompted him to undergo analysis almost 50 years previously was still present and had not developed despite numerous psychotherapeutic and psychoanalytic treatments. He had originally sought consultation as he was beset by difficulties with academic inhibition, experiencing a block in any "examination"-type situation. His thoughts become blocked; he is then no longer able to concentrate, nor demonstrate his knowledge. In his professional life, he has "bypassed" the obstacle of study by becoming an "inventor" and by creating his own business specializing in all kinds of connection and joining systems. He sold his company, and once retired, fortune made, he decides to travel and learn Italian. It is at this point, during his lessons, that he "discovers" that his symptom from back in the beginning is still present.

He comes to see me "as a last resort" and after having read my books (he reads widely in psychoanalysis). During the first interviews, it appears that he is "off topic", a formula which came to mean his fear of not telling me what he needed to and that I had understood, with the strong sense of a major difficulty in being subject, the "becoming-subject" appearing then as the central issue of the cure.

His psychoanalytic treatments having been numerous, and not very productive judging by what he tells me, I suggest at first a "test treatment" of a few months face to face, to explore my possibility of bringing something to him. Then after two months, after reviewing the situation with him and in view of the fact that unlike his former treatments "it's working here", a sensitive transference for him is established and we commence treatment of one then two then three and four sessions per week as different time slots progressively become available.

He comes across as very lively, as are those with high intellect; he is very inventive, the sessions and his associativity are accompanied by a degree of hypomania, he talks very quickly, peppered with non sequiturs, frequently departs ("losing" me) in painstaking and drawn out descriptions of problems of "joining" which he is specialized in, of the machines needed to make these joins, of his "recouping" strategy so as not to run to unnecessary expenditure on the materials or tooling machines required. But at the same time, when he talks and explains all this to me, he also appears cut off from contact with me. He speaks but – at least during the early part of the treatment – does not seem to wait for an echo "response" or reaction on my part, which suggests to me a form of process "cut off" from the other and of an autistic type. He will allude incidentally rather quickly to feeling alone and as if in a kind of "bunker", protected from contact but completely alone, without any links with others.

He has dedicated his life to inventing ways of "holding objects together", objects of all kinds and doing so in the most cost-effective way. (*It would take me some time to understand that these evocations represent "his solution" to the rigid character of his early environment and to the ruptures of link which suffused his early history*).

For some time during treatment, he thus spoke "in the void", convinced that I understood nothing, even that I wasn't listening, which was congruent with the tendency of his historical relational experience that was marked by a feeling of failure of the encounter with the other. He feels he is "losing" me in the midst of his associative stream, of being "off-topic", which then allows itself be understood in connection with a certain, and fairly defensive, mode of "false-self" functioning.

But I do not let him do it, and I intervene often to ask him to explain such and such a mechanism of the machines referred to, such and such a technical point he is addressing and which I am unfamiliar with and so on. And he has the repeated experience, over the months, of my effort to adjust my listening to his associative search. Little by little, his impression changes, and he begins to get the sense of my presence and of an encounter with me during the sessions. This feeling is in fact a little frightening for him, but one that at the same time arouses a certain curiosity: what happened with the other psychoanalysts he encountered, who incidentally remained silent or even fell asleep, or looked like they were falling asleep, does not happen with me. The clinical picture then changes little by little and we can even begin to make connections between his retreat into the bunker with early losses of contact with an asthmatic mother, who would spend a great deal of time withdrawn into herself. He begins to feel more of a link with me and even begins to make links between one session and the other.

The following sequence is one that I would particularly like to focus upon. It comes after the return from the holidays, and in my view, it encapsulates the question of the early forms of symbolization which we alluded to earlier.

He begins the session by referring to the representation of a baby in his cradle who hears his mother coming to see if he is asleep, without revealing herself, remaining at the foot of the cradle. The baby is not asleep, and upon hearing the sound of a presence, writhes in every direction to try to see who is there (he mimes the scene).

Then, after a time, "He had dreams that show that he feels better".

Dream 1. There are two halves that join together. (*the first formal signifier*). He comments: "that usually doesn't join up". "That's good, that shows he's doing better, besides he feels good about it and that's why he wants to continue. It's clearing up within him.

Deep inside him, it is as if there is a swamp with waters that stagnate with methane bubbles stuck at the bottom. There the bubbles come unstuck and burst up to the surface and that brings relief (*another formal signifier: 'a bubble rises to the surface and bursts'*). It isn't very pleasant but it brings relief, it is nice that it brings relief. His intestines are improving too, there also the gases (he laughs a belly laugh), the gases *brrrpp…* (he mimes by touching his stomach, holding his belly between both hands). No, it's better the gases come out, it doesn't hurt as much, it brings relief".

He had another dream.

Dream 2. "Two boards slot together" (*another formal signifier*) forming a kind of sledge, and he gets on the sledge and slides. But after a while, he stops the sledge and he can go back up, he can go backward.

Here this also shows that he is doing better, otherwise, before, he would slide (he shows it slipping from arms) and it didn't ever stop. In this case, he was able to go back up, go backward, and that is a sign.

Several formal signifiers are present in this sequence.

"Two halves join together", from the first dream, is a formal signifier even if it is a "positive" formal signifier, whereas Anzieu has chiefly described formal signifiers which accompany pathological movements. This is a formal signifier of "primary symbolization", a dreamed form of the encounter, the "placing together" of the Greek sumbolon. The processes of symbolization, as we have mentioned above, may also be represented in the form of formal signifiers. But note here that scenification in the dream is minimal; there is no subject or object, only a movement, an action. What came to mind during this session was that this was indeed a session after the return from the holidays, and that in a sense the dream was the enactment of "our reunion": "two halves join together".

Then a bodily impression is evoked in association and translated into another formal signifier: *"a bubble rises to the surface and bursts"*. This is once again taken up in the onomatopoeia *"brrrpp"*, enacting the movement of the bodily impression in verbal prosody. This is a formal signifier of "abreaction", of discharge, linked to the experience of satisfaction. But it also gives form to a return of subjective experiences "stuck" in the depths of the psyche and which come back to the psychic surface in a self-representational process of the psychic process of the "return of the split-off" coming to "join in the conversation" (Freud 1994) and to progressively complexify the work of psychic construction underway. This will become more apparent in the second dream.

In the second dream, two formal signifiers are present; there is the *"two boards slot together"* which is of the same form as that of the first dream, and *"it slides"*. But the dream combines the two formal signifiers, adding a subject, and the presence of a subject makes it possible to control the "sliding" of the formal signifier and of the process it gives form to. Construction and psychic complexification continue.

The first dream and the first formal signifier, the first formal process, calls for a work of scenification to reveal him "telling" that an encounter, the result of the work carried out with me over the months preceding the dream, is now possible. By introducing subject and object, according to the method of construction put forward earlier on, I could have said if I had felt the need, "Now you are able to meet with me and we are able to join together and re-encounter one another after the holidays". I could have "scenified" or set the scene of the formal signifier, contextualizing it and thus inscribing it in a representation, a scenario, of "reunions possible after absence". But I did not feel the need for this intervention, nor would I have had the time if I had felt the need, for that matter, as the second dream soon arrives which complexifies the scene.

The second dream returns to the coming together of the two parts, but with the aid of another formal signifier, constructs a more complex scene where the subject appears. "It slides" enacts a threat of endless falling ("it wouldn't stop before"), a fall linked to separation, to the experience of abandonment, of being dropped or more specifically of being let slip, according to a frequent schema with this patient, but a fall stopped in its tracks by the fact that a subject "takes control", clings on and stops "being let slide" unlike what would normally occur. A reflexive process then emerges and forms a return loop, a recovery or repeat loop.

Let us return to the rest of the session, where he continues:

"There is also another dream but in this case he does not know how to interpret it".

Dream: He must manage to connect all the twisted wires but which have been cut (he mimes the twisted cable molding and shows that the twists of the first wire are offset in relation to those of the other half of the wire, offset by a quarter), he accepts to attempt it. (*I suspect another formal signifier but I do not understand this; I note however that here the encounter is no longer possible*).

He goes on to make the following remarks: "You cannot connect the wires like that (he shows the gap of a quarter with the flat of his hands) because of the twisted cable molding (he shows the twisting with a hand gesture); you must connect strand by strand. You must remove the molding, flatten it out (he shows all of this by gesturing, he 'removes' the molding, 'flattens' the wire and mimes the superposition of the two flattened wires which he places next to each other"). In any case you cannot connect them in a cost-effective manner, it's too expensive, for my old-fashioned hovel of a workshop", (and he moves into complex technical explanations about tools, necessary machinery; this lasts for quite a while and I am a little lost).

I think of the twisting he shows me and I make the link with what he showed me of the baby at the beginning of the session, where he had mimed a baby in his cradle, writhing and twisting to attempt to catch sight of his mother who has surreptitiously walked into the room from behind. I then say to him (also with a certain voice mime) that babies turn toward the source of investment. Like sunflowers following the sun. So they may twist to remain in contact with the mother; they can twist around. But the link is difficult when the torsion is too great and it may break. (*Thus I attempt to open up the formal signifier by revealing a subject and the response of the object and its effect*). Here the implied formal signifier would therefore be less that of encounter than that of rupture, of "breakage" ("*it twists and it breaks*"). This is implicit to his description and it is I who introduce it as historical experience by contextualizing and scenifying it.

Equally noteworthy is that the process of re-linking – the challenge of the dream – may only be effectuated "strand by strand", part by part. This also points to what he is placing "on the agenda" for the coming sessions after the return from the holidays. If "it has been rejoined" it has only been partially rejoined and the work does not stop here.

The relevance of such a sequence is that it makes it possible to articulate the formal signifiers and the work of the dream; it makes it possible to inscribe the clinical exploration of formal signifiers within a more traditional and already well delineated psychoanalytic work.

In the example, I have just given the point of departure is the emergence of a formal signifier and the work of the dream, or failing that the work of the clinician, where the work will be to construct a scene around the formal signifier, bringing into relation a subject and an object within a context, one able to be inscribed within a pertinent and meaningful narrative form.

It is at times necessary to carry out the work the other way round, and to extract from within an associative chain the formal signifier that organizes it in secret. This calls to mind a text in which S. Leclaire[6] brings to light in his patient the presence of what he calls "the letter", in the form of the verbal signifier "pordjelli" which appears in several of his patient's associative chains. Another example taken from the treatment of a young woman, and within a transference conjuncture marked by an experience of disappointment which was repeated in various situations of "hand outstretched" toward the other, without a satisfying response; it is the emergence of the formal process, "a hand stretches out toward an object that pulls away" which gave form most effectively to the clinical sequence taking place.

I return to the underlying theme of Mr. M's cure, to explore another aspect of primary symbolization. The presentation of the sessions from the beginning of the year focused upon listening to primary symbolization at work particularly based on formal signifiers appearing in the patient's dreams and associations.

I shall now present further clinical material focused this time upon another aspect of primary symbolization: a singular form of the *malleable medium* (M. Milner)[7] considered as the thing-presentation (and thus a form of primary symbolization) of the process of symbolization. To enable a sound grasp of the type of work effectuated, and to account for primary symbolization and its articulation with the more classical psychoanalytic work, I am obliged to contextualize the clinical sequence that I wish to talk about.

The last sessions before those I will talk about were marked by the patient's numerous associations on his eating habits, particularly the fact that he eats a lot and that he always feels obliged to finish everything, even if it means making himself ill and taking a long time to digest. Not least, he eats whole salads of a form of very strong "bitter" chicory that he sources from a grower who "keeps it aside" for him. But this chicory plays havoc with his digestion.

These eating habits have been gradually linked to the "bitter" meals of his childhood and his father's demeanor. He was often less than sober and would throw considerable fits of anger at the table, at times directed against the food (which was too meager as his mother would try to save money owing to the fact that a significant portion of his father's pay – as an engineer – would go toward the purchase of his own materials for his inventor's workshop), but also against the Germans (the childhood context of the last World War), indeed against more or less everyone including the children seated at the table. Reproaches directed against the children without any specific content (as they are in any case terrified of their father, even of their mother, and they are not allowed to speak at table) directed at no-one in particular, reproaches "soaring" over their heads, without any particular "culprit".

Within this context, the patient's attitude was, taken as a whole, a form of avoidance; he would concentrate on the food and would eat, he would eat a lot and would finish the dishes in an attempt to turn away from the scene of paternal verbal violence unfolding at the table. This was a form of desperate attempt to metabolize the "bitterness" of the situation, to try to digest it, be that to the detriment of his digestive apparatus.

The question of his father's fits of rage and his attitude in response has therefore been at the center of recent sessions. Here is the verbatim account of one session.

> He has thought over what was said in the session in relation to his father's fits of rage, he agrees he has many memories of his father's rages which come back to him, always at table… He has also thought about numerous links between what he does or has done and what his father did, in his professional activities. He would go into his workshop, he was forbidden to do so, but he would watch his father doing his experiments (his father was also trying to invent technical systems).

Progressively during the session he becomes angry with himself for the various inventions that have been stolen from him: he refers in detail to an invention of *a blocking system for gas pipes* (see his digestive problems mentioned above!). Twisting the pipe was enough for it to block, but also for it to unblock (he explains all of this in detail and in particular how he had not thought to emphasize, in the patent filed, that there could not be twisting over several meters – (*I do not understand everything as he mixes his explanations with invectives against himself, with gestures; he shifts very quickly from one idea to another, I am taken by associations on the twisting and the gas pipe-intestine in connection with his digestive problems*).

But above all he is angry with himself because of some news he has just received regarding a patent that he filed 18 months previously (so before the beginning of the resumption of analysis with me). Here again he enters into complicated explanations in which I manage to grasp that he filed an incomplete patent, in particular he did not make it sufficiently clear that the system he invented possesses folding properties (a double system of wire drawing and stranding from what I understand) which enables it to be used for banding or strapping.

He pointed out the lightweight feature of the product he invented (over five times lighter than traditional systems, but with the same resistance qualities, etc.). But all of these qualities only have meaning because it can be folded and used to bind pipes and keep objects together in place. He had written this in pencil but had forgotten to include it on the final form. *I am providing these details deliberately to give a sense of the particular climate of the sessions and how the "primary" material appears in context, always mixed with rather more customary or standard material, for example here the link with the paternal interdiction of going into the workshop.*

The Swiss agents of the patents service drew his attention to this oversight and asked plenty of questions. His lawyer told him that he would need to re-file a patent (he explains to me the need for a lawyer for this type of matter) but that would cost 2,700 euro, and it was indicated to him that the answers to the questions would suffice, to save money; the lawyer told him in no uncertain terms, but he did not listen. The important thing is what is in the wording of the patent, and his, without these clarifications, is declared "irrelevant". It was published as such and anyone may make use of it. All anyone would have to do would be to think of folding it for his invention to be stolen from him.

The question of his creativity is therefore at the center of the session and with it, how the "found" expropriates the created.

He is in a violent rage against himself; he asks himself why he keeps on persisting with this invention that has taken him at least 20 years now. I feel the need without really knowing why to "save" his invention. I explore how he can rescue the situation, such as the patent has only been published for three weeks and there is the possibility of filing a new patent as soon as tomorrow (it is the date of filing which is authoritative), and all he would have to do is send the corrected version of his patent for him to minimize the damage. He gets angry with me, "for someone like you it's possible but for a crackpot like me…" and his anger is directed once again toward him.

RR. You are angry with yourself like your father could be.

My intervention calms him in part. He returns to the fact that he had written the part concerning the folding properties of the type of metal product he had designed (drawn and stranded stainless steel) in pencil. Why had he forgotten that?

RR. You spoke about your father's fits of anger at the beginning of the session; you seem to be angry with yourself like he was angry with you, perhaps because this question of folding or bending was difficult for you.

Faced with your father's rages, you also had to bend or yield, but at the same time, you must have had an urge to revolt within you.

"Now that's great... yes it must be that, that's it... he was always bent over, (com)pliant towards everything. Yes revolt, it must be that".

The session has finished, and as he leaves he says to me on his way to the door, "Lacan would have said, 'that'll be a thousand euros'". (This is a reference to the fact that, according to him, Lacan would charge a different price according to the quality of the session).

Leaving the session, I ask myself why I wanted so much to protect his invention. The thought comes back to me that while he was explaining his invention, I was watching his hands and I said to myself that he is playing, that this was his game, his inventions and the modifications he subjected the metal to in order to render it pliable.

And then I understood, thus after the session, what I had not yet been able to say to myself but what was underlying my desire to save his invention; not merely his game, but the capacity he had had to transform a rigid environment into a "pliable", that is to say a "malleable" environment. To subject an object to the folding and bending that he himself had been subjected to, and in so doing to triumph over it, to transform a rigid and unusable early environment into a malleable environment he could make use of to construct links.

At the same time, the "forgotten" function of this invention became clear: to maintain the link, and the link with his "rigid" father (upbringing through fits of "you must", "you mustn't", etc.) that is to say, also with an aspect of the symbolizing function (see the beginning of the session and his remarks on the numerous links he made between his activities and those of his father).

And finally, the idea came to me that his repeated and numerous allusions to his inventions represented "his [historical] solution" and that in such a way he transferred this in the sessions of analysis for his "solution" to be recognized but also overtaken by another "solution" which subsequent sessions would quite roundly confirm.

I have examined this sequence in some detail in order to convey the sense of relevance in hearing a piece of clinical material, otherwise almost inaudible from a psychoanalytic classic point of view, based on the question of the primary symbolization at play during the course of the session. The first clinical sequences that I began by mentioning focused on the emergence of formal signifiers in the sessions and in the patient's dreams. This relates to the progressive work of construction of the representational scenario starting from a representation of action or movement "without subject or object" which is gradually understood as a narrative form of "schemes-of-being-with" (Stern 1983),[8] as the way in which the subject relates his experience of primary encounter with the object.

The second sequence is increasingly focused upon one aspect of the primary forms of symbolization, that of transformation, namely, transformation through sensory-motor play. Here we find another aspect of the process of primary symbolization, one that is no longer centered only upon one proto-narrative form of history gone by, but focused instead upon the transformation of the historic order into a useable form so that the subject may "become subject" and appropriate his own history. Between the two we have also underscored the importance, in the primary forms of symbolization, of a self-representation of the psychic processes and in particular of the psychic processes of transformation, which confers Freud's hypothesis regarding the significance of primitive animism with its essential character. In this respect, it is probable that primary symbolization and the subjectivation process go hand in hand and are essential to the process of "becoming subject" of the young infant and thereafter of any subject.

Since 1983[9] (and again in 1991)[10] I have maintained that symbolization and the processes of psychic transformation that this implies rest upon the thing-presentation of a *malleable-medium* object, derived from the encounter with a sufficiently adaptable and transformable maternal environment to adjust to the psychic needs of the newborn. Whenever the early environment appears rigid and unadaptable, it tends rather to bend the baby and after the subject to its own imperatives rather than adapting to its needs, thus when the primary relationship tends to invert the necessary elements, primary symbolization flounders. The subject's effort to "become subject" will thus be an effort "at all costs" to render this rigid environment "malleable".

This is what, for example, the work of sculpture makes clear: starting with a hard material and transforming it until it may accommodate a representation. But this is certainly also an identifiable challenge in various craft forms using solid and rigid materials to accomplish them. But when this work of "rendering malleable" a rigid environment fails, the subject then withdraws within himself; he withdraws within an internal bunker; he seeks to protect himself from the encounter with an object upon which no effect seems possible.

In any creative work, we must be able to identify this process at work; perhaps it even signals that which characterizes creative work, which always, when substantial, meets with a form of resistance of the material to be transformed. A bridge must be established therefore between the work of primary symbolization and the subject of creativity and creation.

To conclude, I would emphasize that primary symbolization is the process that moves from "the raw material" of experience, the perceptive mnemic trace – the instinctual impulse, or even the psychic drive representation, according to Freud – which carries the sensory-motor trace of the impact of the encounter of the subject with a still poorly differentiated, poorly identified object, confusing part of the subject and part of the object, to a possibility of scenification able to "become language", able to be narrated to another subject, to thus be shared and recognized by another subject to in turn become assimilable into subjectivity. But such a process, if it can over time become autonomous, may only be accomplished in the earliest stages if there is an "already-subject" there to share and to recognize the process taking place. Mr. M had to compulsively attempt to modify the rigid environment of his early history, unaware of what was at stake in his life's "passion", until analysis places him in a position to be able to more fully appropriate the meaning of what has represented the greatest endeavor of his life.

I would like to propose now a hypothesis and a model to try to syn-thetize the question of the link to the invested object. The hypothesis concerns the issue of the interpretation of the absence, of the perceptual rupture of the link with the object. I think that what the absence, the rup-ture, reveals "speaks" of the way in which the object was encountered, of what was played out in the encounter with it and of the way in which this experience served to configure the internal representation of the object. One cannot think of separation independently of the conditions of the encounter.

In addition, I propose a model of the link with the object organized as a braid of three unconscious "contracts" with the object. The following chapter is intended to attempt to shed light on this configuration.

Notes

1 Bion, W.R. (1970). *Attention and interpretation*. London: Tavistock. [(1984). London: Karnac.]
2 Winnicott, D.W. (1970). *Playing and reality*. London: Routledge.
3 Fraiberg, S. (1989). Ghost in the nursery, Clinical Studies in Infant mental Health, US.
4 Winnicott, D.W. (1970). *Playing and reality*. London: Routledge, 1999.
5 Anzieu, D. (1987). *Les signifiants formels et le moi-peau, Les enveloppes psychiques*. Paris: Dunod, 1–22.
6 Leclaire, S. (1975). *On tue un enfant*. Paris: Ed Seuil.
7 Milner, M. (1987). *The suppressed madness of sane men: Forty-four years of explor-ing psychoanalysis*. London: Routledge.
8 Stern, D. N. (1985). *The interpersonal world of the infant: A view from psychoanaly-sis and developmental psychology*. London: Karnac Books, 1998.
9 Roussillon, R. (1983). "La réaction thérapeutique négative : du protiste au jeu de construction". *Revue Française de Psychanalyse*, 1985, no. 2: 597–621.
10 Roussillon, R. (1991). *Paradoxes et situations limites de la psychanalyse*. Paris: PUF.

10 Rupture/separation as an analyzer of bonding

Introduction

If "rupture" is often a difficult situation to live through, its elaboration depends to a large extent on the issues at stake in the relationship and the bonds or ties that are severed. From this point of view, "rupture" seems to be a kind of "natural analyzer" of bonding and the braiding of the components that constitute it. Drawing on diverse clinical situations involving difficult ruptures, I will try to identify three of these components organized as forms of "contracts" which are partly conscious but also to a large extent unconscious. The diverse clinical situations referred to will draw particular attention to the primacy of one or the other of the contracts which represent the way the bond is organized and how it is regulated.

These three contracts are:

- the "narcissistic contract" which represents the basis of the relationship and condenses its narcissistic value; it is characterized by a certain number of traits that define its narcissistic "style";
- the "libidinal contract" which regulates the libidinal transactions between the diverse subjects involved in the bond and the forms and limits of its transactions; it is characterized by specific instinctual interests and a style of "conversation between bodies" in sexuality;
- and finally, the "symbolic contract" which condenses and determines the "right conditions" thanks to which the narcissistic contract and the libidinal contract are regulated and can be elaborated at the moment of separation or, conversely, on account of which this elaboration fails.

The three contracts are always present in every relationship, but their quantity and organizing value in the bond are variable; it is their articulation that gives its particular "color" to the bond established, and thus, at the same time, to the separation and its effects.

DOI: 10.4324/9781003198710-10

The braiding of link

The theme of rupture, and widely kind of separation, is far-reaching: ruptures/separation themselves have multiple forms and can concern all the fields in which human beings are involved, whether in the social field – homeless people dropping-out, exile and revolutions are forms of rupture, but there are also invisible ruptures – or in the domain of ideas – L. Althusser[1] spoke of an "epistemological break", thus of an epistemological or paradigmatic rupture – or in the domain of human relations, and, in particular, those that are based on love in one form or another.

But though the manifest forms of rupture/separation are diverse, one can only speak of rupture "for a subject"; the rupture is only such as it is because it affects, regardless of its field and its causes, singular subjects and the relations between singular subjects. And the way in which the rupture is experienced or decided and put into effect also depends on the meaning that this or that incident or circumstance acquires.

At any rate, it is from this point of view that I have decided to reflect on our theme, thus resolutely as a clinician of bonding and relationships. My reflections and argument will be based on the following proposition: rupture is an *analyzer* of the nature and constituents of bonding. Often invisible aspects of the bonds linking or uniting subjects are revealed through and in the experience of rupture.

To explore this hypothesis, I will begin with a clinical situation.

A clinical history

Myriam had asked me for an urgent appointment following the break-up of a relationship; she had been referred to me by a young woman colleague who was a friend of hers.

I met a beautiful and elegant woman in her 50s, who very swiftly collapsed into tears as soon as she tried to explain to me what was happening to her. Since breaking up with her friend, she had lost her courage, spent her time crying, and even her work, which she was normally very interested in, left her feeling relatively indifferent at the moment.

She had already been married twice and had initiated the first two separations which she had coped with very well. But this time she thought that this man would be the right one, and their relationship had been going well for two years. They met each other while she was on a professional assignment in a far-off country, and during the first year, they only saw each other periodically owing to her being away a lot.

As things were going very well between them, she had decided a year ago to come and live in Lyon, where she was born and where her family was currently living, in order to live together with him. They had bought a house together, and everything had been going well until the last few months when violent conflicts had appeared between them, particularly in connection with her youngest son who was living with them.

Her friend had begun showing signs of jealousy and was very critical of the relationship she had with her son, and the conflict had got constantly worse until one day, in the middle of the night, her friend suddenly left the house they owned together. Even though they had seen each other several times, she could not get over it: "Something's broken", she said.

Myriam was referring, then, to an "internal" rupture affecting her relationship with her friend.

The two years of regular clinical sessions that followed made it possible to clarify, in part, what had happened within her; in any case, they were enough to help her emerge of the depressive slump into which this form of rupture had plunged her.

The two divorces in her love-life that preceded her relationship with her current friend had become inevitable for her when she realized that both these men, who were not without qualities and charm, were unable to fulfill their paternal function.

She had met the first after leaving the family home at the age of 18, because she could no longer tolerate living in close proximity with her father, who was a highly intelligent and eminent scientist, but behaved in private like a sort of domestic tyrant and was unlivable with on a daily basis. With this man whom she had met during her medical studies, she went on many mountain races Escalation and shared several passions. But as soon as they had a son, their relationship deteriorated rapidly.

This man invested very little in his "job as a father" and also turned out to be a mediocre doctor, without much professional ambition, whereas she herself was enjoying a very successful career in international bodies responsible for population health.

Myriam had married her second husband without being passionately in love, and mainly so as not to have to bring up her children alone. He turned out to be just as disappointing as the first when it came to providing the children with the educational support she expected from him, and when, for professional reasons, she had to go away for a long period of time anyway, she finally decided to leave him.

It was only later, when she had more or less given up the idea of getting married again or of forming a lasting relationship, that she met her current companion. It was quite quickly a case of "love at first sight" for a brilliant, ambitious and funny man who, like her, was Jewish, and whose family, like hers, had experienced the horrors of genocide. Though she had doubted that it would ever be possible for her to fall in love again, she had lived a cloudless idyll for almost two years that was probably even marked by a form of passionate love.

As, in all three cases, the relationship had broken up over the question of the relation of her men and lovers to the paternal position, I thought it was worth exploring this question with her in greater depth.

The first rupture had occurred with her father when she left the family home at the age of 18. It was a genuine rupture in the sense that, for many years thereafter, she had no further contact with her father and only maintained communication with her mother.

I evoke with her that there might be a connection between her conflict with and separation from her father and the subsequent difficulties she had with men. She accepted this link, and taking this as the starting-point for our analytic work, a certain logic in her history began to emerge.

Through her relationships with men, she was also trying to repair the bad relationship she had had as a girl with her father, and it was when she was faced, each time, with the failure of this project which was "superimposed", as it were, on the love affair itself, that the relationship broke up. It was as if the bond of love with men was established in and through the superimposition of her current relationship with a man, and the "transference" onto this relationship of her former relationship with her father, the prototype of the first relations with men. The rupture with men – the point at which things "broke inside her" – was provoked by the rupture within her of the superimposition of these two relationships, by their dissociation.

Her despair, when her last relationship broke up, was linked to the fact that this man, who was from the same country and of the same religious confession as her, and whose family had experienced a history of community break-up that was similar to her own – and, I let me add, who also had a complex relationship with his own father – seemed like a sort of "double" of herself. A double, a similar other, with whom she had thought she could share the same project and establish a sort of "narcissistic contract" of reparation. She was no doubt also more "torn apart" by the present rupture to the extent that the woman in her was also still very much in love with the man that he was.

Primary construction of the bond of love

Diverse levels of the bond of love seem to be involved in this clinical sequence which I am going to use as a central clinical theme for my considerations. They contribute to creating the first bond, which results from the superimposition of the diverse factors involved in the formation of the relationship, but also to all the factors that participate in its stabilization.

In the choice of a love partner, when it is really a "choice", different elements and levels of investment are involved.

There are of course the parameters specific to the love-object, its bodily and relational qualities and particularities, thus its own alterity. But these are only invested in conformity with internal ideational complexes constructed partly on impressions of childhood, of adolescence and of the young adult's life.

This ideational complex produces an internal "object-presentation" that is mingled with, and more or less superimposed on, the actual perception of the object. This superimposition produces an "effect of illusion" at the heart of the state of love. Illusion, here, is in no way meant pejoratively or to deny the "reality" of love: it is the term that designates the superimposition of an invested (loved) internal representation and the perception of a more or less ideal object. It is this background of illusion that is destroyed in the case of rupture.

If the superimposition is very good, it produces the first effect of "love at first sight": the awaited object is "encountered", as if there were no gap between the internal "ideal" representation and the real object. The greater the gap between the representation and the perception is, the less intense the state of love, at least at the beginning of the relationship, will be.

Against this background the relationship will develop gradually, become more complex and, in a certain way, will also "put to the test" the solidity of the background: diverse "contracts" that are more or less conscious and deliberate will be established to stabilize the primary bond. It is these "contracts" that will structure the bond and that will be torn apart when ruptures occur.

The libidinal contract

I would call the first of these contracts "libidinal" in the sense that it is woven with sexual attractions and a mode of object-relating based on a mode of organization of drive life and of the libido which fixes both the reciprocal postures and the levels of reciprocity of these postures and modes of investment. The libidinal relation to the object is organized by an unconscious fantasy activity which itself configures the rules of the increase of libidinal tension and the type of "language of the sexual" wished for between the partners. It is thus a form of contract that is established between the lovers, a contract that is largely unconscious, even if certain aspects can be in broad daylight, a contract that consists of expectations, prohibitions, of more or less obligatory "passages", of a sexual dialog and "conversation". It is a contract made up of libidinal transactions that must be respected in order to maintain the attraction, and whose transgressions are also partly regulated.

I have very little information about the mode of the "libidinal contract" concluded between Myriam and her current friend; she never spoke to me about her sexuality except to tell me "that it worked very well between them" and that it was satisfying, in contrast with what it had become with her two husbands. I do not think that it was at this level that the relationship broke down.

But in the course of certain analyses, it is not unusual to observe that, as the libidinal economy of one of the partners changes, the "libidinal contract" is undermined and that the sexual life of the couple becomes unsatisfying to the point of causing a breakdown of the relationship. The opposite is fortunately not uncommon either and, with the lifting of certain repressions and the reconquest of certain sexual freedoms, the sexual life of the couple and their "libidinal contract" is enriched and diversified.

The basic narcissistic contract

This first contract is linked to a second contract for which I will take up the term "narcissistic contract", forged by P. Aulagnier[2], though in a different sense to the way she uses it. It is linked to the libidinal contract insofar as sexual life, in the broad sense of the drive engagements in the relationship, contributes to the subject's narcissistic economy, but it is not superimposed entirely on the "libidinal contract" insofar as the regulation of an individual's narcissistic economy, his or her level of self-esteem and self-respect, for example, does not depend only on the use of his or her sexuality, even understood in the broad sense.

The narcissistic contract also concerns the self-image that the partner reflects by what he is himself; as if at a certain level of the relationship, the other was also a "mirror" of oneself. Aesthetic criteria thus play a role in the narcissistic contract, along with diverse other components ranging from the social stature of the partner to his relationship with the truth, including his self-assurance or sense of ease in social relations and many other components intervening in the narcissistic economy of the subject.

The alchemy of the narcissistic economy of the relationship is very complex and also depends in part on the specific difficulties of the subject, the partner realizing "for the subject", and on certain conditions, what the subject himself cannot realize or in relation to which he is in difficulty.

But what I consider to be the decisive level for the subject is that aspect of the "narcissistic contract" which depends on what the partner reflects, less by what he is himself than by the conscious messages that he addresses to the subject. Of course, here again, this level is linked up with the libidinal contract and the relationship as a whole will be affected by the mode of drive engagement and of the object-relation that organizes the latter. It is difficult, for example, to imagine a form of sexuality established on anal sadistic bases which would not leave traces in the other sectors of the relationship, and a certain degree of "sadism" or a certain degree of depreciation is likely to be present in the partner who is dominant at a given moment. This does not preclude, of course, a form of reciprocity or of vengeance from establishing itself which inverses, in the ordinary context of relations that are not directly sexual, the postures of sexuality. Everything depends, then, on the types of contracts and on how the question of reciprocity is regulated within the couple.

Invested human relationships, but no doubt also any interpersonal relationship marked by basic empathy, always comprise a level at which the other is also "a same", another oneself. It is the basis on which social relationships are established; it is the basis on which society establishes itself; indeed, it is the basis of elementary social psychology.

The narcissistic contract is sometimes established on the basis of an experience of sharing a "common skin", where each partner has the other "under his skin" to the point that a large part of the relationship is devoted to diverse maneuvers aimed at finding a space of differentiation, even though this is often impossible. The impasse in which certain couples find themselves, one that family therapists have often drawn attention to and translated by the paradoxical alternative, "separating kills us, living together is deadly", can be recognized here. Separation, the rupture of the bond, is then experienced as a form of tearing off of the skin as D. Anzieu has shown so clearly, one partner leaving with the common skin, while the other feels he or she has been skinned alive. What has been described by Anzieu[3] concerning the experience of having a common skin can also pertain to any part of the body or the Ego, as several authors have pointed out.

I can recall one of my patients who was incapable of having sexual relations, and whose analysis showed that in her fantasies, she and her mother had had a "common womb and genital organs" since her earliest childhood. The analysis had made it possible to link this fantasy – an "operative" fantasy which functioned as an internal reality – with a traumatic experience linked to her mother's repeated pregnancies and to the way in which the latter disinvested the precedent child with each new pregnancy. The fantasy of sharing a "common womb and genital organs" seemed to be an attempt to "preserve" the bond with her mother in the face of the menace of disinvestment, and thus to avoid a psychic breakdown. The elaboration of this traumatic infantile situation gradually made it possible, so to speak, to "unstick" their respective "wombs and genital organs" and helped her to envisage a "libidinal contract" with a man – which nonetheless retained perceptual and "geographical traces" of her father.

In the transactions between Myriam and her companion, this problem unfolded at two levels.

The first concerned the question of knowing *who* was separating, who *was leaving* the other. The one who left took with him the protective "skin" that covered the one who triumphed. But the other one, now exposed, multiplied maneuvers and seductions aimed at reconstructing the relationship so that he or she could then be the first to leave, leaving the other in distress. One can well imagine the stormy character that the relationship took on, the "passionate" hesitation waltz that then unfolded.

The other level, which was already less directly stormy and allowed for the intervention of a legal third party, concerned their "common property": the house. Each of them claimed the right to keep it, neither of them being able to envisage abandoning it to the other. The question of knowing who could or was going to pay the other his own share then took center stage. This also was the source of a raging battle, but social laws provided a means of mediation in a conflict that was otherwise insoluble.

When love-relations break up, it is not uncommon for an object to incarnate particularly the central object of the passionate relationship, functioning as the symbolic equivalent of the common skin, of the common narcissistic object.

A narcissistic contract always involves the construction of a common object, of a common zone, of a "common language", which stand in for the "skin object" of the common skin. It is from this common part that it is difficult to separate in a situation of rupture, that it is difficult to detach oneself, and this is why one of the central figures of rupture is tearing or wrenching apart (*arrachement*).

In the case of parental couples, children embody the "common object" that has welded the narcissistic contract of the couple in love and are thus often at the center of the passionate conflicts of separation.

In the regulation of the "narcissistic contract", there is another aspect which I have often observed to be decisive; it concerns the quality of exchange and communication. In the narcissistic contract, there is a "clause" which concerns supporting the other partner when he or she is in difficulty. The quality of listening, being receptive to the difficult states of the other person and narcissistic solidarity with him or her are also an integral part of this clause of narcissistic support for the other, of the reciprocity that it implies.

But this contract is sometimes perverted so that it loses its character of reciprocity and only works "in one direction": one partner has to support the other without the contrary being true, or rather one of them may be instrumentalized to become the narcissistic complement that is indispensable to the other. Here we can recognize relationships which tend to reproduce the primary forms of "narcissistic contracts", those uniting the parent and child.

Any rupture in such a mode of bonding appears to be a catastrophe for the partner who had hitherto found in the other his or her indispensable complement, in whom a part of him or herself had been deposited vicariously, and with which the other is now threatening to leave.

Separation is thus always experienced as a threat of a rupture of identity; it is then always lived in a state of passion which points, beyond what is at stake strictly at the level of love, to what is at stake "narcissistically" in the bond.

The symbolic contract

The third cement of the bond of love that is apt to produce an experience of rupture is organized around what I have proposed to call the "symbolic" contract: it is this contract which, in a certain way, gives the bond its "framework", gives it its meaning.

A relationship is established within a social "framework" which defines the expectations, rights and duties of the partners of the relationship; this social framework produces a form of contract that is unwritten, except in the fabric of the daily life of the relationship. For example, between children and parents the "symbolic contract" implies a certain type of behavior from the parents which defines the archetype of what a "Mother" or a "Father" is in the educational relationship with their children.

Even if it is difficult to clarify all its aspects, we all know more or less intuitively when a father or a mother does not behave as such and fails to keep the symbolic contract of parenting. It is thus not a question here of a father's or mother's "particular style" but of what underlies this position. It is clear, for example, that everything that pertains to incest refers to a rupture of the "symbolic contract" of parenting, but beyond incest proper, any form of instinctual or narcissistic "abuse" on the part of the parents breaches or undermines the contract. But the "symbolic contract" presents less manifest and spectacular aspects; it operates quietly, in an almost silent manner or one that is only marked by its effects. An example taken from the famous story by J.M. Barrie[4], the creator of Peter Pan, will help us understand this type of silent structure.

Peter Pan, a pre-adolescent child, lives in "Never Never Land", the land of children disappointed by the world of adults, the land of children who have experienced a rupture of the "symbolic contract" uniting them with their parents. In this world, there is only one adult who embodies and "represents" someone who does not respect the parental symbolic contract, and who has clearly himself been hurt by life, for he bears the emblematic mark of it in his "hook grip-hand". He is egoistic, nasty, potentially murderous, the only one who counts in his eyes, and thus embodies the "narcissistic" parent.

From time to time, at nightfall, Peter Pan returns to visit the world that he has left and to observe the other children, those who are still living with their mothers and fathers in the quietness and security of family life. This is how he makes the acquaintance of Wendy, a nice little girl, "prim and proper", good and reasonable, but helpful – she repairs the shadow, the narcissistic double of Peter Pan, evoking right away the question of the wounded self-image that children who are in "Never Never Land" have suffered, and which is awakened when they emerge from their posture of total refusal. Peter Pan invites Wendy and her brother, John, to come to the land of the "lost children". Wendy, who is still good and confident in the world of adults, who is still linked to them by a solid "symbolic contract", refuses his offer. Peter Pan leaves again, somewhat repaired by this encounter but promises himself he will return. End of the first scene.

In the second scene, the parents of Wendy and Joey have returned home and it's time to put the children to bed. John has to take his potion before going to bed, a sort of cod liver oil which opens up the question of one of the great paradoxes of education: transcending primary sensoriality in the name of a higher good. The potion is "good for the health" but tastes bad. Joey is reticent: it is difficult for him to grasp the paradox of what is bad but "good"; he refuses and doesn't want to know anything about it.

To avoid a situation of confrontation and impasse, Wendy suggests that her father should "set an example", one of the situations making it possible to put to work the aporia of the saying, "Do as I say and not as I do". Her father must also regularly drink a potion for his health that clearly tastes unpleasant. He tries to get out of the situation by declaring that he would gladly do so, only his bottle of potion has disappeared. Wendy goes to look for it and brings it to him saying that she had found it behind the bathroom cupboard, which begins to create an element of confusion: how on earth did it end up in this astonishing place? Cornered, and with a certain theatricality and a certain solemnity – that which might be fitting when the father is in the symbolic function of the "Father" – Wendy's father prepares the spoon of potion and is about to put it into his mouth. And the scene suddenly changes, he gets hold of the dog that is passing by and shoves the spoon into its mouth, laughing. Shocked, all Wendy can say is, "Oh Dad!"

The scene is apparently innocuous, there is no incest here, no manifest violence, no spectacular trauma which might move the population when related in the newspapers; it is even almost ordinary. But during his next visit, Peter renews his invitation to Wendy and John to come with him to the "Never Never Land", and this time they follow him.

Of course, it is a fictionalized story, life is undoubtedly more complex, but it seems to me to be a good example of a silent rupture of the "symbolic contract" of the bond between Wendy and her father. One may imagine, moreover, that it is not the first time that such an incident had occurred in the relationship between Wendy and her father, but that this time the incident had occurred "once too many times", rocking the relationship and provoking a form of disappointment that results in losing hope in it. Peter Pan's role as a "tempter" should no doubt not be overlooked either: it represents a possible response to disappointment, an extreme and radical response, an alternative to submission. It represents rebellion carried out in the name of the symbolic contract itself, in its most intransigent and infantile form. But children are often like that; they are infantile and experience in "all or nothing" terms the impact of the breaches of the conditions of symbolization.

Our example concerns the parent-child relationship, where the ruptures of the symbolic contract can most easily be highlighted and separated from the forms of narcissistic contracts.

In relations between adults, within the bond of love, things are often more mixed up and narcissistic and symbolic contracts assume an entangled form.

For Myriam, for whom the narcissistic issues at stake in the breakdown of her relationship were no doubt decisive in the way she experienced the internal rupture of the bond, the symbolic breach is present each time in her observation of a non-paternal attitude in the different men from whom she separated. Narcissistic issues are here closely bound up with symbolic issues. What she told me about the attitude of her current friend toward her son – behavior that was the source of many conflicts that erupted between them just before they broke up – shows that he was incapable of behaving in an adult and parental way toward Myriam's son. He was jealous, was constantly in rivalry with the adolescent, never stopped belittling and criticizing him, etc., while placing himself "at the same level" as the adolescent, in an exclusively narcissistic relationship of rivalry with him. This attitude repeated her father's attitude toward her when she was an adolescent; it therefore did not "repair" her own adolescence, but attacked the symbolic contract that should unite a substitute father with an adolescent.

The danger that was thus posed to an aspect of the symbolic contract of their bond was compounded in the period leading up to the rupture of the internal bond by another danger. As I have said, Myriam is a beautiful woman, she is often courted by the men she meets and is quick to charm on account of her manifest qualities. But she has always rejected advances and, without much effort, has remained entirely focused on her relationship with her friend. In the final period leading up to the separation, her friend, on the other hand, had begun to spend quite a lot of time with one of his female colleagues at work. A bit too much for Myriam's liking, with the result that she began to question his fidelity. On several occasions, when they had planned to have lunch together, he had cancelled the appointment at the last moment to stay and work – and have lunch – with this colleague. A certain number of professional questions that they had been in the habit of speaking about together were now also "transferred" to the relationship with this colleague. Without being excessively jealous, Myriam found it very difficult to tolerate the presence of this other woman behind the scenes of her friend's professional activity; the question of his fidelity was involved and with it another aspect of the symbolic contract.

The symbolic contract defines a type of relationship of "symbolic belonging". Beyond the "social contract" established by laws, it defines and is defined by a sense of belonging which manifests itself when one says "my" wife or "my" husband, "my" child, but also "my" country or "my" company. It is important not to confuse, as in relations marked by mastery, belonging and the sense of ownership. Belonging is defined by a "symbolic contract" which is based on the respect of a certain number of characteristics.

The groups or entities to which we "belong" also belong to us; the relationship of belonging is reciprocal. Belonging defines rights concerning the entity to which we feel we belong; it defines a sort of "right to have one's say" about it; and it also defines the obligations of our belonging.

It is based on inter-recognition: "my wife" is only my wife if I am "her husband", and I am only "her husband" if I respect certain rules within the couple. A child can be "disinherited" symbolically by his or her father: "You are no longer my son" signifies that I no longer recognize you as such, and this is true even if, in practice, the actual inheritance, which is governed by social laws, is not really concerned by this form of symbolic banishment. In some cultures, a woman can be "repudiated" as such, not only in social law but also in the internal symbolic inscription itself.

These rules can vary depending on the couples, the families, and the social groups, but there are always rules that define belonging. When one of these rules is transgressed, one of the fundamental rules of the bond of belonging, a breach of the symbolic contract occurs. For example, in certain couples, fidelity is one of the clauses of the contract, and infidelity is a *casus belli* which results in its "rupture" or termination. In other couples, which are organized differently, infidelity is not totally unacceptable in itself, but the fact that it is manifest and made public will be. Everything depends on what constitutes the basis of the sense of belonging for a particular subject, and thus on what will undermine his or her singular sense of belonging.

By way of conclusion

I can scarcely go any further within the limits of this chapter; what I have already said will suffice, I hope, to show the complexity of what can be involved in the situations of ruptures, "real" ruptures coupled with an "internal sense" of rupture.

The three types of "contracts of bonding", which in reality are closely interwoven, but which I have tried to differentiate in an attempt to clarify the issues at stake, make it possible to configurate different aspects of the situations of rupture which affect our relations with the other. The three types of contract appear to be the components of any relationship: they are always present but, of course, in variable quantities depending on the subjects, the types of bonding and the nature of the "frame" which contains and gives them their meaning.

The way in which rupture and its effects are experienced depends on the type of contract – libidinal, narcissistic or symbolic – that is broken by the situation that provokes it, but also on the way in which the three contracts are interwoven, on their particular combination. Thus, there can be situations of rupture without an actual rupture: nothing happens in reality, but something changes in the subjective sense of the bond with the other, something "breaks" without there being any manifest, "official" effects.

Notes

1 Althusser, L. (1965). *Pour Marx*. Paris: La Découverte, 1996.
2 Aulagnier, P. (1975). *La violence de l'interprétation*. Paris: PUF.
3 Anzieu, D. (1974). "Le moi-peau". *Nouvelle Revue de Psychanalyse*, 8: 195–209. NRF.
4 Barrie, J.M. (1811). *Peter Pan and Wendy*. Simon & Schuster.

Index

For Product Safety Concerns and Information please contact our EU
representative GPSR@taylorandfrancis.com
Taylor & Francis Verlag GmbH, Kaufingerstraße 24, 80331 München, Germany

www.ingramcontent.com/pod-product-compliance
Lightning Source LLC
Chambersburg PA
CBHW050608280326
41932CB00016B/2960

9 7 8 1 0 3 2 0 5 6 8 7 6